TEACHER EDUCATION PREPARATION FOR DIVERSITY

TEACHER EDUCATION PREPARATION FOR DIVERSITY

Edited by
Tony J. Manson

Mellen Studies in Education
Volume 68

The Edwin Mellen Press
Lewiston•Queenston•Lampeter

Library of Congress Cataloging-in-Publication Data

Teacher education preparation for diversity / edited by Tony J. Manson.
    p.   cm. -- (Mellen studies in education ; v. 68)
    Includes bibliographical references.
    ISBN 0-7734-7186-3
    I. Title. II. Series : Mellen studies in education (Lewiston, N.Y.) ; v. 68.

This is volume 68 in the continuing series
Mellen Studies in Education
Volume 68 ISBN 0-7734-7186-3
MSE Series ISBN 0-88946-935-0

A CIP catalog record for this book is available from the British Library.

The Edwin Mellen Press
Box 450
Lewiston, New York
USA 14092-0450

The Edwin Mellen Press
Box 67
Queenston, Ontario
CANADA L0S 1L0

The Edwin Mellen Press, Ltd.
Lampeter, Ceredigion, Wales
UNITED KINGDOM SA48 8LT

Printed in the United States of America

Dedication

I dedicate this book in loving memory to *Mr. James C. Manson and Mr. Melvin A. Ashley*. These two men provided me with the model of manhood that will always be appreciated and cherished. I want to also dedicate this book to my wife, Bonita, and my sons, Tony Jr. and Gregory. All of you have done more for me than words could ever say. Thank you for your presence in my life. It is I who has received the gift!

I want to also dedicate this book to a group of outstanding men. Even though I do not have any known brothers, these men have served in that role from time to time. I have grown extremely in our relationships. These men are; *James Reynolds, Charles Spann, Bobbie Grier, Freddie Goss, Floyd Jamison, and James Cunningham*. These **Great** men have given a great deal toward my development as a man. They have also shown great attitude, leadership and work ethic. Thank You for Everything!!

Table of Contents

THE DILEMMA OF DIVERSITY
Blanche Jackson Glimps, Ph.D.
Theron Ford, Ph.D.

A RATIONALE FOR MULTICULTURALISM AND DIVERSITY IN COLLEGIATE EDUCATION: HOW THE DEBATE IS FRAMED AND WHY IT CONTINUES TO BE CONTROVERSIAL
Blanche Jackson Glimps, Ph.D.
Theron Ford, Ph.D.

Foreword

<u>"The person who is truly effective has the humility and reverence to recognize his own perceptual limitations and appreciate the rich resources available through interaction with the hearts and minds of other human beings."</u>

This passage is from Daily Reflections For Highly Effective People by Stephen R. Covey.

When Dr. Tony Manson asked me to write the foreword for *Teacher Education Preparation For Diversity*, I was very pleased for three reasons. First of all, Tony is a very good and long time friend of mine. We have been friends for many years and I have participated with him on several other successful projects. The second reason is that his work as an educator has proven to outstanding. The above stated passage embodies the efforts and the contributions of all the contributors to this book. Many of the chapters in this text cut to the core of what diversity means to the teacher educators, counselor educators and school administrators.

The issue of sensitizing teachers and other school personnel to the need for multicultural education is one of particular importance, since most students in teacher education programs are predominantly Anglo or European Americans from middle to upper class backgrounds. The concepts and strategies included in multicultural education as they pertain to teacher education programs are rarely carried over to the classroom.

The book chapters reflect the findings from several studies based on changing awareness and attitudes towards diversity. This research became an effective vehicle to allow teachers to integrate ideas of diversity, tolerance and acceptance into an already overstuffed curriculum. Teachers actively embrace combining their existing practice with a newly trained eye towards multiculturalism they achieved the goal of increased awareness and appreciation of diversity within the demands already placed on them. In addition, the research indicates an untapped opportunity for increased school connections around issues of diversity and literacy through the use of quality teacher education programs.

Diversity has many different definitions. In recent time it has taken on many faces in our society. Diversity in education also has several different meanings. This text tries to bring into focus on what some college professors, grade school instructors and counselors believe diversity means to them. The third reason I am excited about writing the foreword is that this book will show everyone the depth and breadth of the thinking that needs to take place to really make our programs strive toward diversity and serve everyone. My hope is that you will gather many thoughts about diversity. Regardless if you agree or not, I hope you read and seriously consider the entire book. In my opinion, in time this book will prove to be one of the outstanding contributions of the day to our profession.

Joseph Jefferson, Ph.D.
Texas Southern University

Acknowledgments and Comments

As I began to think of all the people to whom I would like to express my appreciation for their support, suggestions, and hard work in making this book possible, the list continues to grow. I would like to name certain individuals for their strong efforts and to offer special thanks for everything. First of all I want to thank my wife, Dr. Bonita Manson, and Gregory and Tony Jr. for providing an environment so the creative juices could flow. I want to particularly thank my friends, Dr. Sheri Trent, Mrs. Bettye Adams, Ms Stephanie Adams, Mr. Brian Shaw, and Mrs. Jennifer Shaw for all their efforts in making this project and previous efforts a success. I want them to know I really appreciate them and all they have done for me. I want to particularly thank the Edwin Mellen publishing company for providing a forum for myself to enter my ideas and thoughts. I would also like to give special thanks to the family, friends, and colleagues on the following list for without you and your thoughts, insight, and prayers this project would not have come true:

Dr. James B. Boyer

Mr. James C. Manson (Deceased) and Mrs. Geraldine Manson

Mr. Will H. Jones Sr. and Joan Jones

Mr. Melvin Ashley (Deceased) and Mrs. Lois Ashley

Sister Marie Faubert

Dr. Ben Smith

Ms. Beatrice Manson

Ms. Helen Norris

Ms. Beatrice Wren

Ms. Hazel Robinson

Dr. Rose Duhon-Sells

Mr. Will Robinson

Mr. Lawrence Cooper

Dr. Frederic Will

Last but not ever least I want to give to Our Lord Jesus for all my strength and inspiration comes from above.

How wonderful it is, how pleasant, for God's people to live together in harmony! It is like the precious anointing oil running down from Aaron's head and beard, down to the collar of his robes. It is like the dew on Mount Hermon, falling on the hills of Zion. That is where the Lord has promised his blessing—Life that never ends. Psalms 133

Each chapter in **Teacher Education Preparation for Diversity** features real-life descriptions and first-person accounts relating to chapter content. These chapters tried to let the readers see some ideas that teachers have about instructing across ethnic and racial lines. The book is to be viewed as a reference to what school life is really like and how teacher reflection and decision-making form professional practice.

Introduction

Teacher education faces a crisis of confidence today unless teacher educators can convince the public that professional teacher education is necessary to the future of public education. Critics of teacher education do not hesitate to assert that teaching is not a profession. The critics claim there is no mystique, no body of knowledge, skills and professional values necessary to effective teaching on which teacher education curriculum may be based. A curriculum that would be analogous to those which characterizes medicine, law, and other learned professions is strongly desired. Teacher educators today are powerless to refute this charge, are unable to demonstrate any differences between graduates of teacher education programs and liberal arts programs. Teacher education programs have become an issue of multicultural education though the need for diversity in not only the teacher education program, but in the classroom.

Historically, teacher education institutions have trained educators to work effectively with only one group: middle-class Anglo Americans. Teachers are products of an ethnocentric curriculum (Banks, 1987) that does not prepare them to deal with students who may come not only from different social, economic, linguistic, and cultural backgrounds, but also from urban and rural cultures. Teacher education programs also have tried to help pre-service as well as in-service teachers to develop positive attitudes toward their own culture and the culture of others. "Such cultural consciousness helps teachers to value their culture without seeing it as normative, and to respect a variety of cultural experiences" (Adams, Pardo, and Schniedewind, 1992, p. 37). Effective teacher/school research has indicated that teacher/administrators who are successful with minority students possess high levels of sensitivity to the needs of those students (Brookover, Lezotte, 1977; Brookover et al., 1981). These teacher/administrators also possess the necessary cultural awareness knowledge to produce high-achieving minority students. Therefore, educators must be trained, to understand individual differences, and build upon those differences to create a learning environment that is effective for all students, regardless of ethnic or racial identity. The philosophical concepts of multicultural education must be integrated into the total teacher education program in order to prepare all educators to work effectively with students who are ethnically and racially different (Larke, 1990).

The preparation of teachers usually consists of three major components: (1) liberal (or general) education, (2) specialized subject-field education, and (3) professional education. A liberal arts program combines the arts and sciences and seeks to give the perspective teacher a board cultural background. The specialized subject-field comprises a cluster of courses in a specific subject area and provides perspective teachers with an extensive preparation in their chosen teaching field. Professional education consists of courses designed to provide knowledge and skills regarding the arts and science of teaching.

It is important that prospective teachers explore what teachers do in the classroom. Teachers have to be able to not only teach, but be able to daily manage their classrooms. Teaching involves a complex series of acts. Teaching must fit the learner, the subject content, and the knowledge or the skill being taught. The behavior of one teacher can seldom be transferred. A technique or an approach that works for one teacher may not be effective for another.

Tony J. Manson, Ph.D.

Chapter 1

Why Not Try Educating All The Children?

Tony J. Manson, Ph.D.
Middle Tennessee State University
Murfreesboro, Tennessee

Introduction

Providing education for children who are not of the dominant culture poses some additional challenges for the classroom teacher. It is the successful management of these challenges to which this chapter addresses.

Accommodation or Assimilation?

Simplistically speaking, there are two official approaches to educating minority children in American public schools: *accommodation* or *assimilation*. However, there are those (Trueba and Bartolome, 1997) who would argue that there is a third approach: simply ignoring them. Webster's defines *accommodation* as "to fit, to adapt, or make suitable", "to supply with conveniences". *Assimilation* is defined as "to make like or alike, to take up and make part of itself or one self."

The professional literature published in this decade does not specifically employ these two terms, with the one exception of the word *accommodation* in reference to providing and adapting services to enable the disabled (of all varieties) to obtain a public school education ("Accommodations", 1999, pp. 1-2). Otherwise, the reader is left to discern the writer's bias, and clearly, *accommodation* is the frontrunner.

Previous generations of immigrants were assimilated into American culture and "everyone" thought that was a good thing. Today the word smacks of racism, ethnic whitewashing, and cultural obliteration. The literature is clear that minority children must be allowed, and encouraged, to maintain their languages, cultures, and traditions within the classroom and public school setting. This is the practical definition of *accommodation*.

The Education of Minorities

Dominating the discussion of educating minority students is the issue of teacher attitude (Burnett, 1993, pp. 1-5; Cazden, 1992, pp. 1-19; Gomez, 1991, pp. 1-4; Trueba and Bartolome, 1997, pp. 1-8). The literature makes it clear what a teacher must do to successfully educate today's minority children. He/She must:

- Provide a warm and welcoming classroom (Kindler, 1995, p. 6; "Highly", 1991, p.1)

- Create an exciting and dynamic classroom environment that is conducive to learning, respects the different abilities of students and their cultural and linguistics differences,

- Avoid cultural, racial, and gender-based stereotypes (Garicia, 1991, pp. 1-11; Gomez, 1991, pp. 1-4).

- Commit to ongoing professional growth (Cazden, 1994, pp. 11-12) and to rid themselves of racial or ethnic biases and prejudices (Trueba and Bartolome, 1997, p. 3).

- Create opportunities for the student's success and avoid tracking within the classroom (Trueba and Bartolome, 1997, p. 3).

- Actively communicate with the parents of his/her students (Chavkin, 1991, p. 3; Garcia, 1991, p. 4; Kindler, 1995, p. 6; Cazden, 1992, pp. 14-15).

Include the family in the educational setting and be a social worker. Social work literature (Craves, 1995; Chavkin and Brown, 1992; Chavkin and Gonzalez, 1995; Guthrie and Guthrie, 1991; Hinkle, 1992; Perry, 1992; Rittner and Sacks, 1995; Schorr, 1997; Wittmer, 1992) is replete with examples of minority families and school disconnectedness. Hispanic, African American, and Asian parents have different attitudes toward education and teachers than do middle class Caucasian parents; consequently, encouraging involvement in the classroom can be the catalyst for the minority caretaker's future empowerment in a public school system that is frequently overwhelming.

Provide positive role modeling from other cultures and languages. Teachers should solicit the volunteer efforts of community and family members and have them teach a lesson, share a cultural activity, or help with ordinary daily classroom activities. This demonstrates respect for the cultures, values, and dialects of the student's home. This approach can be very effective for minority students with significant language delays (Garcia, 1991, p. 1). Be bi-lingual and utilize more than one language in the classroom (Cazden, 1992, 1992, pp.1-19; Lankard, 1994, p. 3).

Allow the use of the child's home language and use it oneself. Experts (Adger, 1997; Ima and Labovitz, 1991; Rickford, 1999) assert that allowing the social use of a child's home language (bidialectalism) and using a teaching compare and contrast techniques in classroom instruction (versus correcting language use mistakes) can ease the student's discomfort. Furthermore, it sends the message that the teacher values what the student values, namely the student's customs, culture, and language.

Teach **all** children how to be citizens of a pluralistic society. An inter-disciplinary multicultural curriculum is important to all children: Caucasian children can learn from the minority caretakers of their minority classmates, thereby learning to value and respect other races and ethnic groups, which can undermine the overpowering messages of racism in America; and the minority students will experience cultural pride and self-pride.

Students learn from the positive role modeling provided by members of their own race or ethnic group, therefore, conferring value and respectability on their race or ethnic group. This concept undermines the soul-wrenching effects of racism on their self-image (Garcia, 1991, pp. 1-11).

- Live in same neighborhood in which his/her students live (Skylarz, as cited in Lankard, 1994).

- Create whole-person, thematic lessons that promote a democratic depiction of all cultures. An attitude of inclusiveness in all subjects can encourage student self-respect and self-confidence (Garcia, 1991, p. 3; Gomez, 1991, pp.1-4; Trueba and Bartolome, 1997, p. 3).

- Believe that every student is a winner and communicate high expectations for success (Cazden, 1992, p. 14; Garcia, 1991, p. 4; Gomez, 1991, p. 3; Kindler, 1995, p. 7; Milk, Mercado, and Sapiens, 1992, p. 4; Trueba and Bartolome, 1997, p. 3).

- Be a positive role model of a minority group (Lankard, 1994, p. 1).

- Have a working knowledge of the social and behavioral characteristics of at least two minority populations (Faltis and Merino, as quoted in Milk, Mercado, and Sapiens, 1992).

Teacher Education Programs

Colleges and universities are coming under attack by the experts to modernize teaching techniques and recruit more minority students (among others, Lankard, 1994, pp. 1-4). The expert assert that teachers and future teachers need professional development programs and degree programs that "model an ideal classroom environment, " help them develop "strategies for fostering team-based approaches to resolving instructional challenges, " and engage them to engage in "an active, introspective process in through which they are, in some manner, transformed...better able to sustain the willingness and ability to effect change in their classrooms" (Milk, Mercado, and Sapiens, 1992, p. 9). Additionally, "mentoring, role modeling, peer guidance, review, and counseling are among methods used to enhance intellectual and personal growth" of minorities who might become teachers (Lankard, 1994, p. 3).

Traditionally, the typical teacher-training program has emphasized the skills needed to transfer information to students via various strategies designed to achieve the school's or the state's educational objectives. Today "the challenge for teacher education is shifting to how to prepare teachers (both beginning and experienced) to move from wherever they happen to be in their current approach to teaching toward becoming the kind of professionals who can create an optimal learning environment for language minority students" (Milk, Mercado, and Sapiens, 1992, p.3).

All teachers, not just the language specialist or the teacher of an ESL or LEP or immersion classroom, must be specially trained. The experts tell us that mainstream classroom teachers "need to be prepared to teach language minority students and to take a more active role in these students' education" (Milk, Mercado, and Sapiens, 1992, p. 3).

There are six important roles or functions that mainstream classroom teachers perform with regard to language minority students. These functions include:

- Mediator and facilitator of content learning;

- Facilitator of the acquisition of English as a second language;

- Model on behalf of the dominant language;

- Mediator of mainstream culture;

- Advocate for student empowerment;

Collaborators (with administrators and other teachers) should provide valuable information about language minority students in their classes and about the content of their classes (Milk, Mercado, and Sapiens, 1992, p. 3).

Demands

The demands placed upon today's teachers require that they engage in life-long training and education. Today's teachers must:

- Read the latest books and journals on related subjects and theoretical discussions; find the best in classroom materials and curricula;

- Work or volunteer at a summer day camp for neighborhood kids, that contribute to a teacher's understanding of where and how her/his students live;

Advocate for in-service trainings about multiculturalism, which "reflect in a more holistic fashion on two fundamental questions: What kind of learning environment would most successfully engage students in the learning process? And, what kind of learning environment would be most conducive to language development for learners who possess unique linguistic and cultural characteristics" (Milk, Mercado, and Sapiens, 1992, p. 3)? The "future lies in understanding how diverse population, in such a situation of risk and vulnerability, can achieve social, educational, and employment competence" (Garcia, 1991, p. 2).

Attend workshops and conferences that utilize the coaching approach: "Coaching typically involves presenting teachers with information for implementing an instructional innovation in the classroom and pairing them to provide non-threatening feedback to each other regarding their effectiveness in applying this knowledge in the classroom setting" (Milk, Mercado, and Sapiens, 1992, p. 7).

Three hundred years ago, America was created by groups of people who wanted to live in a country where they could be different. As America builds on Its' history and become increasingly more different, more diverse, teachers must educate "children about other groups or countries...lifestyles, languages, cultures, and points of view" (Gomez, 1991, p.3). Mutual respect (accommodation), not whitewashing (assimilation), is the key to "fitting" together the multicultural pieces of the American mosaic. If teachers employ strategies that "acknowledge, respect, and build upon the language and culture of the home" (Garcia, 1991, p. 6), then minority children can succeed academically and secure rewarding futures of financial promise, thereby planting the seeds of success for future generations of minority students.

REFERENCES

Accommodations for disabilities. (1999, February 13). Washington, DC: American Council on Education. Available: http://www.acenet.edu/calec/ged/disability-accom-TT.html.

Adger, C. T. (1997, January 12). Language policy and public knowledge. Washington, DC: Center for Applied Linguistics. Available: http://www.cal.org.

Burnett, G. (1993). The assessment and placement of language minority students. New York, NY: ERIC Clearinghouse on Urban Education. Available: http://eric-web.tc.columbia.edu/digests/dig89.html

Caves, R.W. (1995). Exploring urban America: An introductory reader. CA: Sage Publications

Cazden, C. B. (1992). Language minority education in the United States: Implications of the Ramirez Report. Washington, DC: U.S. Department of Education, Office of Educational Research and Improvement (OERI). Available: http://www.ncbe.gwu.edu.

Chavkin, N.F., & Gonzalez, D.L. (1995, October). Forging partnerships between Mexican-American parents and the school. Eugene, OR: ERIC Clearinghouse on Educational Management. Available: http://www.ed.gov/databases/ERIC_Digests/ed388489.html.

Chavkin, N.F., & Brown, K. (1992, July). School social workers building a multi-ethnic family-school-community partnership. Social Work in Education, 14, 160-164.

Chavkin, N. Fl. (1991, May). Family lives and parental involvement in migrant students' education. Charleston, WV: ERIC Clearinghouse on Rural Education and Small Schools. Available:

http://www.teleplex.net/docotrv/pages/11666927.htm

Cross, B.E., & Reitzug, U.C. (1995-1996, December-January). How to build ownership in city schools. Educational Leadership, 53, 16-19.

Garcia, E. E. (1991). The education of linguistically and culturally diverse students: Effective instructional practices. Washington, DC: U.S. Department of Education, OERI Available:

http://www.ncbe.gwu.miscpubbs/ncrcdsll/eprl/

Gomez, R. A. (1991). Teaching with a multicultural perspective. Urbana, IL: ERIC Clearinghouse on elementary and Early childhood Education.

Available: http://www.ed.gov/databases/ERIC_Digests/ed339548.html.

Guthrie, G., &Guthrie, L. (1991, September). Streamlining interagency collaboration for youth at risk. Educational Leadership, 49, 17-22.

Highly mobile students: Educational problems and possible solutions. (1991, June). New York, NY: ERIC Clearinghouse on Urban Education. Available:

http://www.ed.gov/databases/ERIC_Digests/ed338745.html.

Hinkle, J. S. (1992, December). Family counseling in the schools. Eugene, OR: ERIC Clearinghouse on Educational Management. Available: http://www.ed.gov/databases/ERIC_Digests/ed3477482.html.

Kindler, A. L. (1995, Fall). Education of migrant children in the United States. Washington, DC: U.S. Department of Education, Office of Bilingual Education and Minority Languages Affairs (OBEMLA), National Clearinghouse for Bilingual Education (NCBE). Available: http://www.ncbe.gwu.edu/ncbepubs/directions/08.html.

Ima, K. & Labovitz, E. M. (1991). Language proficiency, ethnicity and standardized test performance on elementary school students. ERIC Clearinghouse on Assessment and Evaluation. Available: http://ericae.net/db/riiiecije/ed341700.htlm.

Lankford, B. A. (1994). Recruitment and retention of minority teachers in vocational education. Columbus, OH: ERIC Clearinghouse on Adult, Career, and Vocational Education. Available: http://www.ed.gov/databases/ERIC_Digests/ed368889.html.

Milk, R., Mercado, C., & Sapiens, A. (1992, Summer). Rethinking the education of teachers of language minority children: Developing reflective teachers for changing schools. Washington, DC: U.S. Department of Education, OBEMLA, NCBE. Available: http://www.ncbe.gwu.edu/ncbepubs/focus/focus6.htlm.

Rittner, B. & Sacks, A. (1995, January). Children in protective services: The missing educational link for children in kinship networks. Social Work in Education, 17, 7-15.

Schorr, L. B. (1997). Common purposes: Strengthening families and neighborhoods to rebuild America. NY: Anchor Books (Doubleday).

Rickford, J. R. (1997, January 22). Letter to Senator Arlen Specter, Chairman, Subcommittee of Labor, Health and Human Services and Education; Committee on Appropriations. Available:
http://www.standford.edu~rickford/ebonics/Specterletter.html.

Trueba, E. T. & Bartolome, L. I. (1997, July). The education of Latino students: Is school reform enough? New York, NY: ERIC Clearinghouse on Urban Education. Avaible:
http://www.ed.gov/databases/ERIC_Digests/ed410367.html.

Wittmer, J. (1992, December). Valuing diversity in the schools: The counselor's role. Eugene, OR: ERIC Clearinghouse on Educational Management. Available:
http://www.ed.gov.databases/ERIC_Digests/ed347475.html.

Chapter 2

So You Say You Want to Teach?

Tony J. Manson, Ph.D.
Middle Tennessee State University
Murfreesboro, Tennessee

Introduction

The purpose of this chapter is to present a review of multicultural education. In this regard, the focus is upon delineating those basic facts and points that are important for beginning teachers to know about the topic.

Multicultural Education

In the period from 1960 to 1975, there occurred several important and major changes in the educational system. According to Banks (1981), these changes were due to several factors, the most contribuitive of which were: the passage of the Civil Rights Act of 1964, the growth of new educational philosophies which stressed student participation in educational planning and the relaxation of institutional controls, and the push, in large part by minority groups, for schools to develop a curriculum better suited to the needs of their particular cultural group.

One of the major changes ushered into the system as a result of the just delineated factors was the call for multicultural education. Perhaps no-where is this call better voiced neither the objectives of multicultural education more succinctly delineated than in what Havighurst (1978) termed his proposed curriculum for a post-industrial society. Specifically, Havighurst (1978) wrote that:

The curriculum should support a constructive and democratic cultural pluralism. This idea could contribute to:

a) Mutual appreciation and understanding of every subculture by the other ones

b) Freedom for each subculture to practice its culture and socialize its children

c) Sharing by each group in the economic and civic life of the society

d) Peaceful coexistence of diverse...(people and their ways)...(pp. 120-121).

The foregoing may be associated with one point which beginning teachers should be well-versed in regarding multicultural education; this point being that teachers need to know the goals of multicultural education, goals which are derived from the postulates listed by Havighurst (1978). Regarding the goals of multicultural education, Sleeter and Grant (1988) have noted that the multicultural approach to education has five primary goals, which teachers need to be both aware of and ready to implement in the classroom situation. These goals are:

• Promoting strength and value of cultural diversity;

• Promoting human rights and respect for those who are different from oneself;

• Promoting alternative life choices f or people:

- Promoting social justice and equal opportunity for all people.

- Promoting equity in the distribution of power among groups.

- A second point which beginning teachers need to understand with respect to multicultural education is that as pointed out by several authors (Stent, Hazard, & Fivlin, 1973; Suzuki, 1984; Valverde, 1977), this approach is based on ideology. This point is aptly made by Sleeter and-Grant (1988) who note that:

The ideology of Multicultural Education ... does not advocate that the world is fine as it is and that children should learn about more of it. Rather it is borne of a concern that society as it exists is unfair and detrimental to many people (p.149).

It can be seen that one obvious perspective of the multicultural ideology is a need for reform in the school curriculum (Baker, 1983; Sadker & Sadker, 1982). The purpose here is to make the curriculum more in line with multicultural goals. An example of curriculum changes might be effect teachers in general and beginning teachers in particular may be seen if one considers the multicultural approach of an English teacher.

The multiculturally oriented English teacher when drawing up her list of novels to be read by students during the school year would do such things as attempting to include novels written by people of various ethnicities and cultural backgrounds; an attempt would also be made to include stories written by females. All too often what has been given to students as "the classics" have been stories and novels written by white males who, regardless of the excellence of their writing skills, simply do not present a wide variety of cultural perspectives in their stories.

Another facet of curriculum reform concerns text materials and instructional displays. In this regard, authors espousing multicultural education (Seaburg, Smith, & Gallaher, 1980) have noted that these materials must be free of stereotyping based on race, ethnic background, religion, or gender. Also, advocates of the multicultural perspective feel that these materials should include concepts and ideas that relate to diverse cultures (Anyon, 1979).

Sleeter and Grant (1988) have stated that:

- If the multicultural education approach is to work and the curriculum is to be provocative and challenging, teachers will need to be guided by certain instructional principles (p.156).
- The principles discussed by these authors may be summarized here:
- Students are curious and can learn complex materials.
- Students each have their own unique learning styles.
- Teachers need to use the conceptual schemes that students bring to class rather than attempt to replace these schemes with new ones; in other words, start with what students know and build.
- Teachers need to have realistic yet high expectations for all students regardless of apparent differences.
- Teachers need to actively attempt to foster cooperation among students.
- Teachers need to be non-sexist in their approach to instruction.
- Teachers need to help students toward increasingly positive self-concepts.

There is one final and extremely important element of multicultural education that must be understood by beginning teachers; and this is that the approach is not without its critics. In order to fully understand the strengths and the weaknesses of the approach as well as possible areas of difficulty, it is necessary for beginning teachers to be aware of what criticism could exists. Therefore, the final section of this chapter presents a summarization of the major criticisms of the multicultural approach to education as discussed by Banks (1986). Specifically, these criticisms are:

1. The multicultural approach is a palliative to keep oppressed groups from rebelling in a manner that will force meaningful change which multicultural curriculum is not.

2. The purpose of education is to disseminate certain basic areas of information; to use the system to promote social ideologies or changes (however lofty or noble) is improper.

The goals of multicultural education are unrealistic. No educational system could actually achieve the social objectives that the approach specifies. Therefore time and monies spent on this approach are wasted.

The multicultural approach is misdirected. It is interpersonal interaction among diverse groups of people (and the learning that comes from said) that will change society in the direction desired by multicultural advocates. Learning about other peoples in a cognitive manner in the artificiality of the classroom situation will not achieve such goals.

18

REFERENCE

Anyon, J. (1979). Ideology and United States history textbooks. Harvard Educational Review, 49, 361-386.

Baker, C.C. (1983). Planning and organizing of multicultural instruction. Leading, MA: Addison-Wesley.

Banks, J. A. (1981). Multicultural education: Theory and practice. Boston: Allyn and Bacon.

Banks, J. A. (1986). Multicultural education and its critics: Britain and the United States. In S. Modgil et al, (Eds.), Multicultural education: The interminable debate. London: The Falmer Press.

Havighurst, F.J. (1978). Common experience versus diversity in the curriculum. Educational Leadership, 36, 118-121.

Sadker, M. & Sadker, D. (1982). Sex equity handbook for schools. New York: Longman.

Seaburg, J. J., Smith, J. C. & Gallaher, J. H. (1980). Building a multicultural education media collection. Viewpoints in Teaching and Learning, 56, 100-104.

Sleeter, C. E. & Grant, C. A. (1988). Making choices for multicultural education. Columbus, Ohio: Merrill Publishing.

Stent, M. Hazard, W., & Pivlin, H. (1973). Cultural pluralism in education: A mandate for change. New York: Appleton-Century-Crofts.

Suzuki, B. H. (1984). Curriculum transformation for multicultural education. Education and Urban Society, 16, 294-322.

Valverde, L. A. (1977). Multicultural education: Social and educational justice. Educational Leadership, 36, 196-201.

Chapter 3

The Multi-Cultural Agenda: Striving For Equity and Justice

Kathleen G. Burriss, Ed.D.
Elementary and Special Education
Middle Tennessee State University
Murfreesboro, TN

Larry L. Burriss, Ph.D.
School of Journalism
Middle Tennessee State University
Murfreesboro, TN

Abstract

This chapter identifies methods of securing equity and justice for diverse students as part of a multicultural agenda. Strategies are provided to assist teacher educators and candidates in gaining insight into the rationale for multicultural education.

Background

In the United States, populations have shifted dramatically from a nonwhite minority to a nonwhite majority. As a result, classroom teachers interact with an increasing number of diverse students. "[I]n urban areas, the teaching force is over 85 percent European American and middle class, while the student population is much more diverse" (Campbell, 1996, p. 69).

In another area, findings show a disproportionate number of minority students are unsuccessful in school (Center for Educational Statistics, 2001; Perez, 1994;

Nel, 1992). As has been traditionally understood, if education is viewed as a way to gain access to the larger society (Stevens and Wood, 1987), then increased school achievement is warranted in order for diverse students to maintain active citizenry. The way in which teacher candidates are instructed during teacher education determines the societal effectiveness or failure of minority students (Nel, 1992). "Educational reform must embrace equity goals, must honor the right of parents and communities, must promote tolerance for diversity, and responsiveness to clients" (Sykes cited in Zeichner, 1991, p.364). Therefore, preparing candidates to teach for justice and equity is integral within teacher education.

In the 21st century classroom, teachers are expected to successfully interact with students significantly different from themselves. Ethnicity, culture, race, religion, socioeconomic status, ability and language will interact and contribute to these perceived differences. An individual's background frames an individual's *Weltanschauung*, and serves as a powerful filter to guide expectations and behaviors. Thus, teachers' and students' different backgrounds will significantly influence classroom activities, expectations, and performance. Determining strategies to promote teacher candidates' commitment to insure a pluralistic democracy begins with self-reflection. With an eye toward understanding and appreciating differences among and between diverse groups, self-reflection will afford opportunities for teacher candidates to consider how their life experiences shape personal values and beliefs.

In addition, it is critical to move teacher candidates to understand how these perceptions will impact their interactions with students who hold different filters. If never questioned, they may not be aware that others hold different, and even contradictory, beliefs from their own. In doing so, while teacher candidates may not agree with their students, their commitment to regard the values and beliefs of others is critical to insuring equitable and just education for minority students.

The Dilemma

Teacher candidates are largely Euro-American women from rural areas, small towns, or suburban communities with little experience or knowledge regarding diverse cultures and who prefer to teach children like themselves (Liston and Zeichner, 1990 cited in McCall and Andringa, 1997). Teacher educators may be no different in terms of thinking about diversity. As a group, they are politically conservative and base their curriculum on the science of teaching (Liston and Zeichner 1990 cited in McCall and Andringa, 1997). They also do not wish to alienate students or public school administrators (Liston and Zeichner, 1990 cited in McCall and Andringa, 1997).

Research indicates teacher candidates are not comfortable with discussions of racism, and their perceptions of racial issues usually confirm their initial prejudices and misunderstandings (Cross, 1993 cited in McCall, 1995). Further research indicates students' definitions of multicultural understanding are minimal and limited to race and ethnicity (Neuharth-Pritchett, Reiff, and Pearson, in press, 2001). Reports also indicate teacher candidates' attitudes and beliefs are not easily altered (Campbell, 1996; Larkin and Sleeter, 1995). Delany-Barman and Minner (1997) contend beliefs will change as a result of experience, and these experiences must occur across time. Particular features in teacher preparation may have a positive influence on teacher development (Larkin and Sleeter, 1995; Zeichner, 1991).

Teacher education programs are successful when a multicultural perspective is infused across the curriculum, professional courses, and field experiences. Also, teachers are better able to reflect on their practices when diversity issues are presented at the beginning of the professional courses (Barry and Lechner, 1995). McDiarmid (1992) recommends an examination of historical developments and their contemporary significance. That is, provide educational opportunities for teacher candidates to learn 'about' history (p.59). Further, McDiarmid (1992) purports if there is a great amount of information to cover, lecture is appropriate. If, however, the attempt is to change attitudes, he suggests appealing to the sense of justice.

Research indicates that multicultural education in teacher education programs may not be a positive influence (Pajares, 1993), and may even contribute to stereotypes of minority students (Derman-Sparks,1989).

Clark, DeWolf and Clark (1992) state "Unwittingly, we were teaching teachers to magnify differences, not to teach understanding and respect for diversity" (p.5). They contend that because of teacher preparation programs, teacher candidates' first inclination to be multicultural is to create units. The example they provide is on "Indians" wherein the unit includes songs (i.e. Ten Little Indians), stories and games. Clark, DeWolf and Clark (1992) describe this approach as a "play kit" and argue it is "culturally assaultive" (p.5). Findings indicate teacher education must move teacher candidates toward more complex constructions of multicultural education through university classroom and field-based experiences (Neuharth-Pritchett, Reiff and Pearson, in press, 2001). They believe it is necessary to assist teacher candidates in examining their personal experiences and recognize natural diversity as being a component of seemingly homogeneous groups. "People don't learn social lessons cognitively; they learn them affectively, by emotionally processing and anchoring lessons learned from intense experiences" (Clark, DeWolf and Clark, 1992, p.6). Then, what university experiences will provoke teacher candidates' cognitive and affective states to promote their receptivity to equity and justice as the multicultural agenda?

Another major problem facing those who would teach others about multicultural education is the process of "getting inside" another person. The myriad of customs, beliefs, morals and traditions make for a bewildering mosaic that is sometimes amusing and frequently misunderstood. A prime example is in the area of body language and gestures. We think nothing of pointing our finger at someone, giving the "v-for-victory" sign or waving our hand. Yet many of these gestures, of which there are more than 700,000, in other cultures can be insulting. You may ask, "Why should pointing my finger at someone, or giving a gift with my left hand, be insulting? After all, it's only a gesture." Well, think of American hand gestures that are considered obscene or insulting. Why should you be insulted if someone uses one of these signs with you? After all, they are only gestures!

In reality, for many of our customs, there is no *real* right or wrong. We make certain words, symbols and gestures right or wrong, but these conversational elements are not inherently anything. They mean whatever we say they mean, nothing more and nothing less. Think of how many traditions we covet or behaviors we minimize "just because." Would your grandmother ever wear white shoes before Memorial Day? Probably not. And if you ask her why not, she would say, "Well, you just don't, that's all." How about plaids and stripes? We may not like the way they look, but there is nothing inherently *wrong* about them.

These problems are exacerbated when we start dealing with transnational expressions, modes of address, use of words and body gestures (i.e. hand gestures, body posture, eye contact). The problem, all too often, stems from the fact that we fail to "get inside" the other person due to fears or ignorance. Thus before teachers may be effective in public schools, teacher educators must mediate teacher candidates' perceptions.

The dynamic interaction shared between teacher and student is critical when promoting individual student achievement. More than the materials or instruction, rapport that occurs between teacher and learner determines effectiveness. What is not recommended is the continued demonstration of songs, bulletin boards, and props as multicultural education. Even the choice of children's literature is critical. Literature may be accurate and insightful but at the same time wrong and superficial. Without the commitment and understanding of the teacher, these are superficial activities. What is recommended is to provide teacher candidates with opportunities that provoke and challenge them on an adult cognitive level. Too often teacher candidates are presented with "how to" strategies to use with children. This approach is linear, and simply providing scores of activities alone cannot demonstrate cultural sensitivity.

The mere action of "doing" an activity is too often misunderstood to convey understanding. Hands-on activities and materials are important only so far as they promote thinking. Promoting teacher candidates to replicate children's activities without understanding the societal rationale for justice and equality will have little effect and may even serve to undermine cultural awareness. Multicultural education is not a collection of discrete activities. Continuance of these practices (i.e. prop boxes, puppets, holiday celebrations, cultural food demonstrations) eliminates opportunities for teacher candidates to take responsibility for their individual biases. In failing to do so, teacher candidates diminish their potential to influence classroom practice for diverse students.

Strategies

Pajares (1993) suggests creating cognitive tension in order for teacher candidates to challenge existing assumptions. Teacher candidates' filters are critical. The identical materials and lessons will impact students' learning differently depending on the teacher candidates' perceptions. Teacher candidates must first be brought to the awareness that they are in a "box" and then helped to move outside of it.

The first day of class, an instructor can help teacher candidates identify their filters by modeling self-reflection. The instructor begins by identifying his or her own filters based on background and perceptions of the world. The instructor asks teacher candidates to jot down indicators or terms which best describe who they are. Teacher candidates should be assured this exercise is for their benefit, and responses will not be collected or reviewed. Allow a few minutes for teacher candidates to write their thoughts. Most frequently, after describing their gender and race, teacher candidate resort to a description of roles: mother, daughter, and friend. The instructor then demonstrates on a board those filters that guide his or her own behaviors and thinking (i.e. white, Catholic, Irish, liberal democrat, middle-class, monolingual, visually-impaired, woman, feminist). Until this time teacher candidates may not have considered these filters as influencing their roles as teachers. For example, teacher candidates who are white and middle class will begin to examine how the course of their life has been different from, and perhaps more privileged than others.

With the increasing numbers of children who hold non-Christian beliefs, another example is the influence of a religious filter. Byrnes and Kiger (1992) refer to religion as the "hidden bias." This religious introspection may be particularly difficult for some regions of the country than others but it is important for teacher candidates to realize they are not being forced to change their personal filters but to understand that, because others (students in their classrooms) think differently, different expectations for behavior can be expected.

Through the semester, the teacher educator will identify how personal filters that may influence particular classroom practice.

Another strategy used effectively to provoke discussion and reflection on personal beliefs is to read *The Giver* by Lois Lowry (1992). The single direction to be provided before reading the book is for the teacher educator to ask teacher candidates to draw analogies between the community in the book and public school practice. Typically, teacher candidates demonstrate frustration during the first chapters because the context of the story is unclear. Further frustration arises when the instructor does not provide interpretation. This is an opportunity for university class members to begin to discuss issues, share voice and build community. To read this book aloud takes time from traditional university instruction. However, the benefits to individual class members is invaluable.

In order for teacher candidates to deal with their misconceptions, assumptions and prejudices, Goodwin (1994) suggests providing opportunities to make beliefs about multicultural education more explicit. Findings indicate that white men and women tend to believe that racism is synonymous with personal prejudice. Since they do not personally "feel prejudiced," they consider racism someone else's predicament (Lawrence, 1997, p.108). While there is an emotional component to prejudice, stereotypic thinking is based on a lack of incorrect facts (Cushner and Brislin, 1996).

The Value of the Other Person and Their Ideas

In his 1859 essay, *On Liberty*, John Stuart Mill (1975) poses four reasons why we need to value opinions, even those that are patently false and wrong. These same principles apply to all human interactions, not just dealing with ideas and opinions, but in all of our interactions. These four principles can be summed up as follows:

1. The other idea may, in fact, be right.
2. Even if the idea is wrong, it may contain either an element of truth, or it may help us discover the truth.

If we hold an idea, but don't know the basis for that belief, then we, in fact, are holding on to a prejudice.

Ideas need to be challenged in order to strengthen them.

Mill is specifically talking about the need to not suppress ideas and opinions, even those with which we disagree. The same principles can be applied to our dealing with the multicultural classroom. For example, you have a Bulgarian child in your classroom. You ask if he brought his book to class. He shakes his head from side to side, but you see the book on the desk. You ask again. Again, he shakes his head. There is obviously something wrong here. The book is in plain sight, but the child is telling you "no." Or is he?

In Bulgaria, moving the head from side to side indicates "yes," and nodding up and down indicates "no." This is just the opposite of the "correct" response in the Untied States. So, the child's gesture is, in fact, correct! Here is a prime "teachable moment" for both teacher and child. To be sure, the child will have to learn the "correct" meaning of nodding and shaking. Effective communication and teaching is based on the shared meanings of symbols. We can't have everyone making up his or her own meanings. There have to be standards. Otherwise, we have anarchy. So, if we tell the child the back-and-forth gesture is "wrong," we are, by Mill's parlance, suppressing the truth. The gesture is neither right nor wrong. It is just different. For the classroom teacher this also means allowing time for the student to learn what the communication patterns are.

Mill's second point was that if we suppress an idea, then we may, in fact, be suppressing the truth, or we may be stifling our ability to find the truth. How many teachers do you think are willing to send their older children to a Nazi, Ku Klux Klan or anti-holocaust web site? My guess is, not many. One of the problems we have with these kinds of web sites and this kind of information is that we are afraid of it for the simple reason that "they" know their material better than we know ours. We "know" the StormFront white supremacist site is wrong, but can we prove it without resorting to the irresolute "well, everyone knows" argument? "Everyone knows" is not evidence, and, as will be argued shortly, is just as much of a prejudice as the perspectives we avoid.

These kinds of web sites can, in fact, actually help us discover the truth if we find evidence to disprove them. For example, there are several convincing web sites that contend the Apollo moon landings are faked. The evidence is compelling, and uses an array of scientific facts and arguments. Can *you* prove they are wrong? Well, you may not be a space scientist, but you can use these sites as a springboard for discussing the nature of evidence and logic. You can then visit sites that specifically address the issues they bring to light. This method uses something that is wrong to make a case for what is right.

Of particular concern is the question, "In our quest for acceptance of others and their beliefs, what do we do with those whose values are contrary to our own?" If we accept other people and respect their beliefs, what do we do about parents and students whose value system stresses the subservience of women? In our culture, these ideas are not acceptable, but they do give us an opportunity to explore other value systems.

A related issue Mill proposes is that we listen to the "other side" in order to better understand what we ourselves believe. By way of example, we may define a prejudice as a belief we hold without just grounds or before having sufficient evidence. Now, we do not like to think we are prejudiced, but do we have a rational basis for all the things we believe? Can we explain *why* we should or should not behave in certain ways? Remember, the answer cannot be "just because" or "everyone knows." Finding a rational basis can strengthen our own beliefs and make it easier to argue against beliefs and values that are inimical to the multicultural classroom.

Finally, Mill argues that by challenging beliefs we strengthen them. We need to periodically step back and say, "*Why* is that a good idea?" Such introspection can be painful, but it is essential to effective teaching, particularly in the multicultural classroom. For example, why should we favor inclusion? Is there any real evidence that it works? What is the opposing evidence, and what if it is right?

A strategy educators in any college department can use makes the point that we need to understand why we believe what we believe and how to strengthen those beliefs. On the first day of class, the instructor asks students to complete a short assignment to be turned in by the next class period. The assignment is to think of a current issue in the educational community (i.e. inclusion, vouchers, school uniforms, prayer in school, teaching diversity, etc.). The assignment is to write two to three paragraphs explaining what the teacher candidate thinks about the issue they choose. This short paper has to take a stand on an issue and should include the statement, "I believe ____ because . . .." The assignment is due the next class period.

Many students will assume this assignment is a precursor to a term paper and will select something they *really* believe in, thinking this will be an easy subject about which to write.

The next class period, the teacher educator collects the papers, then announces, "Here is your term paper topic: I want you to take the *opposite* position from what you have written, and prove it. Find evidence to support the opposite of what you believe. The first fifteen pages should support this position. In the last five pages, you can provide evidence for what you really believe if your evidence directly refutes the opposition." After the moaning and complaining has died down, the teacher educator explains that anyone can blindly argue what they believe, but, too often, these beliefs have no rational basis. They are mere prejudices because the students don't know *why* they believe what they believe. Taking the opposite stand will compel the student to examine other evidence and force them into a period of self-reflection. And after all, isn't that what education is supposed to be all about?

Another, similar exercise, involves using the World Wide Web. In case you have never seen one (afraid to look, perhaps?), here are a few anti-holocaust and white supremacist sites.

- http://www.codoh.com/ads/adschallenge.html (A Revisionist Challenge to the U.S. Holocaust Memorial Museum)
- http://www.lebensraum.org/index.html (A general list of anti-holocaust sites)
- http://www.stormfront.org/ (White Nationalist Resource Page)
- http://kids.stormfront.org/ (Stormfront for Kids)

Here is the classroom assignment: assume one of your students comes across one of these pages and asks you what it is about. Without using the phrases "Everyone knows they are wrong," or "Those aren't very nice people," answer these two questions from your student: "How do you know they are wrong," and "What if they are right?"

Mill would urge you, rather than ignore wrong ideas, to find relevant evidence (can you find the Southern Poverty Law Center site?) to refute them. And remember, the people who run these sites (and innumerable others) already know what you are going to say, and they already have answers to refute your arguments. For example, the anti-holocaust sites already have a reply to your statement, "There are photographs of the concentration camp ovens."

Remember, reflection does not mean just spending time congratulating yourself on your correct point of views. It also means being able to refute wrong ideas. And to do that you have to reflect on what "they" are saying and doing.

Conclusion

Teacher educators must also take time for self-reflection. In doing so, we consider the purposes for which public schools were originally created. The role multicultural education plays in this pursuit may alter the direction of teacher education. Literature is complete with recommendations for public school reform. However, before changes can occur with classroom teachers and children, teacher education must take a different approach. Teaching methods are important with respect to ensuring professional development, but methods implemented without cognitive and affective reflection are not capable of individualizing classroom practice. That is, until teacher candidates are challenged to be critical about themselves and their practices, classroom scholarship is not possible without equity and justice. We begin with teacher candidates developing a sense of their place in a pluralistic nation. Once accomplished, their role as future classroom teachers to insure democracy will come as a consequence of their *membership* in a democracy.

34

REFERENCES

Barry, N. H., & Lechner, J. V. (1995). Preservice teachers' attitudes about and awareness of multicultural teaching and learning. *Teaching and Teacher Education*, 11(2), 149-161.

Byrnes, D. & Kiger, G. (1992). *Common Bonds*. Wheaton: Association for Childhood Education International.

Campbell, D. (1996). *Choosing democracy: A practical guide to multicultural education*. Englewood Cliffs: Prentice-Hall.

Center for Educational Statistics (2001), "Digest of Educational Statistics," http:/nces.ed.gov/pubsearch/pubsinfo.asp?pubid=2001034.

Clark, L. DeWolf, S. & Clark, C. (1992). Teaching teachers to avoid having culturally assaultive classrooms. *Young Children, 47*(5), 4-9.

Cushner, K. and Brislin, R. (1996) Intercultural Interactions: A Practical Guide, 2nd., Thousand Oaks, Calif.: Sage Publications.

Delaney-Barmann, G. and Minner, S. (1997). Development and implementation of a program of study prepares teachers for diversity. *Equity and Excellence in Education, 30*(2), 78-85.

Derman-Sparks, L. (1989). Anti-Bias Curriculum: Tools for Empowering Young Children. Washington, D.C.: National Association for the Education of Young Children.

Goodwin, A. L. (1994, March-April). Making the transition from self to other: What do preservice teachers really think about multicultural education? *Journal of Teacher Education, 45*(2), 119-131.

Larkin, J. M. & Sleeter, C. E. (1995). *Developing multicultural teacher education curricula.* New York: SUNY Press.

Lawrence, S. (1997). Beyond race awareness: white racial identity and multicultural teaching *Journal of Teacher Education, 48* (2), 108-117.

Lowry, L. (1992). *The Giver.* New York: Dell Books.

MccCall, A. L. (1995). Constructing conceptions of multicultural teaching: Preservice teachers' life experiences and teacher education. *Journal of Teacher Education, 46* (5), 340-350.

McCall, A. L. and Andringa, A. A. (1997). Learning to teach for justice and equality in a multicultural social reconstructionist teacher education course. *Action in Teacher Education, 18*(4), 57-67.

McDiarmid, G. W. (1992, March-April). What to do about differences: A study of multicultural education for teacher trainees in the Los Angeles United school district. *Journal of Teacher Education, 43* (2), 83-93.

Mill, John Stuart (1975) *On Liberty.* New York: Norton.

Nel, J. (1992, Fall). The empowerment of minority students: Implication of Cummins model for teacher education. *Action In Teacher Education, 14* (3), 38-45.

Neuharth-Pritchett, Reiff and Pearson (2001) Through the eyes of pre-service teachers: Implications for the multicultural journey from teacher education, *Journal of Research in Childhood Education* (in press).

Pajares, F. (1993). Preservice teachers' beliefs: A focus for teacher education. *Action In Teacher Education, 15*, 45-54.

Perez, S. A. (1994). Responding differently to diversity. *Childhood Education, 70* (3), 151-153.

Zeichner, K. (1991). Contradictions and Tensions in the Professionalization of Teaching and the democratization of schools. *Teachers College Record, 92* (3), 363-379.

The Perfect Teacher

Author Unknown

I imagine that all of us building-level administrators often wonder what our schools would be like if we had so-called "master teachers" in every classroom. It starts you thinking about the traits and teaching styles that make some teachers stand out. You begin to conjure up an image of a perfect teacher.

I believe I've had the opportunity, in 22 years as a teacher and administrator, to have worked with a few people who would fit my image of the perfect teacher. What impressed me most about them was that they lived to teach. Their lives were built around finding ways to do a better job of teaching the children assigned to them.

They spent their summers pursuing academic studies or attending workshops to improve themselves, and by reading or creating educational materials that would make their classroom instruction more effective.

These teachers had a penchant for creativity, demanding much from themselves and from their students. Every moment of their time in the classroom seemed to involve some worthwhile activity demanding constant on-task performance by students.

I vividly recall one such teacher. Her classroom always held a few surprises both for the principal and the students, changes designed to transform the classroom atmosphere and to stimulate learning. Before classes began each morning, the teacher worked with small groups of students who needed extra help. Yet everything was ready so that learning began without a moment of wasted time once the bell rang.

Even while standing in a cafeteria lunch line, this teacher would read a story to some of her students, or reinforce skills being taught that day.

The perfect teacher is the one that parents talk about when they report "the children don't want to stay home even on days when they are ill." This is the teacher who maintains a constant dialogue with parents through notes, phone calls, and conferences.

The perfect teacher is likely to write a letter to the parents of every student at the beginning of the school year, introducing himself or herself and providing a home phone number that can be used as an alternative to the normal procedure of leaving a message at the school office.

The perfect teacher strives to be an equal partner with the parent and child in the educational process. The parents are always viewed as a positive element in a child's learning process and the teacher tries to involve them in school activities whenever possible.

The perfect teacher is always very positive. Teaching, to such a person, is a mission based on the belief that every child can and will learn. The teacher provides individual students with the opportunity to learn by the use of a wide variety of learning materials and teaching styles. In fact, the perfect teacher demands that students learn. They will not be emotionally satisfied until there is measurable progress demonstrated by every child.

Chapter 4

Before We Enter The Classroom: What Do We Believe?

Tony J. Manson, Ph.D.

Middle Tennessee State University

Murfreesboro, TN

Introduction

This chapter takes a look at the extent and impact of various social, cultural and ethnic differences on the perceived cognitive abilities of the school-aged child. This chapter will also look at the beliefs that teachers and student teachers hold before they enter the classroom. It also looks at the power that these beliefs have on the teacher's ability to teach children of diverse cultural, social and ethnic backgrounds. It also considers the options that are available for teaching students of varying backgrounds and how to implement them.

Numbers

In 1987, the number of teachers of color decreased as the number of students of color increased (Perkins, as cited in Kailan, 1994, p. 170). This trend is expected to continue until the percentage of African American teachers drops to as low as 5 percent by this year (2000) (Perkins, as cited in Kailan, 1994, p. 170). This has brought about an increase focus on preparing teachers to teach a student body with diversity in their background (Banks, as cited in Tatto, 1996, p. 155; Zeichner, as cited in Tatto, 1996, p. 155). To further complicate the situation, Perkins (as cited in Kailan, 1994, p. 170) found that white candidates showed no desire to teach in the inner city schools, where the vast majority of the minority students are to be found. There are many teachers teaching students from cultures and backgrounds different from their own, the effect that their prior beliefs have on the students they teach is important (Kailan, 1994, p. 170). The beliefs that are being passed down from the educators of student teachers are also important.

Currently, many educators are beginning to introduce multiculturalism into their school systems. Some schools system are changing their curriculums to meet the backgrounds of their students, and they want to expose teachers to the variety of cultures that they are teaching. However, the result is actually that teachers end up separating themselves more from their students. As this happens, teachers are unable to relate to their students. They are unable to speak a language that students understand. Furthermore, the differences in culture are seen as problems. The focus in turn is on the differences between educators and students instead of the similarities. Teachers are not being taught to relate to students in any way. In fact, they are being taught to treat students differently. What then happens is that students are seen to have different learning abilities because of their backgrounds, and expectations for their success are dropped, substantially.

Thoughts

A teacher may have preconceived notions of a child's ability to learn and behave on his/her own experience or lack of experience with people who share a common background (Cabello & Burstein, 1995, p. 285). Since people tend to believe their cultural norms and beliefs it's usually very difficult. Naturally, the student is not prepared to follow rules that she has never been taught; the student is seen as being wrong. In many cases, the student's bad behavior is ignored because of a false belief that it is normal for someone of his/her background. When things get too far out of hand, the student is blamed and then removed from the classroom. He no longer has the educational opportunity he needs to change from a lower-income bracket. In many cases, the student may well find that behavior or beliefs that are acceptable at home may not be acceptable in the school (Cuban, Payne, Patton, Kauffman, Brown, &Payne, as cited in Cabello & Burstein, 1995, p. 286).

These misplaced beliefs are not necessarily confined to teachers of a different ethnic background than that of their students (Cabello & Burstein, 1995, pp. 288-89). For example, in a study that followed the effects of a teaching program on student teachers, an African American teacher clearly had misplaced beliefs concerning her students. She had grown up in the same neighborhood as her students and had gone to the same school that she was teaching. Therefore, she believed that she would be able to understand and react to their behavior in school. Yet, very early in the study, she realized that this was not the case at all. While she often felt sympathy for the students, she had a hard time understanding much of the behavior that they were exhibiting. She realized that the neighborhood has changed, and, as drugs had entered the community, her students were experiencing problems and emotions that she never had to face when she was growing up. The result was that she has a class in which children were hitting one another, and she had to take care of a variety of discipline problems. She grew frustrated by the differences between her and her students and looked to an outside source to blame for her inability to reach these students.

When teachers make assumptions about how teachers are supposed to teach and students are supposed to learn, using the differences in students to a positive end is difficult (Tatto, 1996, p. 156). In fact, such teachers very often use the difference to justify a student's poor performance in school. Harold Kelly's work (as cited in Tatto, 1996, pp. 170-71) shows that teachers tend to attribute a student's success to inward qualities such as ability or enthusiasm. On the other hand, he also shows that perceived failure tends to be attributed to outward factors such as the student's home life or poor teaching. This attribution tends to send a message to the student that he/she can blame outside forces for his/her lack of success. In this way, the student transfers low expectations by a teacher to their own expectations. As the expectations decrease, performance naturally also decreases.

Throughout the decades, many have complained that white teachers have stereotyped children of color and have not given them the same attention that they have given to their white counterparts (Clarke, as cited in Kailan, 1996, pp. 170-71) .In many cases, this lack of attention has resulted in low test results, with students fighting and winding up in prison. This stereotyping has been brought on by false beliefs about the students, and these beliefs tend to be self-perpetuating.

Solutions?

So what is the solution? There are many differing answers to this question. Some believe that good teaching practices can teach anyone (Grant and Sleeter, as cited in Kailan, 1996, pp. 170-71). Others (Nieto, as cited in Kailan, 1996, pp. 170-71) suggest that teaching should emphasize the various backgrounds and cultures of the students. Collier (as cited in Cabello & Burstein, 1995, p. 285) suggests that the student should be looked at as a whole individual and that her needs and skills should all be taken into consideration as a plan is made to educate her. This plan takes into account the fact that the main difference between people is how they are treated (Kailin, 1996 p. 169). Teachers often assume that students have only one way of learning, and therefore only one way of teaching is needed. The traditional method of teaching is for the teacher to give the student the information that he has, with the student absorbing it in a uniform way. In this manner, a teacher assumes that a student who does not succeed in picking up the knowledge has a learning problem. Outside sources are looked at to determine the problem (Prawat, as cited in Tat to, 1996, p. 156). Since teachers are still treating students differently based on preconceived beliefs.

So what should be done to change this? The first thing to do is look at what the beliefs of the teachers are toward their students and where these beliefs originate. Beliefs tend to grow out of a person's experience, background, culture and even social standing. Since experience is an extremely powerful teacher, changing these beliefs is often extremely difficult (Pajares, as cited in Cabello & Burstein, 1995, p. 286). Students tend to reject information that does not coincide with their already existing beliefs. The only way they would consider changing those beliefs was after long sessions of attempts to convince them, and that was only as a last resort. Therefore, the effort to change the beliefs that teachers have as they enter the classroom is not an easy one. The belief system has been in place for a long time and is difficult to replace. However, the teacher must make changes in beliefs and images about teaching in order to grow (Kagan, as cited in Cabello & Burstein, 1995, p. 286). *Since* the conditions in which they are teaching continue to change, they must be able to change with them. Kagan (as cited in Cabello & Burstein, 1995, p. 286) insists that the teacher do constant fieldwork. Since experience is what created the beliefs, experience will change the belief. This should be done over a long period so that teachers can have enough time to assimilate the information and work it into their belief system. Many teacher education programs are created with this goal. Yet fieldwork alone will not change the belief system of a teacher (Bondy, Schmitz & Johnson, 1996, p. 62). Course work must also go with the experience in the field, or the teacher is more than likely to have an extremely negative experience.

A Teachers (Justine) View

Teachers should look at their personal beliefs in a very analytical way. One way this is done is through testing (Tat to, 1996, p. 167). In this way, the teacher educator can look at the beliefs that a student teacher brings into the classroom. This is a way to gauge the expectations that a teacher would have of a student who is thought to be a slow learner, and it also gives a good idea of how teachers would handle the situation. For example, in the preparation program (Cabello & Burstein, 1995, p. 289), Justine, a first-year Euro-American third grade teacher is asked about her first thoughts about working in an inner city school. She says that the teaching conditions are bad, and she seems to attribute the deficiencies of the children to this problem. On the other hand, she also takes responsibility for the welfare of the children and sticks to the belief that all children can be taught.

The student then participates in a program that believes that teachers must be able to draw on their knowledge of an individual student's needs in order to teach them (Kennedy, as cited in Cabello & Burstein, 1995, p. 287). Thus, the teacher needs sensitivity to the cultural, economic and social background of the student. As she takes this course, she is exposed to cultural differences, out of which she is able to acquire new techniques for her teaching lessons. She brings these new techniques to class as she learns them and gets to look at the results. The program takes two years to complete, thus providing time for the student to digest the material and change the previous belief system.

Justine reports that she is making her teaching techniques more flexible. The basic technique stays the same, but she is able to adjust it to meet the needs of her students. Although Justine does not see the change in herself, she has started to refer to the environmental problems that her students have as being differences. This kind of change occurred because of the positive results that she got from trying out new teaching techniques. When a person is getting positive results, she no longer needs to look for a source of blame. Thus, the solution for teaching a classroom of students of diverse backgrounds is in the school system itself. When Paula reported the success of one of her students, it occurred from a change that took place within her (Cabello & Burstein, 1995, p. 289). No change was reported in the child's family life. Drugs were still a part of society. She had allowed him to stay in at recess, and this gave him a chance to open up to her. She had maintained a positive attitude, and the little boy's attitude changed along with hers. She re-enforced his positive behavior.

As she did this, he began to feel good about himself, and that created room for change to take place. Programs such as these should include the development of opportunities within them (Tatto, 1996, p. 176). Dialogue among the teachers is needed so that they can relate their experiences with one another. They must be coherent. The structure must be strong in terms of follow-up and mentoring by experienced teachers to the novice. In this way, new teachers have an opportunity to learn how to teach students in any situation.

Contradictions (Conclusion)

The problem with this study is that it is inherently contradictory (Kailan, 1996, p. 182) Teaching that is anti- racist in a society that continues to have a race that dominates another is not possible. Like school integration, many of these efforts are attempts by a dominant race to appease the minority. However, much good can still come from these suggestions. The effort to put forth a program that can educate students at all levels can only be looked at in a positive light. In this sense, the issue of racism has been side stepped so that students of all races might have equal opportunity for success through education. Although the issues of racism clearly exist, these programs allow students to get an education that is not so strongly hindered by racism. In this way, the minority has the potential to combat the oppression of racism and go on to greater success.

REFERENCES

Bondy, E., Schmitz, S., & Johnson, M. (1993, Summer) .The impact of coursework and fieldwork on student teachers' reported beliefs about teaching poor and minority students. Action in Teacher Education, 55-62.

Cabello, B. & Burstein, N. D. (1995, September-October). Examining teachers' beliefs about teaching in culturally diverse classrooms. Journal of Teacher Education, 285-294.

Kailan, J. (1994, March). Anti-racist staff development for teachers: Considerations of race, class and gender. Teaching & Teacher Education 169-184.

Tatto, M. T. (1996, Summer). Examining values and beliefs about teaching diverse students: Understanding the challenges for teacher education. Educational Evaluation and Policy - Analysis, 155-180.

Chapter 5

The Teacher Education Program - Is There A Vision And Can They Accomplish It For Minorities?

Tony J. Manson, Ph. D.
Middle Tennessee State University
Bonita Manson, Ph. D.
Middle Tennessee State University

Introduction

The profession of teaching is faced with a crisis. Teacher educators must make an attempt to convince the American public that teacher education is necessary to the future of public education. The critics believe that teaching is not a profession. Some believe there is no mystique, body of knowledge, skills or professional values needed to make teaching effective, especially in the urban setting. The teacher education curriculum is not analogous to other professions that may be more exact and measurable. Teacher educators are unable to demonstrate any differences between graduates of teacher education programs and those of liberal arts.

Historically, teacher preparation institutions have trained educators to work effectively with only one group, the middle-class Anglo Americans. However, education has changed drastically. It is necessary for the teacher education programs to train perspective teachers for diversity. Diversity has been defined in many different ways depending upon what region of the country you are located. Too few teacher education programs have incorporated positive attitudes toward other cultures or ethnicity/race in their pre-service and in-service teacher training. Not even the recent violent outbreaks in our schools, have given the programs a different focus. The argument would be that the school violence has not been racial nature. It is not known yet that if a minority teachers presence could have change the outcomes, but we should agree that the students viewed themselves as being different from everyone else.

Preparation

The preparation of teachers usually consists of three major components: (1) liberal (or general) education, (2) specialized subject-field education, and (3) professional education. A liberal arts program combines the arts and sciences and seeks to give the perspective teacher a board cultural background. The specialized subject-field comprises a cluster of courses in a specific subject area and provides the perspective teacher with an extensive preparation in their chosen teaching field. Professional education consists of courses designed to provide knowledge and skills regarding the arts and science of teaching. It is important that perspective teachers explore what teachers do in the classroom. Teachers have to be able to teach, manage their classrooms daily. Teaching involves a complex series of acts. Teaching must fit the learner, the subject content, and the knowledge or the skill being taught. The behavior of one teacher can seldom be transferred. A technique or an approach that works for one teacher may not be effective for another.

Previously teaching was thought of as an art, but more recently it has moved in the direction of becoming a science due to the advances of research. There are a number of discernible things a teacher should have knowledge of to be successful. Over the years, I have been able to mentor new and student teachers who want to make a difference, but do not know how.

It is believed there are nine basic functions that teachers should be required to do. They are as follows:

1. The management of instruction

2. The management of student behavior

3. Instructional presentation

4. Instructional monitoring of student performance

5. Instructional feedback

6. Facilitating instruction

7. Communicating within the educational environment

8. Having a firm knowledge of culture and diversity

9. Performing non-instructional duties

These basic functions provide an overview of the major sets of knowledge and skills persons planning to become a teacher should learn, practice and be able to perfect in order to become successful in teaching.

The teacher education programs at institutions of higher learning have on the most part tried to fulfill the needs of both school districts and even more importantly the perspective teachers. Yet, there are not enough teachers to meet the needs of the districts. New graduates who endure the rigors of the teacher education programs are often unprepared for what schools need. Perspective teachers know subject matter, but most know nothing about working with diversity and classroom management. Now there could a greater need to fill for our schools that even our teacher educators cannot remedy.

Universities should institute field experience early in the teacher education program. This will give perspective teacher an opportunity to redirect their studies if teaching does not suit their needs. In fact, a small number of universities that have a similar program did have some perspective teacher to change their area of study. Teachers need to be dedicated to the field of teaching, but at the moment dedication may not be enough to rally the unsure. The recent school violence has put into question everything aspect of teaching as career.

Minorities and Urban Teaching

The teaching profession has changed, perhaps not as quick as our society or demographics. The demographic change has created a student with a very different family background. The students we face today come from a broader diverse background with many cultural differences. There is a growing need for the teacher education programs to attract the minority ethnic and racial groups into the teaching profession, which could target urban areas. Students need to be able to identify with persons that look like them which may be a reason why there are not many minority teacher educators seen by students that may become perspective teachers.

There is extensive research on how students learn. Teachers who believe that the way to deal with culture or diversity/race is to individualize learning tasks are unlikely to create opportunities for pupils to learn from one another. They sometimes view those who beliefs are different from their own as being inadequate teachers and educators. There is a continued outcry for minority teachers, but the minority population who attend our colleges and universities are continually not going into the teaching profession.

Could the reason be, what students see when they look at education as a profession?

A teacher education program should do everything possible for students to experience early teacher-student interaction in the classrooms (even confrontational ones). The program should recruit and retain as many minorities as possible. Even though very little can be done regarding salaries or teaching conditions, the programs can sale teaching to the nations outstanding high school students. Minorities on the teaching faculty can greatly help the teacher education program. Minority students need to see persons like themselves as role models. These students who believe they can be successful, will be attracted to the teaching profession. They can become what might be needed to reshape the next generation of learners. The visibility of the minority educator can encourage retention among minority students. Experienced teacher at school sites can help sale their student on the teaching profession and show them how new creative ideas are needed for the future.

Teachers need to be better educated and prepared for the challenges they will face in our schools now and in the future. Of course, the recent school violence events do not help. The teaching profession must meet all of the challenges ahead. The vision of a teacher education program has to approach these concerns with enthusiasm and vigor.

52

REFERENCES

Ashton, P. & Webb, R. (1986). Making a difference: Teacher's sense of efficacy and student achievment. New York: Longman.

Good, T. L. & Brophy, J. E. (1994). Looking into classrooms (6th ed.). New York: Harper Collins.

Manson, T. J. (1998). Cross-ethnic, cross-racial dynamics of instruction. (Eric Document Reproduction Service No. ED 429141)

Morrison, G. (2000). Teaching in America (2nd ed.). Needham, Heights, MA: Allyn and Bacon.

National Council for Accreditation for Teacher Education. (1995). A vision of the future: The new professional teacher project. (Brochure.) Washington, DC: Morrison, George

Zehm, S. J. & Kottler, J. A. (1993). On being a teacher: The human dimensions (pp. 5-15). Newbury Park, CA: Corwin Press.

Chapter 6

Teacher Education Preparation for Diversity

Tony J. Manson, Ph. D., Assistant Professor

Middle Tennessee State University

Introduction

Teacher education faces a crisis of confidence today. Unless teacher educators can convince the public that professional teacher education is necessary to the future of public education. Critics of teacher education do not hesitate to assert that teaching is not a profession. The critics claim there is no mystique, no body of knowledge, skills and professional values necessary to effective teaching on which teacher education curriculum may be based. A curriculum that would be analogous to those which characterizes medicine, law, and other learned professions is strongly desired. Teacher educators today are powerless to refute this charge, are unable to demonstrate any differences between graduates of teacher education programs and liberal arts programs. Teacher education programs have become an issue of multicultural education through the need for diversity in not only the teacher education program, but in the classroom.

Teacher Preparation

Historically, teacher education institutions have trained educators to work effectively with only one group: middle-class Anglo Americans. Teachers are products of an ethnocentric curriculum (Banks, 1987) that does not prepare them to deal with students who may come not only from different social, economic, linguistic, and cultural backgrounds, but also from urban and rural cultures. Teacher education programs also have tried to help pre-service as well as in-service teachers to develop positive attitudes toward their own culture and the culture of others. "Such cultural consciousness helps teachers to value their culture without seeing it as normative, and to respect a variety of cultural experiences" (Adams, Pardo, and Schniedewind, 1992, p. 37). Effective teacher/school research has indicated that teacher/administrators who are successful with minority students possess high levels of sensitivity to the needs of those students (Brookover, Lezotte, 1977; Brookover et al., 1981). These teacher/administrators also possess the necessary cultural awareness knowledge to produce high-achieving minority students. Therefore, educators must be trained, to understand, individual differences, and build upon those differences to create a learning environment that is effective for all students, regardless of ethnic or racial identity. The philosophical concepts of multicultural education must be integrated into the total teacher education program in order to prepare all educators work effectively with students who are ethnically and racially different (Larke, 1990).

The preparation of teachers usually consists of three major components: (1) liberal (or general) education, (2) specialized subject-field education, and (3) professional education. A liberal arts program combines the arts and sciences and seeks to give the perspective teacher a board cultural background. The specialized subject-field comprises a cluster of courses in a specific subject area and provides the perspective teacher with an extensive preparation in their chosen teaching field. Professional education consists of courses designed to provide knowledge and skills regarding the arts and science of teaching.

It is important that prospective teachers explore what teachers do in the classroom. Teachers have to be able to not only teach, but be able to daily manage their classrooms. Teaching involves a complex series of acts. Teaching must fit the learner, the subject content, and the knowledge or the skill being taught. The behavior of one teacher can seldom be transferred. A technique or an approach that works for one teacher may not be effective for another.

Previously teaching was thought of as an art, but more recently it has moved in the direction of becoming a science due to the advances of research. There are a number of discernible things a teacher should have knowledge of to be successful.

It has been stated previously in the previous chapter that it is believed there are nine basic functions that teachers should be required to do. They are as follows:

1. The management of instruction
2. The management of student behavior
3. Instructional presentation
4. Instructional monitoring of student performance
5. Instructional feedback
6. Facilitating instruction
7. Communicating within the educational environment
8. Having a firm knowledge of culture and diversity
9. Performing non-instructional duties

These basic functions provide an overview of the major sets of knowledge and skills persons planning to become a teacher should learn, practice and be able to perfect in order to become successful in teaching. The teacher education programs at institutions of higher learning have on the most part tried to fulfill the needs of both school districts and even more importantly the prospective teachers. Yet, there are not enough teachers to meet the needs of the districts. New graduates who endure the rigors of the teacher education are often unprepared for what schools need. Prospective teachers know subject matter, but most know nothing about working with diversity and classroom management

Universities should institute field experience early in the teacher education program. This will give prospective teachers an opportunity to redirect their studies if teaching does not suit their needs. In fact, a small number of universities that have a similar program did have some prospective teacher to change their area of study. Teachers need to be dedicated to the field of teaching, but at the moment dedication may not be enough to rally the unsure. The recent school violence has put into question whether students want to pursue careers in teaching.

G. Williamson McDiarmid and Jeremy Price (1990), both of Michigan State University, gave pre- and post-program questionnaires to and interviewed a group of seventeen student teachers. The group was drawn from five Michigan universities. The authors tried to influence the views of the culturally diverse learners both before and after a three-day workshop. The authors implied that multicultural presentations had little effect on prospective teachers' beliefs about the capabilities of learners labeled "high" and "low" ability, about the use of stereotypes in making teaching decisions, or about providing genuinely equal opportunities to learn any given subject matter. The authors suggest that teacher educators may need to rethink both the content and pedagogy of opportunities to learn about teaching socially and culturally diverse learners.

The project was called the Accepting Behaviors for Cultural Diversity for Teachers (ABCD). The purpose of the evaluation was to find out what student teachers who participated in the ABCD training believe about learners, learning, teaching, subject matter, and the content in learning and teaching and how some fundamental beliefs were influenced by the program.

The greatest paradox in looking at the results not only of the ABCD project but more broadly at teacher education is that students are exposed to increasing amounts of information about children who are culturally different from themselves, yet the proportion of those who subsequently recognize and reject stereotypes does not increase and may decrease. Most teacher-education students have not had the opportunity to explore their own beliefs about student differences and the role these play in teaching and learning. More commonly, teacher education students, who are predominately white, may become unsure about how to think about diverse children. On the other hand, they are taught to be suspicious of any generalizations about a group of people. The teacher-education student does encounter materials that in fact make generalizations about normative values, attitudes, and behaviors among different groups.

Research Agenda: Issues for Multicultural Education in Teacher Education

Multicultural Education grew out of the ferment of the civil rights movement of the 1960s. During this decade, African Americans and other minority groups started a quest for their rights that was unprecedented in the United States. The major goal of the civil rights movement of the 1960s was to eliminate discrimination in public accommodations, housing, employment, and education. This was unpleasant for all people no matter what their ethnic or racial group.

The first response of schools and educators to the ethnic and racial movement was hurried. Courses and programs were developed without the thought and careful planning needed to make them educationally sound or to institutionalize them within the educational system.

Changing demographics has made society take notice to the need of a multicultural component for our schools. We now are faced with the challenge of trying to train all teachers to teach students who are Asian, Black, Hispanic, Native American or other ethnic group that shows up at our schools.

There are several obstacles that have been institutionally set up to hinder minorities from entering the teaching field. One such obstacle is testing. Through the constraints of NCATE, our universities are mandated to test. Testing is not the absolute way of choosing future instructional staff, but it places a roadblock between those who would be teachers and the profession. Tests, in many cases act as a deterrent rather than a helping hand. We should be mandated to provide alternative avenues for minorities to enter teaching, and if at all possible, guide students through the process with care. Our teacher education programs must be allowed a degree of flexibility to develop required courses for those minorities who choose to enter the education arena. These courses will give a teacher education student a chance to develop sensitivity to certain problems that may arise throughout his/her teacher education career. These courses should be two separate appropriate multicultural courses provided by a teacher education program. One course can be offered at the undergraduate level, such as, Teaching in a Multicultural Society and another one, Multicultural Programming course at the graduate level. These components should be clinical and theoretical in nature. Colleges of education must be involved in the necessary research and development of multicultural studies to make it work.

There are many multicultural concerns, but the most pressing concerns are those that are in opposition. In the American School Board Journal, Hitz, R. and Schmidt, J. (1996) pointed out three reasons for opposition to Multicultural Education. The first one is that multicultural education has failed to emphasize properly our common American culture. They cite that in educators eagerness to affirm cultural differences, they may have neglected to ask the pluralistic questions about how people are alike and how they can work together cooperatively in a democratic society. The point here that can be expanded over time is the definition and dimension of research in multicultural education. While both qualitative and quantitative data supports and provides greater insight in the academic area, earlier research trials were only profiles.

The second reason for opposition to multicultural education might come from a misunderstanding of the nature of culture itself. The thought here is that our society may be broken in to sub-cultures and these sub-cultures may be inter-related in some way.

The third opposition, the scholars pointed out is that society's tolerance does not extend to some sub-cultures and types of diversity. In fact, they have identified many children as being unacceptable. This researcher believes that the concept of sub-cultures and how educators perceive these cultures is the next phase of multicultural education. Many educators have studied their experiences with minority students. The next phase of research should be the interactions educators have with students of different ethnic and racial backgrounds.

The quest as an educator is to promote a better understanding of multicultural education through our teacher education programs. The researchers believe we can have an appreciation and understanding of our commonalities as well as our differences.

Some researchers would like to heighten the awareness and the appreciation for multicultural education at the school and university levels. There is a new look in the research categories that lend themselves to multicultural educational research but rarely get the attention of educational practitioners:

Historical Research - builds a chronology of persons, groups, or issues not normally studied by traditional researchers in the professional educational research community (Boyer, J.B. and Baptiste, H.P., 1996).

Descriptive Research - defines a reality and offers findings that do not readily lend themselves to quantitative reporting though they may contribute to professional understanding of teaching, learning, or consumer issues (Boyer, J.B. and Baptiste, H.P., 1996).

Creative Research - is the result of compositions in educational theater, music, art, drama, photography, or other areas including poetry (Boyer, J.B. and Baptiste, H.P., 1996).

In the future, multicultural education concerns will include friendly confrontations with assumption that historical, descriptive, or creative research designs have equal merit in attempting to generate new knowledge on which to base professional practice.

According Banks J. (1991), multicultural education is at least three things: an idea or concept, an educational reform movement, and a process. Multicultural education incorporates the idea that all students--regardless of their gender and social class and their ethnic, racial, or cultural characteristics-should have an equal opportunity to learn in school.

Multicultural education should include provisions for the teaching of racial balance and ethnicity, the effects of socioeconomic status, equity among all people, cooperation for the masses, and elimination of racism. Multicultural education absolutely must address the significance of pluralism and group heritages. A culturally diverse population also has diverse learning and communication styles. Therefore, the programs instruction, and /or educators and its educators should be extremely sensitive to population differences. The instructors should be in diverse instructional methods and have knowledge of cultural differences. If multicultural education efforts are to be successful schools should make an attempt to accept the social, cultural; and educational issues need to be addressed. Cultural differences should be viewed as an asset rather than a liability. Also, cultural differences cannot be viewed as problems that are too great to be attended to. Initially, it has been extremely complicated and difficult for schools and other agencies to step forward and begin building the necessary organizational and instructional paradigms for accommodating the demographic changes in the society.

Multicultural issues to be addressed are:

- Acceptance of differences: The theory of the Salad bowl versus the Melting pot.
- Adjustment of learning styles: an environment in which students are taught how to learn and appreciate differences within our society.
- Dismantling racism: Diversity should be guarded as a positive element in society.

These issues lend themselves to possible research questions for educators:

- How can prospective educators examine their own cultural and gender bias before entering the classroom?

- Why is it important for an educator to be extremely sensitive to the differences in learning styles of all people regardless of culture or gender?
- What types of classroom practices can the educator employ that will lead to the elimination or reduction of stereotyping practices?

To implement multicultural education, it is this researchers intent to move into the next and much larger phase Cross-Gender Instruction. This is necessary to inform and try to eliminate gender bias in the classroom. Educators must transform the way they think about the nation's past, present, and future.

Teacher Professionalism

Teachers are going through a transition, which threatens their very existence as professionals. Recent efforts to remedy some of the historical problems are embedded in teacher education via the Holmes Group (The Holmes Group, 1986). This group is made up of approximately 100 deans from colleges of education at research-oriented universities. The Holmes Group's answer is a reform proposal that focuses on the goal of teacher professionalism. In recent time was compared to the view of the Carnegie Task Force. The Carnegie Task Force was a 14-member group consisting of business leaders, governors, chief state school officers, journalists, leaders of teacher unions, and other leaders in the field of education. Their main purpose is to restructure the teaching force into four categories: licensed teachers, certified teachers, advanced certificate holders, and lead teachers. A National Board for Professional Teaching Standards would determine the knowledge and skills essential for teachers at each level and would certify individuals who meet those standards (Carnegie Task Force, 1986). The Holmes Group (1986) argues that teachers need to receive an extensive and intensive professional education much like that accorded medical doctors and lawyers.

The Holmes Group (1986) and the Carnegie Task Force (1986) agree that teacher education needs to be dramatically changed, or restructured. The groups agree that colleges and universities must face the fact that undergraduate majors in the arts and sciences often provide better preparation for graduate study than for teaching in the secondary schools. The groups are troubled by the increasing standards for entry into the teaching profession and they both predict a teacher shortage in the 1990's and extended beyond. The fear is that school districts will respond by hiring warm bodies to watch over students day by day.

The Carnegie Task Force devotes some time in their report towards the special problems of minority students and the desperate need for minority teachers. The Holmes Group (1986) addresses the same issue, but not to any great detail. The Carnegie Task Force (1986) seeks to meet the expected need of approximately 50,000 to 60,000 new minority teachers each year during the 1990's and beyond, but the report does not propose a national plan for recruitment (Carnegie Task Force, 1986). The Holmes Group does plan recruitment of minorities, but they also do not have direct solutions.

The Holmes Group would like it known that the quality of education will not improve unless the quality of the educators' education is improved. They also contend that this task will not be accomplished without changing the universities, the credentialing systems, and the schools themselves. The function of these institutions cannot be independent of each other. The two groups agree that the licensing apparatus and the professional certification must all be changed together so that both documents mean that same thing to everyone.

The main difference in the two groups is what price would be paid for the reform. The Carnegie Task Force says that, "Improving the rate of return on our current investment in education requires additional investment because education is a highly labor intensive enterprise heavily dependent on the quality and performance of the teaching force" (Carnegie Task Force, 1986). The Holmes Group made no calculations concerning cost but committed itself to reform within the state legislative chambers by working for changes in the policies that shape the teaching profession.

The Holmes Group (1986) is more committed to the reform because it is a direct part of the profession. The things they propose are directed to the future professors and educators of teachers. The Holmes Group stated five major goals, which start with the idea of making the education of teachers intellectually sound. Competent teaching is a compound of four kinds of knowledge: 1) a broad general and liberal education, 2) the subject matter of the teaching field, 3) the literature of education, and 4) reflective practical experience. The Holmes Group (1986) sees a mastery of the liberal arts as essential in the preparation of teachers. The second goal of the Holmes Group is to recognize differences in knowledge, skill, and commitment among teachers. The group feels that the commitment among understanding that the rewards and opportunities for professional advancement would increase substantially. The third goal of the group is to create honest standards of entry into the profession of teaching. The Holmes Group (1986) sees that to help create a profession that is representative of the pluralistic society, the main problem is in regard to minority undergraduate enrollments and minority entry into teaching. As a result, the teacher force has been mainly composed of people from the majority background and teaching students who are primarily from minority backgrounds. The fourth goal is to connect schools of education with schools. This theory ties in with the development of teaching strategies for a broad range of children with different backgrounds, abilities, and learning styles. There are some teaching strategies that include teaching across ethnic and racial lines. The fifth goal of the group includes making the schools better places in which teachers can work and learn. The current working conditions of teachers is the division of authority between administrators and teachers. The problem is that the school districts feel that the level of guidance and supervision should be greater at different levels to be true professionals. These goals of the group suggest that the Holmes Group would help to free teachers from subordination within schools and more important, would enable teachers to provide students with the kind of empowered learning that would allow them full participation in a democratic society.

The Holmes Group would like to see a true profession created through its plans. Over a period of years they feel the problems that exist with diversity and other concerns can be addressed. They have increased their membership to span through five regions of the United States. As we worry ourselves with these types of problems, which must be addressed, the issue in which the researcher is proposing still exist and seemingly a more urgent issue than the professionalism problem. The researcher does not wish to diminish the dilemma of the teachers' professional status in the community, but classes are being taught every day and students are in class expecting a quality education as we speak.

California, in contrast to other states, has adopted a testing format to identify prospective teachers. Passage of the California Basic Skills Test (CBEST) and the National Teacher Examination (NTE) are necessary before entering into the teaching profession. California's testing program, like other states has come under harsh criticism. The criticism has come from groups who are concerned about the problems confronting prospective teachers from minority backgrounds. A serious problem is developing with minority students contemplating teaching careers who learn that they are often judged not good enough to teach. Teacher education students lose confidence in their own abilities and conclude that the teaching profession is off-limits to minorities. The state of California insists that all teachers must demonstrate mastery of basic skills in mathematics, reading, and writing. Many argue that the CBEST is culturally biased and heavily directed towards the pupils from middle class homes. The teachers' outlook on how they teach after different types of preparations has a direct bearing on how they perceive students.

What is the Vision for Minorities? Minorities and Teaching

The teaching profession has changed, perhaps not as quickly as our society or demographics. The demographic change has created a student with a very different family background. The students we face today come from a broader diverse background with many cultural differences. There is a growing need for the teacher education programs to attract minority groups into the teaching profession. Students need to be able to identify with persons that look like them which may be a reason why there are not many minority teacher educators seen by students that may become prospective teachers.

There is extensive research on how students learn. Teachers who believe that the way to deal with culture or diversity/race is to individualize learning tasks are unlikely to create opportunities for pupils to learn from one another. Other scholars offend many teacher educators or persons who would like to see someone other than the majority race as teachers and teacher educators. There is a continued outcry for minority teachers, but the minority population who attends our colleges and universities are continually not going into the teaching profession.

Could the reason be, what students see when they look at education as a profession?

A teacher education program should do everything possible for the students to experience early teacher-student interaction in the classroom (even confrontational ones). The program should recruit and retain as many minorities as possible. Even though very little can be done regarding salaries or teaching conditions, the programs can attract outstanding high school students to teaching. Minorities on the teaching faculty can greatly help the teacher education program. Minority students need to see persons like themselves as role models. The top minority students, who believe they can be successful, will be attracted to the teaching profession. They can become the needed images to reshape the next generation of learners. The visibility of the minority educator can encourage retention among minority students. Experienced teachers at school sites can help sell their student on the teaching profession and show them how new creative ideas are needed for the future.

Teachers need to be better educated and prepared for the challenges they will face in our schools now and in the future. Of course, the recent school violence events do not help. The teaching profession must meet all of the challenges ahead. The vision of a teacher education program has to approach these concerns with enthusiasm and vigor.

68

BIBLIOGRAPHY

Adams, B. S., Pardo, W. E., & Schniedewind, N. (1992). Changing the way things are done here. Educational Leadership, 49, 37-43.

Appleton, N. (1988). Cultural pluralism in education: Theoretical foundations. New York: Longham.

Banks, J. A. (1994). Multiethnic education: Theory and practice (3rd ed.) Boston:Allyn and Bacon.

Banks, J. A. (1987). Teaching strategies for ethnic studies (4th ed.). Boston: Allyn and Bacon.

Baptiste, P. H., Baptiste, M. L. (1980). Multicultural teacher education: Preparing educators to provide educational equity. Washington, D. C.: American Association of Colleges for Teacher Education.

Book, C., Byers, J., & Freeman, D. (1983). Student expectations and teacher education traditions with which we can and can not live. Journal of Teacher Education, 34, 9-13.

Boyer, J. B., & Baptiste, H. P. (1996). Transforming the curriculum for multicultural understandings - A practioner's handbook (p. 200). Caddo Gap Press.

Boyer, J. B. (1993). Cross racial instructional dynamics: Instructional interaction. EDCIP- 9 10 Multicultural Programming, (November 4, 1993).

Brookover, W. et al. (1982). Creating effective schools. Homes Beach, FL: Learning Publications.

Brookover, W. & Lezotte, L. (1977). Changes in schools characteristics coincident with changes in student achievement. College of Urban Development of Michigan State University and Michigan Department of Education.

Brown v Board of Education (1), 347, U. S. 483, (1954).

Carnegie Task Force on Teaching as a Profession. (1986). A nation prepared: Teachers for the 21st Century. New York: Carnegie Forum on Education and the Economy.

Ciscell, R. E. (1989). Ready or not: The career perspectives of preservice teachers. Issues in Education, 2, 1, 8-17.

Feiman-Nemser, S. & Buchmann, M. (1986). The pitfalls of experience. In J. D. Raths and L. D. Katz (Eds.). Advances in Research on Teacher Education, 2, 61-74.

Friedrich, G. W. (1978). Effect of teaching behavior on the acquisition of communication competencies. Paper presented at the meeting of the American Educational Research Association, Toronto.

Garcia, R. L. (1982). Teaching in a pluralistic society: Concepts, models strategies. New York: Harper and Row.

Grant, C. A. & Sleeter, C. E. (1989). Turning on learning: Five approaches for multicultural teaching plans for race, class, gender, and disability. Columbus, OH: Merrill.

Green, M. F. (1989). Minorities on campus: A handbook for enhancing diversity. Washington, D. C.: American Council of Education.

Gudykunst, W. B., Ting-Toomey, S., & Wiseman, R. L. (1991). Taming the beast: Designing course in intercultural communication. Communication Education, 40, 271-285.

Hadaway, N. L. & Florez, V. (1988). Diversity in the classroom: Are our teachers prepared? Teacher Education and Practice, 4, 25-30.

Hitz, R. & Schmitz, J. (1996). Three reasons in opposition to multicultural education. American School Board Journal, 6, 34-37.

Kendall, F. E. (1983). Diversity in the classroom: A multicultural approach to the education of young children. New York: Teachers College.

Kleg, M., Ford, S., & Karabinus, R. (1993). Elementary students attitudes and perceptions of select racial, religious, and ethnic groups. The Journal of Social Studies Research, 16-17,2, 31-36.

Larke, P. J. (1990). Cultural diversity awareness inventory: Assessing the sensitivity of pre-service teachers. Action in Teacher Education, 12, 5-11.

Larke, P. J., Wiseman, D., & Bradley, C. (1990). The minority mentorship project: changing the attitudes of pre-service teachers for diverse classrooms. Action in Teacher Education, 12, 5-11.

Lortie, D. (1975). Schoolteacher: A sociological study. Chicago: University of Chicago.

Manson, T.J. (1995). Cross-ethnic, cross-racial dynamics of instruction: Implications for teacher education. Dissertation Abstracts International. (University Microfilms No. 9614276)

McCroskey, J. C. (1992). An introduction to communication in the classroom. Edina, MN: Burgess Publishing Group.

McDiarmid, G. W. (1990). Challenging prospective teachers' beliefs during an early field experience: A quixotic undertaking? Journal of Teacher Education, 41 (3), 12-20.

Pang, V. 0. (1994). Why do we need this class? Teachers. Phi Delta Kappan, 76, (4), 289-292.

Phuntsog, N. (1993). Multicultural teacher education curricula: Educators' perceptions of the importance of a multicultural curriculum in selected elementary teacher preparation programs (Doctoral dissertation, University of Massachusetts, 1993). Dissertation Abstract International, 54(08), 298A.

Richmond, V. P. & Gorman, J. (1988). Language patterns and gender role orientation among students in grades 3-12. Communication Education, 37, 142-149.

The Holmes Group. (1986). Tomorrow's teachers: A report of Holmes group. East Lansing,

Chapter 7

Let's Take A Look At Gender Equity in the Classroom

Bonita Manson, Ph.D.
Middle Tennessee State University

Introduction

Gender equity has become a priority in the school curriculum. One reason is that women have been asked to learn the experience of men and accept them as representative of all human experience. When they are unable to do this (match this masculine knowledge to their own lives), the women not the facts, theories, and curricula have been termed deficient (Kohlberg 1981; Vaillant 1977). The challenge is to change the schools and curricula to reflect the perspectives of all students. This step may help to eliminate bias that might occur when the masculine experience is the standard.

The Past

In the past, women used legislation to help prioritize change. Title IX of the Educational Amendment Act of 1972, the Women's Educational Equity Act in 1975 and the Vocational Amendment Act of 1976 as well as other legislation from 31 states prohibited sex discrimination in primary and secondary school programs receiving federal funds. The legislation precipitated some changes, but researchers such as Myra Sadker (1989), surveyed practitioners' who viewed the educational movement as doing very little to promote educational equity or even close the gender achievement gap. Today, we must teach equity in the classroom. Without equity in schools, students will not experience true educational excellence. The goals of gender equity are:

- To protect students' rights to an equal educational free of discrimination on the basis of sex, marital and/or parental status;

- To help students free themselves from limiting, rigid sex-role stereotypes and sex bias;

- To assist students to explore and participate in a broader range of educational programs and activities leading to higher paying or more satisfying careers;

- To help students understand, think about, and prepare for a future characterized by change, especially in male and female roles, relationships, and in careers.

- To evaluate students personal and social economic changes, by traditional socialization of male and females, or those which affect girls and women disproportionately (Rodenstein, 1990).

Goals

The educator's goal is to make sure that all students have a fair chance to learn and develop as a person. Any practice that discriminates or reinforces competitive individualism must be changed. The female omission from the textbook sends the wrong messages to females. This message is intensified when the teachers do not point out or confront the omission. Furthermore, according to Sadker (1994) when teachers add their stereotypes to the curriculum bias in books, the message becomes even more harmful. Our daughters learn that to be female is to be the absent partner in the development of our nation (Sadker, 1994). An interesting study was conducted in Michigan, with approximately 2,000 students, about what it was like to be male or female at school. The students interviewed felt that girls were treated differently in schools and by high school this number had increased to 76 percent. The question becomes, what can we do to provide equitable education to all students so that they will have a positive experience in school?

The school curriculum can be changed to reflect the needs of all students. It is no longer okay to limit the expectations about abilities, interest, skills and temperament by gender. We can no longer say gender roles are biologically inherited because there is no scientific proof (Klein, 1985). Gender biased thinking that has resulted in the lack of awareness and expectations for women must be counteracted. The goal is for all persons to be independent rather than dependent in their daily lives and to be truly financially self-sufficient. Creating better options, skills, and expectations opens the door to newer better opportunities.

Boys and Girls

Girls start out ahead of boys in speaking, reading and counting. The academic performance is equal to that of boys in math and science in the early grades. However, as the girls progress in school, their achievement in these subjects significantly declines (Sadker, Sadker and Long, 1993). In fact, many girls do not even take courses in math when they reach high school. The gender gap in mathematics performance and attitudes was attributed by several authors to course enrollment in high school (Lindbeck and Dambrot, 1986). Many areas in college require a math background. Thus when females lack mathematical background, they limit their opportunities to participate in areas requiring math in college and later in the job market. A question asked in recent research is, "Why are women less interested in taking mathematics courses, especially at an advanced level?" Several researchers, (Betz, 1978; Fennema, and Sherman, 1977; Gressard and Loyd, 1987; and Lindbeck and Dambrot, 1986) have all suggested that math anxiety is an inhibiting factor in both the participation in and learning of mathematics. Fennema (1980) suggested that the anxiety level along with low self-confidence in math courses is an important factor that explains the sex related differences.

Women have also been deterred from math because it has been stereotyped as a "masculine subject" (Shashaani, 1995). It is this stereotypic view about math and science that parents and teachers support (Shashaani, 1993; Jacobs, 1991). Further research by Sells (1990) found a strong relationship between taking advanced mathematics in high school and the support and encouragement shown by parents, teachers and peers. A model by Eccles and colleagues (1983) was developed to determine academic achievement behavior. According to this model, students' career choice is influence by (1) socio-cultural environment including socialization forces, gender-role beliefs, and cultural norms; and (2) psychological factors such as expectations for success, short and long range goals, subjective task value, and perceptions of task difficulty (Shashaani, 1995). Sometimes females are very successful in math and science courses but they are not provided the same feedback that the males receive. Sadker (1994) concluded that teacher response to the male students in his physics class who had scored less than the three female students on an exam, "Boys, you are failing. These three pretty cookies are out scoring you guys on every test," (Sadker, 1994). Not only did the teacher not compliment the girls, but he did not even address them as females or by their name. Both teachers and parents are influential in encouraging students to take more math or science courses. If encouragement is not given, students tend to not further their studies in this area.

Parents seem to have lower levels of educational expectations for their daughters, especially in the areas of mathematics and science (MacCoby and Jacklin, 1973; Eccles et al., 1983). Yee and Eccles (1988) reported that parents attributed their daughters, math success to effort and their sons' math success to talent. Parents are children's first teacher and their role is very powerful. It is important that they send out positive messages to their children. Children do not need to feel that they are different just because of their gender. Gender bias such as this, discourages girls even though their grades are as high as boys on math tests. Many myths exist between males and females as to which group actually gains the favor of the academic world, but what educators need to do is to examine the areas of specialization that males are in as opposed to those of their female counterparts. Teachers and counselors often advise stereotypical careers to their students. This behavior may result in less potential for females, while offering greater potential for males. The goal is to eliminate roadblocks by providing equity for all. If females choose not to study math or science, they are filtered out of careers that remain overwhelming and solidly male.

Careers

The career connection is also made through sports in high school. Athletics is important in shaping the lives of the male students by providing leadership, self-confidence and courage. Sports are seen as a vehicle for shaping boys into men who will lead society. This same concept should apply to girls. However, girls have been historically barred from sports until recently. Their only experience in sports was in segregated classes with poor equipment and fewer resources. After the passage of Title IX in 1972, female participation in interscholastic sports programs has increased but it still lags behind the male participation.

Teachers need to expand the examples used in the classroom and go beyond the traditional world of males in their discussion. This sometimes can be difficult because attitudes are hard to change. James Banks, (1989) introduced a six-part curriculum of articles that provided future and experienced teachers with knowledge, insight, and understanding needed to work effectively with both male and female students, with exceptional abilities from various social classes, ethnic, religious, and culture groups. James Banks says, "A major assumption is that, substantial reforms must be made in schools to give each student an equal chance to succeed academically" (1989). Teachers also need to provide young women with a curriculum that values them and teaches them about their contributions in history. Through learning all students can draw on the full range of life experiences that both men and women bring to the classroom. Teachers need to acknowledge the relevance of gender equity. Women have their own unique history, training and concerns just as men do.

The American Association of University Women ("How Schools Shortchange Girls", 1992) and Bartholomew and Schnorr ("Gender Equity: Educational Problems and Possibilities for Female Students," 1991) suggest some possible strategies for providing an equitable, gender fair education to all females: (1) mentor programs; (2) non-traditional roles models; (3) curriculum revisions; (4) Curriculum innovation; (5) teacher/counselor training; (6) parental-male peer awareness; (7) mathematics and science course emphasis. Davis, and Nfemiroff (1992) define a gender-fair education as seeking to enable students to develop a critical perspective toward all knowledge, and to empower all students to become equitable and active participants in the critical educational process. Davis and Nemiroff critiques five pedagogical models, such as,

(1) "Talking Head" pedagogy, which' seeks to reproduce the common wisdom of established knowledge;

(2) "Humanistic Education", in which learners and teachers interact to produce knowledge;

(3) "Critical Pedagogy", in which teachers and learners produce knowledge through a collective examination of their socio-economic situations;

(4) "Early Feminist Pedagogy, which emphasizes the collective production of knowledge, focusing on gender and sexism as universals;

(5) "Critical Humanism", which combines the thinking of humanists, critical pedagogues, and feminist educators, and centers the problems of race, social class, ethnicity. These types of strategies would have a major impact in education if totally implemented.

Research

The quality of life of young people is also effected by gender bias as shown in current research on gender differences in date rape, adolescent violence, adolescent suicide, alcohol and drug abuse, eating disorders, childhood sexual assault, sexual abuse and reasons for dropping out of school (Young, 1992). This behavior sends a disturbing message about women and sends a message out that men are eliminated from these social ills. Research on gender and its effect has focused mainly on health concerns, self-concept, achievement and sex roles attitudes and behavior, but very little on the social implications. Administrators and teachers can no longer look the other way if there is a suspicion of sexual harassment. There is very little tolerance for the assumption that "boys will be boys" (Sadker, 1994). Society can no longer encourage aggressive and domineering behavior from males, while asking females to be more accepting of the status quo. Educators need to retrain children against stereotypical roles. The gender difference in classroom communications is more than a mere counting game of who gets the teacher's attention and who doesn't. Teacher attention is a vote of high expectations and commitment to a student. Decades of research show that students who are actively involved in classroom discussion are more likely to achieve and to express positive attitudes toward schools and learning (Flanders, 1970). The account of why women don't respond in class discussions at the college level is that they are afraid. They often attribute their success to external factors such as luck, rather than to internal factors such as ability (Frieze et. al, 1975). There are trends toward a single sex school setting, but trends in recent times suggest coeducation, encouraged by such laws as Title IX. A single sex school setting was thought to be a benefit to the achievement of the female student. There are also thoughts that these types of schools would harbor feelings of self-doubt. Questions about capabilities and intellectual competence would be made more evident in single sex schools. Of course, there are exceptions to some of the feelings held by educators, but it seems the research bear out different feelings. A major, multi-year study of Harvard undergraduates (Light, 1990) supports the claim that women do harbor more self-doubt than men do, despite educational achievement, success, or satisfaction. When the Harvard women experience failure, they were quick to doubt themselves. They attributed their problems to self-limitations and personal inadequacies. In sharp contrast, their male peers put the blame on others or on circumstances. The Harvard study is powerful when we consider that the gender findings were unanticipated. It showed that the Harvard women excelled in academic environments. They were successful in making the grade. They had little experience of academic failure. Yet, these highly selective women still carried doubts and questions about their intellectual capabilities. It is believed from this study that social forces combined to make women doubt themselves. It is also believed that it is easier for women to gain approval and attention for their bodies and physical attributes than for the quality of their minds (Light, 1990). The time has long come to ignore these stereotypes and still remain feminine.

Conclusion

In conclusion, an African proverb says it takes the whole village to educate a child: this includes grandparents and parents, teachers and school administrators, lawmakers and civil leaders. It will take everyone from our American village to join forces; they can transform our educational institutions into the most powerful levers for equity, places where girls are valued as much as boys, daughters are cherished as fully as sons are, and tomorrow's women are prepared to be full partners in all activities of the next century and beyond (Sadker, 1994). Educators and parents can no longer have their heads buried in the sand. There is a need for equitable education for males as well as females. Society is changing. Everyone needs to be assured that they will have the same opportunities to be all they can be. In fact, they have every opportunity to do as well as they can in the entire school curriculum without disturbing thoughts of bias looming in the air.

BIBLIOGRAPHY

Bigelow, B, Christensen, L. Karp, S., Miner, B., Peterson, B., Levine, D. & Miller, L. (1994). Rethinking our classrooms teaching for equity and justice. Montgomery, AL: Rethinking School, Ltd.

Corelli, A. 0. (1988). Sex equity in education. Springfield, IL: Charles C. Thomas, Publisher.

Flanders, N. (1970). Analyzing teaching behaviors. Reading, MA: Addison-Wesley.

Fennema, E. (1980). Mathematics education research: Implications for the 80s. Alexandria, VA: Association for Supervision and Curriculum Development; Reston, VA: National Council of Teachers of Mathematics 1981.

Fennema, E. & Sherman, J. (1977). Women and mathematics: Research perspectives for change. Washington: U.S. Department of Health, Education and Welfare, National Institute of Education, Education and Work Group 1977.

Frieze et al. (1975). Women and sex role: A social psychological perspective. New York: Norton.

Gallos, J. V. (1995). Gender and silence implications of women's gays of knowing. College Teaching,413 pp. 101-105.

Klein, S.S. (1985). Through education. University Press. Handbook for Achieving Sex Equity. Baltimore, MA: The Johns Hopkins.

Kohlberg, L. (1981). The philosophy of moral development: Moral stages and the idea of justice (1st ed.). San Francisco: Harper & Row.

Light, R. (1990). Explorations with students and faculty about teaching, learning, and student life: The first report. Cambridge, MA: The Harvard University Assessment Seminars.

Lord, S. B., Wyman, L., Scott, N. & McLoughlin, X. E. (1979). The female experience in America a learning/teaching guide. Newton, MA: U S Department of Health and Welfare.

MacCoby, E. E. & Jacklin, C. N. (1973). The psychology of sex differences. Sanford, CA: Sanford University Press.

Manning, M. L. (1993). Cultural and gender differences in young adolescents. Middle School Journal, 13-17.

Noddings, N. (1992). The gender issue. Educational Leadership, 65-70.

Rodenstein, J. M. (1990). Children at risk a resource and planning guide. Madison, WI: Wisconsin Department of Public Instruction.

Sadker, M. & Sadker, D. (1994). Failing at fairness how America's schools cheat girls. New York, NY: Charles Scribner's Sons.

Sadker, M., Sadker, D., & Long, L. (1993). Gender and educational equality. In J. A. Banks and C. A. Banks (Eds.), Multicultural educational issue and perspectives (pp. 11-128). Needham, MA: Division of Simon & Schuster, Inc.

84

Shapira, J., Kramer, S., & Hunerberg, C. (1981). Equal their chances children's activities for non-sexist learning. Englewood Cliffs, NJ: Prentice Hall, Inc.

Shashanni, L. (1995). Gender differences in mathematics experiences and attitude and their relation to computer attitude. Educational Technology, 35 32-38.

Tetreault, M. K. T. (1993). Classrooms for diversity: Rethinking curriculum and pedagogy. In J. A. Banks and C. A. Banks (Eds.), Multicultural educational issues and perspectives (pp. 111-128). Needham, MA: A division of Simmon & Schuster, Inc.

Vaillant, G. E. (1977). Adaptation to life (1st ed.). Boston: Little, Brown.

Young, Wathene. (1992). A-gay-yah a gender equity curriculum for grades 6-12. Tahlequah, OK: WEEA Publishing Co.

Chapter 8

The Quest for Bountiful Supervision: Questions for Emerging Counselors

Dale Elizabeth Pehrsson Ed.D.
Oregon State University
Corvallis, OR

Michael A. Ingram, Ed.D.
Oregon State University
Corvallis, OR

Introduction

According to Corey, Corey & Callahan (1988) it is imperative that new counseling graduates seek out and receive supervisory assistance in order to be effective, avoid unethical practice and professional burn out. A review of the literature revealed that there are multiple factors to consider when seeking a new a supervisory relationship

(Bernard & Goodyear, 1998; Borders & Leddick, 1987). These supervisory factors include the following: Education, clinical training and field experiences (Gladding, 2000); theoretical orientation or philosophy (Aponte & Johnson, 2000); prior supervisory experiences (Pehrsson, 2000); multicultural/diversity awareness (Fukayama, 1994; Ingram, 2000); goal clarification (Borders & Leddick, 1987); supervision style and techniques (Bradley, 1989) and practical matters (Pehrsson, 2000).

It has been well documented that strong supervisory relationships provide essential professional support and rich learning experiences for both supervisors and supervisees (Bernard & Goodyear, 1998; Borders & Leddick, 1987). Yet, many emerging counselors often feel unprepared to find or establish supervisory relationships once they leave their protected educational and clinical training environments. These neophyte counselors are at risk of entering the overwhelming and "real world" of counseling practice without established professional support systems (Schmidt, 1999). In the following article, it is our intent to provide a set of tangible questions for emerging counselors (i.e. supervisees) to ask of supervisors as they attempt to find the appropriate person to provide counselor supervision.

Education, Clinical Training and Field Experiences

According to Gladding (1992), the counseling profession is distinguished from other mental health disciplines in its history, clinical training, curricula and present emphases. To illustrate, the counseling profession focuses on the prevention of serious mental health problems through education and short-term treatment. In contrast, social work deals primarily with the social and legal aspects of assisting individuals. Other professions such as psychiatry and clinical psychology concentrate primarily on the treatment of persons with severe emotional disorders. Therefore, it is imperative that emerging counselors question potential supervisors about their education, clinical training and field experiences. Beneficial questions to ask include the following: Where did the supervisor earn their degrees? Was the institution accredited by CACREP or by an equivalent accrediting body? What was the clinical focus of the supervisor's training program? What was the length of their training? What other counseling related experiences have the supervisor engaged in? In addition to these questions, the supervisee should also engage in self-reflection and ask the following: Will I learn from this person? Is this person clinically competent? Does this person understand my field? Is this person genuinely interested in me? Most importantly, am I comfortable with this person? These questions and others will aid the supervisee in making informed decisions before establishing a supervisory relationship.

Theoretical Orientation or Philosophy

Supervision models and theories are often categorized into four broad categories:

(1) psychotherapy-based theories,

(2) developmental models,

(3) social role models and

(4) eclectic and integrationist models (Bernard & Goodyear, 1998).

According to Aponte and Johnson (2000) each model operates under different assumptions, directs the supervisory process into different paths by empathizing different psychological processes, and places varying degrees of importance on the supervisor-supervisee-client relationship (p. 269). Therefore, emerging counselors should ask potential supervisors questions that include the following: What is their counseling theoretical orientation, philosophy of change and supervision model? Do they embrace or utilize a model? Furthermore, how does the supervisor actualize their orientation into practice. Emerging counselor should be wary if the person cannot articulate these concepts. They may find that the supervisory process with this person has the potential to be muddled, confused and unfocused. Thus, hindering the possibility of developing a strong working alliance in the supervisory relationship (Bordin, 1983).

Prior Supervisory Experiences

Supervisors and supervisees have varied and rich experiences and stories (Monk, Winslade, Crockett & Epston, 1998). The exchange and interaction of all these processes has the potential for tremendous learning and growth for both parties. Therefore, it is advantageous that both parties discuss their prior supervision experiences and how these experiences might impact the supervisory relationship (Perhsson, 2000). For example, supervisors who have negatively experienced students from particular programs may have preset views of how the supervisee may perform. These views can hamper relationship building, trust and rapport. Hence, questions that pertain to prior supervisory experiences may prove useful in determining the potential success of the relationship. Instrumental questions might be: What were the supervisor's clinical and supervisory experiences? Describe rewarding supervisory experiences? What disappointments have they experienced? What concerns do they have about prior supervisory experiences?

Multicultural/Diversity Awareness

According to Helms and Cook (1999) the unspoken assumptions regarding the racial and cultural natures of the participants in supervision and therapy may influence every aspect of supervision. Racial and cultural factors potentially influence establishment of supervisory relations, supervision expectations, client assignments, client conceptualization, treatment planning, recommendations for client referrals and evaluation of supervisees. As demographics shift and the need for counselors with strong multicultural competencies emerge, questions such as the following are critical: Does this person understand my population? What is their definition of diversity? What are their experiences in a multicultural environment? What is their conception of social advocacy? And finally, do they practice in a manner that demonstrate empathic understanding of cultural, ethnic and spiritual differences? (Ingram , 2000).

Goal Clarification

According to Pehrsson (2000), supervision is the balancing and blending together of two perspectives. Therefore, it is important for the emerging counselor and supervisor to establish common criteria for expectations and outcomes of the relationship (Bradley, 1988). Only when goals are clearly articulated can both the supervisor and the supervisee fully actualize the supervision process. To illustrate, a supervisor's goals may include enjoyment of the mentoring process, ethical commitment, personal growth or financial gain. Therefore, it is critical for the supervisee to ask befitting questions that pertain to the supervisor's goals for entering into the relationship. Moreover, it might be helpful for the supervisee to engage in self-reflection and consider the following questions: What is my motivation for seeking clinical training from this supervisor? Is my goal to gain certification, licensure or advanced certificates/registrations? Or is my goal personal development? When appropriate questions are asked, the supervision process can unfold and both parties can achieve awareness and insight from the experience.

Supervision Style and Techniques

It is worthwhile to understand the supervisory style and techniques that will be employed during the lengthy relationship of supervision (Bernard & Goodyear, 1998). Neufeldt (1999) adds, that theories and styles of both participants need not be identical but there should be a comfortable fit. If the differences in theoretical frameworks or style impede growth and development, it is advisable to probe for clarification and possibly reconsider the relationship. If these differences and other concerns are discussed in the beginning of supervision, both parties can formulate a solid plan that avoids confusion, alleviates anxiety and prevents disappointment. Discerning questions to consider include: What learning styles are both individuals comfortable with in the supervision process? Is the supervisor's process more like a conversation, a formal interview, a consultation or a lesson with specific objectives? Does the supervisor request audio transcriptions, tapes or case analysis? The supervisory relationship is a challenge. It is the merging of diverse backgrounds and ways of being. As a consequence, the supervisee may feel discomfort within themselves, and with the supervisor's way of being. One invaluable strategy to deal with this discomfort is to review the meeting and journal feelings, thoughts or questions for later clarification or self-reflection.

Practical Matters

According to Pehrsson (2000) defining practical matters in supervision are essential to success. Practical matters include those tangible factors that constitute the supervisory relationship. Effective questions that pertain to these factors may include the following: What are the financial arrangements necessary for supervision? Who will negotiate costs? What are the rates? What benefits are included in the price? What will be the allotted meeting time? What is an acceptable meeting place? Is the supervision process group or individual? Which costs more? What are the financial consequences when an appointment is cancelled? Who is responsible for supplying audio or video equipment? Who pays for copies and supplies? Are future reference letters an extra fee? Practical matters may be deemed inconsequential but resentment is reduced if attention is paid to these seemingly small details in the formulation stage of the supervisory process.

Summary

As we know, a considerable amount of time and energy is expended in the quest for a suitable supervisory match. It is both, critical and fruitful for neophyte counselors to ask relevant questions of potential supervisors. As previously stated, these questions should address the areas of education, clinical training and field experiences; theoretical orientation and philosophy; prior supervisory experiences; multicultural and diversity awareness; goal clarification; supervision style, techniques and practical matters. The emerging counselor's quest for bountiful supervision can be less daunting when equipped with these and other questions.

REFERENCES

Aponte, J.F. & Wohl, J. (2000). Psychological intervention and cultural diversity 2nd Ed. Needham Heights: Allyn and Bacon.

Bernard, J.M. & Goodyear, R.K. (1998). Fundamentals of clinical supervision, 2nd Ed. Needham Heights: Allyn and Bacon.

Borders, L.D. & Leddick, G.R. (1987). Handbook of counseling supervision. Alexandria, VA: Association of Counselor Education and Supervision.

Bordin, E.S. (1983). A working alliance model of supervision. Counseling Psychologist, 11, 35-42.

Bradley, L.J. (1989). Counselor supervision: Principles, process and practice 2nd Ed. Muncie, IN: Accelerated Development:

Corey, G., Corey, M.S., & Callahan, P. (1988). Issues and ethics in the helping professions, 3rd Ed. Pacific Grove: Brooks/Cole Publishing Company.

Fukuyama, M.A. (1994). Critical incidents in multicultural counseling supervision: A phenomenological approach to supervision research. Counselor Education & Supervision, 34, 142-147.

Gladding, S.T. (2000). Counseling a comprehensive profession 4th Ed. Upper Saddle River: Princeton-Hall.

Helms, J.E. & Cook, D.A. (1999). Using race and culture in counseling and psychotherapy: Theory and process. Boston: Allyn and Bacon

Ingram, M.A. (2000). Empathic understanding of cultural differences in the supervision process. (In process).

Monk, G., Winslade, J., Crocket, K. , & Epston, D. (1997). Narrative therapy in practice: The archaelogy of hope. San Francisco: Jossey-Bass.

Neufeldt, S. (1999). Supervision strategies for the first practicum, 2nd Ed. Alexandria, VA: American Counseling Association.

Pehrsson, D. E. (2000). Supervision: Finding the perfect in the imperfect. (In process).

Schmidt, J.S. (1999) Counseling in schools: Essential services and comprehensive programs, 3rd Ed. Boston: Allyn and Bacon

Special thanks to Kathy Biles, Setsuko Nakajima & Dale Pehrsson

Chapter 9

The School Counselor's Challenge of Collaborating With Students, Parents, and Teachers: Strategies and Strengths

Michael Anthony Ingram, Ed.D.

Oregon State University, Corvallis, OR.

Collaborative relationships between school counselors, students, teachers, and parents are important to the overall success of any school environment (Kameen, Robinson, Rotter, 1985; & Myrick, 1993). Yet in many instances, a mutual lack of understanding precludes these groups from working together in an optimal fashion. Often, parents do not trust teachers or school counselors, teachers do not trust parents or school counselors, and students do not trust anybody! Therefore, poor communication patterns exist and the school community operates in a less than ideal manner.

Nonetheless, one of the responsibilities of the school counselor is to help develop working relationships with students, teachers, and parents (Kottler & Kottler, 1993). This chapter examines the school counselor's role and challenge of building these working relationships; discuss current perceptions of school counselors by students, teachers, and parents; and provide strategies that can be utilized to strengthen collaborative efforts and enhance student performance.

The School Counselor

The school counselor has a multiplicity of responsibilities within the school environment (Clark, 1995; Murray, 1995). According to the American School Counselor Association (ASCA, 1992), these duties include: (1) facilitating students educational, personal, vocational, and social development; (2) promoting curricular and environmental conditions appropriate for the school and the community; (3) promoting educational procedures and programs to meet student needs; and (4) providing a systematic evaluation process for guidance and counseling programs, services, and personnel.

Yet, due to budget cuts and other administrative concerns, the school counselor often is relegated to performing duties that are less relevant and more peripheral in nature. Assignments such as class scheduling, bus duty, and discipline are some of the additional responsibilities that often are carried out by the school counselor. Although important to school functioning, these duties are not essential to the school counselors' identity. Consequently, many school counselors question the importance of their role in the school infrastructure (Ratts, personal communication, May 20, 1999). Furthermore, many question the importance of a position that is often misunderstood by students, teachers, parents, administrators and other key personnel (Schmidt, 1996). Still, one role is rarely questioned –the role of serving as an intermediary in conflicts, conferences or consultations between the aforementioned groups. This role requires that school counselors possess many of the following proficiencies: (1) a working knowledge of the differences, as well as similarities that exist in each group (Davis & Garrett, 1998; Helms & Ibrahim, 1985; Wilgus & Shelley, 1988); (2) the ability to provide feedback that will be helpful in building better communication patterns between each group and ultimately enhance students performance levels (Schmidt, 1996); and (3) empathic understanding of the feelings behind the experiences of students, teachers, and parents (Kottler & Kottler, 1993; Zehm & Kottler, 1993).

Students

Much has been written about the key role of students in the school environment (Bleurer & Schreiber, 1989). Simply stated, schools are designed to foster the growth and development of their student populations. Yet, concerns are growing that schools are not equipped to meet the needs of their constituents. Despite changes instigated by the education reform movement, student performance levels are decreasing and dropout rates are increasing (Boyd & Raffel, 1990; Griffin, 1994). These are pressing concerns that continue to produce considerable consternation within the educational community.

In other words, schools no longer holds any promise for many students. These young people, lacking opportunities to experience genuine success in the classroom, often feel unchallenged, unmotivated, and unsure about their futures (Ingram, 1997). The college aspirations of these students evaporate further with low scores on state proficiency tests, college entrance exams, (such as the Standardized Aptitude Test (SAT), the Advanced Placement Test (AP), and the American College Test (ACT). These young people often feel uncertain about whether they can handle the college environment. If students are not productive, the chances diminish for the school's long-term survival as well as for academic achievement. Many young people end up dropping out of school and finding themselves ill prepared for adult life and its many challenges. Their academic achievement, which should continue into high school, often gradually fades away after the elementary and junior high years. To illustrate, a report revealed that " . . . of the three million students who began public school in 1990, 25 percent would not make it through high school" (Martin, 1991, p. 23). As adolescent students approach adulthood, increased peer pressure, drugs, alcohol abuse, school-related violence, teen pregnancies, and unchallenging coursework serve as well-documented catalysts for early school withdrawals.

According to Safer (1986), " . . . students who exhibit repeated behavioral difficulties, frequent absenteeism, and serious academic deficiencies are generally vulnerable throughout their formal educational careers" (p. 407).

Evidence further suggests that psychological, emotional, and societal stressors are antecedents, which cause many students to strike out against the very people who can provide the greatest assistance -- school personnel. School counselors' working relationships with students, in particular, are thwarted by misconceptions of the counselors' role in the school and by their perceived inability to assist or change the circumstances that cause frustration and angst in students' lives.

Teachers

Collaborating with teachers also can be a complex challenge for school counselors (Blum, 1986). Teachers often have negative attitudes about school counseling in general. These unfavorable opinions may be attributed to a lack of understanding of school counselors' roles and how counselors affect the overall structure of the school experience (Nelson, 1992). Many teachers feel that a school counselor is the person who pulls students from class and interrupts the educational process. Some also may have had negative experiences with counselors during their own years in school; therefore, they are less inclined to cooperate or help their colleagues do their jobs. To be in a school that does not value the role of the school counselor is an unenviable assignment. If teachers do not support the work of the school counselor, the goals of the position can be very difficult to accomplish.

Additionally, teachers who struggle with increasing numbers of students and worsening discipline problems generally have insufficient access to professional training programs to help them cope. The opportunities that would likely re-energize creative thought processes and instill a deeper level of pride in the vocation often are absent. Given all of the above, it is little wonder that students do not receive the educational, emotional and physical support necessary for success (Ingram, 1997). Rising rates of poverty (Reed & Saulter, 1990, p. 3), school-related violence (Martin-Shore, 1996) and growing apathy (Nunn & Parish, 1992) about the school experience make it increasingly more difficult for schoolteachers to do their job effectively. Further, the school counselors' challenge of collaborating with teachers intensifies when their roles are misunderstood and teachers themselves feel unsupported and frustrated in their own positions.

Parents

Parental involvement is very important in the social and academic success of students (Torbert, 1998). A review of the literature revealed that parental involvement is tantamount in helping students achieve a level of support and security in the school environment (Smith, E P, Connel, C.M.; Wright, G., Sizer, M., Norman, J.M., Hurley, A., & Walker, S.N. (1998). Parents who are active in the educational process are better able to understand the needs of their children as well as the needs of the school (Griffith, 1997). School counselors realize that supportive parents are key to the success of the school experience (Timmins & Dunkley, 1991). Yet, the relationship between parents and school counselors often is fraught with obstacles. For example, some parents question whether the school counselor is truly an advocate for change who understands the child's dilemma or is really just the spokesperson for the administration or teachers who would like to label the child (Vickers & Minke, 1996). Further and potentially more damaging to the psyche of parents is the expectation that school counselors will challenge their parental competence. Mandatory reporting of child abuse often creates a climate of suspicion around the school counselor and can preclude open and honest dialogue about child discipline, behavior patterns or family dynamics (Roberts, 1985). Combating these perceptions is proving a very difficult task for the school counselor. In a number of school systems, school counselors have designed and implemented innovative programming to increase parental participation as well as improve student performance and behavior. Nonetheless, these well-intentioned and initially well-received programs often meet with parental resistance, soon lose focus, and thus fail to effect positive changes (Ingram, 1997).

Strategies

As described previously, developing a collaborative relationship between school counselor, students, teachers, and parents is often daunting and can be fraught with difficulty. There are a number of strategies, however, that can be incorporated to assist with the challenge. One strategy, for example, is to conceptualize the collaboration as a working alliance between the aforementioned groups. The following discussion of this specific approach integrates principles from therapeutic models of working alliances (Halstead, Brooks, Goldberg & Stone Fish, 1990; Kivlighan, 1990; Kokotovic & Tracey, 1990). The working alliance commonly refers to the coming together of different participants to reach a common goal of fostering growth and development. From its origins in psychoanalytic theory, the alliance construct was broadened by Bordin's work during the 1970s (1974, 1979). Bordin postulated that three components were central to the success of the working alliance: (1) goal, (2) task, and (3) bonds.

According to Kokotovic and Tracey (1990), "goal" pertains to the client's and the counselor's agreement on the treatment objective. "Task" pertains to their agreement on the steps to achieve these goals. "Bonds" pertains to the development of a personal attachment between the counselor and the client. Halstead, Brooks, Goldberg, and Fish (1990) further suggest that the effectiveness of the alliance depends on how well the elements of goal, task, and bonds are incorporated within the counseling relationship. Kokotovic and Tracey also revealed that working alliance effectiveness is ascertained by the quality of past and present interpersonal relationships, level of adjustment, and type of presenting concern. All of these have direct applicability to school counseling practice.

To illustrate, a parent/teacher conference is called to address a student behavior problem that frequently occurs in the classroom. The school counselor can begin to develop a working alliance between student, teacher and parent by helping them set a mutually agreed upon goal for the meeting.

Next, the school counselor can facilitate the group in a process of brainstorming tasks or steps to goal attainment. Finally, and perhaps most importantly, the school counselor can cultivates a bond of trust and rapport among members by acknowledging and validating the feelings behind their respective experiences as well as by listening actively and responding to attitudes and other nonverbal cues that could hinder or help the collaborative process. When school counselors conceptualize their role with students, teachers, and parents as developing goals, setting tasks, and creating bonds, they provide a structured and thoughtful way of producing tangible outcomes regardless of the situation.

As previously stated, working alliance principles can be applied to the school counselor's capacity for building collaborative relationships. Application of these tenets would also depend on the school counselor's willingness to challenge preconceived notions about their role and to risk closer involvement working with students, teachers, and parents to create an environment that is safe and conducive for all concerned.

In summary, the outcomes of a strong working alliance can include improved student performance, increased teacher support, and enhanced parental involvement as well as opportunities for the school counselor's true integration into the school environment.

REFERENCES

American School Counselor Association. (April, 1992). Ethical standards for school counselors. The ASCA Counselor, 29(4), 13-16.

Bleurer, J. C., & Schreiber, P. A. (Eds.). (1989). Counseling young students at risk. Ann Arbor: ERIC Counseling and Personnel Services Clearinghouse.

Blum, L. (1986). Building constructive counselor and teacher relationships. Elementary School Guidance & Counseling, 20(4), 236-239.

Bordin, E. S. (1974). Research strategies in psychotherapy. New York: Wiley.

Bordin, E. S. (1979). The generalizability of the psychoanalytic concept of the working alliance. Psychotherapy: Theory, Research and Practice, 16, 252-260.

Boyd, W. L., & Raffel, ? (1992). Urban education today. Journal of Planning Today, 5(1), 23-24.

Clark, A. J. (1995). Rationalization and the role of the school counselor. The School Counselor, 42(4), 283-291.

Davis, K., Garrett, M. T. (1998). Bridging the gap between school counselors and teachers: A proactive approach. Professional School Counseling, 1(5), 54-55.

Griffin. D. (1991). Educational incentive programs and at-risk students: An integration of research and an initial examination of once incentive program, Project Choice. Dissertation Abstracts International, 55(06), 146A. (University Microfilms No. 9429098).

Griffith, J. (1996). Relation of parental involvement, empowerment and school traits to student academic performance. Journal of Educational Research, 90(1), 33-41.

Halstead, R. W., Brooks, D. K., Goldberg, A., Stone Fish, L. (1990). Counselor and client perceptions of the working alliance. Journal of Mental Health Counseling, 12(20) 208-221.

Helms, B. J. & Ibrahim, F. A. (1985). A comparison of counselor and parent perceptions of the role and function of the secondary school counselor. The School Counselor, 32(4), 266-274.

Kameen, M. C., Robinson, E. H., & Rotter, J. C. (1985). Coordination activities: A study of perceptions of elementary and middle school counselors. Elementary school guidance and counseling, 20, 97-103.

Klivlighan, D. M. (1990). Relation between counselors' use of intentions and clients' perception of working alliance. Journal of Counseling Psychology, 37(1), 27-32.

Kottler, J. A., & Kottler, E. (1993). Teacher as counselor. Newbury Park: Corwin Press.

Kokotovic, A. M., & Tracey, T. J. (1990). Working alliance in the early phase of the counseling. Journal of Counseling Psychology, 37, 16-21.

Martin, L. (1991). Improving student attendance with recognition, rewards. NASSP Bulletin, 75, 111-122.

Martin-Shore, R. (1996). Personalization – Working to curb violence in an American high school. Phi Delta Kappan, 77(5), 362-363.

Murray, B. A. (1995). Validating the role of the school counselor. The School Counselor, 43(1), 5-9.

Myrick, R. D. (1993). Developmental guidance and counseling: A practical approach (2nd ed). Minneapolis: MN: Educational Media Corporation.

Nelson, R. (1991). The counselor as reinforcer. The School Counselor, 39(2), 68-76.

Nunn, G. D., & Parish, T. (1992). The psychological characteristics of at-risk high school students, Adolescence, 27 (106), 435-440.

Reed, S., & Sautter, R. C. (1990). Children of poverty. Phi Delta Kappan, 71 (1), 1-12.

Roberts, H. (1984). Uncloseting the cumulative record: A parent, student and counselor conference project. The School Counselor, 32(1), 54-60.

Safer, D. (1986). The stress of secondary school for vulnerable students. Journal of Youth and Adolescence, 15(5), 405-417.

Schmidt, J. J. (1996). Counseling in schools: Essentials services and comprehensive programs. Boston: Allyn and Bacon.

Smith, E. P., Connell, C. M., Wright, G., Sizer, M., Norman, J., Hurley, A., & Walker, S. N. (1997). An ecological model of home, school and community partnerships: Implications for research and practice. Journal of Educational & Psychological Consultation, 8(4), 339-360.

Timmins, P., & Dunkley, D. (1990). Steps towards a partnership with parents: A self-organized learning perspective. Educational and Child Psychology, 7(2), 61-70.

Torbert, E. (1998). Redefining parental involvement in a diverse society: A socio-cultural perspective of African American families and how it affects their children's social and academic success. Unpublished doctoral dissertation, University of Cincinnati.

Vickers, H. S., & Minke, K. M. (1995). Exploring parent and teacher relationships: Joining and communication to others. School Psychology Quarterly, 10(2), Summer, 133-150.

Wilgus, E., & Shelley, V. (1988). The role of the elementary counselor: Teacher perceptions, expectations and actual functions. School Counselor, 35 (4), 259-266.

Zehm, S. J., & Kottler, J. A. (1993). On being a teacher: The human dimension. Newbury Park, CA: Corwin Press.

Chapter 10

Business as usual: another look at racism in teacher preparation

Eugenio A. Basualdo

State University of New York

College at Oswego

Oswego New York

Stephen C. Fleury

Le Moyne College

Syracuse New York

Our discussion concerns the efforts of educators in an Upstate Central New York State College and large City School District to "transform the culture of teacher preparation" to better serve the needs of urban school districts. The needs of the urban school district were defined as (1) recruiting, preparing and retaining more teachers from traditionally underrepresented minority populations and (2) to better prepare teachers to work with high numbers of students who are at-risk of academic failure. Similar to the situation in many urban school districts where students of color make up the majority of the student population, teachers of color compose only a fractional proportion of the teacher population.

The State College is typical of many rural colleges in the northeastern United States. The overwhelming majority of college students and instructors are white. A perfunctory rhetoric of diversity exists in course outlines, catalog excerpts and college mission statements, yet the cultural thrust is defined and supported by a mainstream curricula that echoes Western Core values and premises in Business,

Teacher Education, and Liberal Arts and Sciences. Administrators and faculty at both the State College and City School District attest to previous attempts at "increasing diversity," but bemoan the disappointing and short-term results.

It is within this context in 1992 that a new President for the State College arrived on the scene with a renewed agenda for diversity. The president had a particularly tough State fiscal environment within which to operate. As he was attempting to gain new and greater positions for minority candidates, governmental support for the State College was decreased form almost 80% to less than 40%. Admittedly, it is difficult to institutionalize equity gains through hiring and recruitment while financial support is being withdrawn, but most of the staffing changes brought about by the President were not lasting, structural ones. Rather, hiring gains were made in lower level administrative positions (such as dorm directors, etc.). The administrative power structure remained intact. One might also question the sincerity of his commitment with his hiring of an Academic Vice-President whose actions and staffing decisions often indicated a strong anti-Affirmative Action position.

One change that did promote the goal of diversity at the State College was the hiring of an African American Dean for the newly created School of Education. The School of Education was a serendipitous result of the need to organize the remaining departments of the Division of Professional Studies when the School of Business was formed. At least two members of the search committee for the new Dean had a strong commitment to ethnic and racial campus diversity and sought high caliber candidates with records to this effect. The candidate hired had a wealth of experiences in urban education, national and local efforts of recruiting students and faculty of color, and with NCATE, the national professional accrediting agency for teacher education programs that requires, among its indicators, a strong action-oriented commitment towards campus and academic diversity.

A nucleus of educators existed at both the State College and City School District committed to the promotion of a more diverse teaching and learning population. Many of these educators were experienced in similar programs in previous times and, all too familiar with the ebb and flow of popular politics, realized how such efforts can be promoted or marginalized, depending on the attitude of the current administration and the political context of the school board.

City School District administrators had institutional and political needs that were similar to those of the new State College president, i.e., to showcase best efforts in rectifying the racial imbalance of the teacher and student populations. The City School District had recently experienced explosive racial divisiveness over the departure of an African American superintendent. In addition, the City School District now has three African American members and, while not a large number when considering that over half of the city's student population was non-white, three sitting board members are able to create a forceful presence to the other board members.

It was within this politically charged context for which the invitation for collaboration extended by the Dean of the new School of Education at the State College was overwhelmingly received. A large contingent of city school district administrators and teachers met at the State College for a full day meeting with the college President, Dean, Chairs, and faculty of the School of Education. The group of about fifty people identified the most desirable characteristics and talents of city school district teachers, and answered their mutual support in working towards creating a teacher preparation program to best prepare graduates to meet the challenges and opportunities of an urban setting. A collaboratively authored position paper describes the co-creation of a Center for Urban Education resulted from this

day-long meeting and served as a prototype for subsequent grant applications.

A number of the participants in the planning group for the Center for Urban Education shared their reflections on the results of earlier teacher preparation programs between the City School District and teacher education programs. Both programs, one in the early 1970s and the other in the 1980s, were intended to enhance the instructional capabilities of new teachers to work with high need students as well as to recruit inner-city candidates for teacher preparation certification programs. Unfortunately, neither program was successful at addressing the racial imbalance between the teacher and student populations in the city district. After the first year, the cohorts were predominantly filled with white candidates. It was for this reason that, once funded with grant support, the staff of the Center for Urban Education (more commonly known as the Urban Teacher Opportunity Corps) were determined to maintain a nearly exclusive focus on recruiting and supporting nonwhite teacher candidates, and refused to utilize an income-based admissions criteria.

Ancillary Projects in Five Years

Scholarship

The Center for Urban Education applied and received a grant from the New York State Education Department to (I) better prepare teachers for urban areas and (2) increase the number of minority teachers through recruitment, advisement, preparation, certification and support. The grant received an "A" minimal over a five year period, it continued to provide moral support and leverage to reallocate college and school institutional resources towards the goals of the urban education project.

For example, the State College president had vowed to provide scholarships for minority teacher education candidates if a Center for Urban Education were established. Ten tuition-based scholarships, accompanied by a $1,000 annual stipend for four years were offered to incoming freshman minority students and transfers from the local urban community college.

The State College President's announcement of the ten scholarships at a national meeting on recruiting and retaining minorities in education was made in a political rush, coming at the end of the academic year. Administrators at the State College, anxious to fill all ten spots immediately, encouraged and awarded the scholarship to many students who in all probability would not have "passed" the usual admissions criteria. Interestingly enough, each of the original ten scholarship winners completed the teacher education program and attained their bachelor's degree with an overall 3.3 grade point average.

Graduates

Beginning the third year of the project, the number of graduates from the Urban Teacher Opportunity Corps has ranged between six and eleven. This may seem a very small number. However, some of these graduates received teaching positions in the City School District, but most have received and accepted offers with other school districts. This phenomenon itself needs analysis. Mutual Professional Development

As the original recruitment project got off the ground, the Center for Urban Education also received a Dwight D. Eisenhower grant for the enhanced professional development of urban teachers in meeting new State curricular standards. The unique aspect of the project was its basis in a social constructivist theory of knowledge, i.e.. rather than providing "top down" expertise, urban teachers, pre- service teachers, and college instructors were involved in exchanging ideas of how best to meet new state standards. In essence, urban teachers and students are providing in service to college instructors. Additionally, the measurable outcome of the success of the grant was the changes in activities of college teacher preparation courses.

Super Summer

Other projects relating to the education of inner-city youth have occurred through the Center for Urban Education. The Super Summer Program, sponsored by the City Housing Authority, and open to all students, regardless of their academic background is now in its fifth year. Approximately 35-40 middle-school youth from the city housing projects spend four weeks on the State College Campus. Students are involved in integrating academic and recreational activities, focusing on the construction of a robot. Many students from the earlier years are now hired as "teaching assistants." Mentoring and Tutoring

Extensive mentoring and tutoring programs have been established in the City School District. Students from the Urban Teacher Opportunity Corp travel twice weekly to the city school district so that they can work with middle and high school students. College students are instructed in various strategies for mentoring and tutoring, and meet weekly to discuss their methodologies and reflections.

Advisement Practices

One of the most effective means for recruiting students of color has been the deliberate targeting of advisement sessions for teacher assistants in the City School District. The State College has provided program advisors for elementary, secondary, and vocational education on a bi-semester basis for three years.

Expanded Center for Urban Education

Over the past five years of efforts to assist in urban education efforts, it is becoming increasingly apparent that more resources and support are needed to effectively change the culture of teacher preparation. We are currently involved in collaborating with two private universities as well as a City Teaching Center to ensure that all higher education efforts, as well as in the city school district, work toward similar goals.

In addition we have enlisted the support of various inner city community groups such as the churches and local businesses who are interested in creating a stronger workforce. The intent of a new expanded Center for Urban Education is to instill a sense of communal crisis. Our belief is that the small but credible successes with the Urban Teacher Opportunity Corps can be greatly expanded and enhanced.

Lessons Learned

In five years of working on shifting institutional State College and City School District priorities towards the needs of an effective urban teacher education. Many of these lessons learned involve identifying subtle resistance to institutional changes that, in essence, amount to the maintenance of institutional racism.

1. *Committed educators always work within a limited window of time.*

Administrators and faculty of the City School District and the State College Teacher Education programs were most enthusiastic about the goals of the Center for Urban Education when both the City School District Superintendent and State College President promoted urban teacher education as their utmost priority. Directors of various administrative (the city school district) departments eagerly sought collaborative projects with college administrators and faculty; college courses were delivered in City School District sites; college faculty and administrators ensured that college advisement and academic support was available on a frequent and regular basis in the school district sites for high school students and teaching assistants; two national conferences for the recruitment and retention of minorities in education were collaboratively sponsored; and the State College President created ten tuition scholarships for graduates of the City School Districts who were going into teacher education programs; selected teachers from the City School District were provided to mentors pre-service urban teacher candidates from the State College; and college students, City District teachers, and college professors collaboratively worked on creating teaching strategies to assist in helping students of the City School District prepare for the new State learning standards.

As with any social movement, the shift of institutional support is a confluence of multiple social., institutional, and political factors, often guided by one or two key leaders. School superintendents and college presidents can lead others by moral suasion and a signaling of value stances through a shifting of institutional resources. But the momentum for change can easily diminish when particular school and college leaders leave their position. When the College President was promoted to a State-level position, the interim President withdrew the original institutional commitment to create ten new scholarships each year for four years to attract minorities into teacher education. In addition, the Interim President requested that the School of Education Dean find alternative funding for the original ten scholarships. Concurrently, the City School District Superintendent retired his position and was replaced by a school administrator who was racked with serious political problems during his two years of duty before resigning. While the original commitments between the State College and the City School District were to be able to be maintained in spirit, the verve and vitality of the cooperative venture was severely diminished.

2. *Personal and institutional commitment is NOT unconditional commitment.*

Educational leaders often use urban initiatives politically to showcase the institutions' mission and intent. Often, the institutional efforts that are selected are those bringing the most "PR" (i.e., public relations) with bringing the least amount of economic difficulty. For example, the ten tuition-based scholarships created by the State College President were named after a high-profile African American who once worked at the college, yet no communication was first made with her family. Additionally, the tuition-based scholarships were in reality less than what they at first appeared. Recipients were required to apply for the State's Tuition Assistance Program and to provide this for the college. In our experiences, most students who are eligible for the scholarship are also eligible for a partial or full tuition support from the State's Tuition Assistance Program, thus requiring little financial support from the State College.

Neither the State College nor the City School District provided much financial support for the National conferences on recruiting and retaining minorities in education, yet both places received top billing in all the promotional literature. Grant writing was encouraged by the administration, yet few curricular sacrifices were asked of our colleagues in the Arts and Sciences. In addition, the City School District backed off previous promises to hire "any and all" graduates of the Teacher Opportunity Corps program. Many of the graduates of the UTOC program were able to take positions in neighboring cities and states.

3. *"Equal" does not mean equity nor justice.*

The City School District's policy provides a "career ladder" opportunity for employees of the district from all races. In the career ladder program, teacher assistants start out at a very low level salary, but some with provisions made for longs periods to time within which to students, but are provided with tuition credit waivers that are able to be used for the participants courses. The career ladder program appears both fair and equitable, yet it is an overwhelming tool of the predominantly white student body. The racial imbalance has been so historically tipped that contemporary counter-weights need to be overwhelming, yet ANY special consideration for minority candidates exists within a "context of fear." There are no special hiring considerations for minority candidates. District officials often explain a "union contract" as protection from change.

4. Not all faculty and teachers share authentic commitment to diversity and/or urban teaching.

Within the college teaching culture, there are at least three identifiable groups: those who historically want to be part; those who are sincere about diversity and supporters, until they realize change will also affect them. The behavior of minority students is judged more harshly than that of whites. Often if a student seeks help, advice received is "quit." If the student misses a class, he or she is usually considered late by the college professors. Seldom considered as a nontraditional student, these students are often the sole family supporters, who work for a low salary, in addition to transportation fee, childcare.

5. No education program can survive without white allies.

Much to the disgruntlement of white members of the teacher education programs, the exclusive and restrictive member criteria for the Urban Teacher Opportunity Corps project is that participants be an African American, Hispanic, or Native American. In reality, students did not challenge this criterion, although to a large degree, it was the Associate Dean, who also was white, who had to clarify the news.

6. Goodwill and rhetoric do not equal cultural change.

Good will and rhetoric do not equal cultural change. Untenured faculty, those most vulnerable to the effects of institutional racism, is often at a disadvantage in openly supporting social causes. Other faculty members may not see similar activities in the same way. For example, when advising, faculty is often unwilling to substitute courses for the college core courses. This often creates serious learning problems for both instructors and students. A serious barrier is that educators in higher education "over-believe" a myth that State Education Department requirements are immutable. Often, teacher educators will concur with proposed changes, but later explain how such changes cannot be completed. A permeating belief is that teacher preparation is linear, absolute, and hierarchical, and therefore, students must learn their "professional" knowledge in an orderly, step-wise fashion. In addition, traditional faculty believe that certain experiences cannot be translated into courses, a belief that curtails both innovation and practicality in teacher education. On the other hand, school personnel misperceive college instructors are free to do anything with their courses. All in all, good will and rhetoric can remain positive. Yet this is still no assurance that desired change in the cultural of teacher preparation will come about.

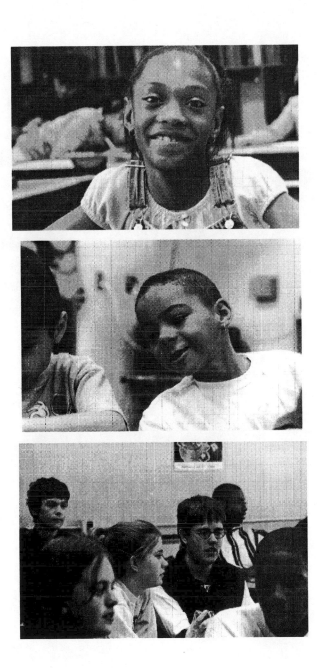

Chapter 11

The Language Differences in the American Schools for the Chicano/ Mexican-American Child.

Dr. Tony J. Manson
Middle Tennessee State University
Murfreesboro, Tennessee

This paper will be focusing on the education of the Mexican-American child in the schools of the American Southwest and West. For the better part of two decades, politicians, parents, educators and political activists have critically examined and disputed the issues related to the education of the Mexican-American or Chicano child. It cannot be said that, after two decades of debate, there is a general consensus among the public or educators concerning the most effective approaches to education of the culturally different child. On the ideological level there is a deeply imbedded sentiment that bilingual and bi-cultural programs do the child an injustice, postponing or perhaps permanently retarding the child's mastery of the English language and thus inhibiting the process of acculturation. (Though this sentiment is regularly associated with the Anglo majority, there are those in the Mexican-American community who share this sentiment.) Others view bilingual and bi-cultural education as an asset and a necessity. Those espousing this view do so for a number of reasons, pedagogical and cultural. At root, they claim, the Chicano child enters school with a language and a culture of a cultural minority and it will take at least a couple of years before the child bi-cultural programs is intercultural communication in the education of cultural subgroups or minorities.

Language and Culture

In his study of the language of the Chicano, Leonardo Hernandez appeals to the authority of a number of specialists in the field, including the well-known Edward Sapir and Benjamin Whorf and Sapir has written: "It is quite an illusion to imagine that one adjusts to reality essentially without the use of language and that language is merely the incidental means of solving specific problems of communication or reflection." Sapir disagrees with this viewpoint, stating: "The fact of the matter is that the 'real world is to a large extent unconsciously built upon the language habits of the group" (in Hernandez: 1979, p. 25). Both Sapir and Whorf note that the complete lexicon of the language can be considered to be "a complex inventory of all the ideas, interests, and occupations that take up the attention of the community."

Hernandez observes that language performs a number of social functions. First, it is a principal tool in the socialization of the child, serving as a means of communication between the youngest and the other generations of the solidarity of the group. Language, in other words, is most instrumental in preserving culture and the cultural group. Second, language plays an important role in the development of the social personality of the individual; language plays a significant role in the interactions of people within the social group. Third, the spoken language identifies the person as a member of a subculture in a pluralistic society (p. 29).

Hernandez, citing the work of the psychologist Uvaldo Palomares, indicates that the Chicano child, born in this country of Mexican-American parents, is at a distinct advantage when entering the Anglo school. In the earliest years of development, the child learns neither pure English nor pure Spanish, but a variant dialect that is referred to Tex-Mex or Spanish. Also, the same can be said for the Western dialect. When the child enters school, he/she is ill equipped to engage in English instructional activities; if he/she speaks English with any fluency at all, it is usually with an identifiable accent. Thus, as Hernandez and Palomares indicate, the Chicano child is at a distinct disadvantage in the crucial early years of schooling: though the child has successfully built up a language by means of which he can interact in the social group and with the world, that language is not the **lengua franca** of the classroom; often it is the case that no accommodation is made for the special language problems of the child and flounders in the confusing tasks set for them in the English-speaking classroom.

From the years of schooling then, the child becomes, as often is the case, a failure. This does nothing for their sense of achievement and self-worth. In addition, if their native language or dialect is depreciated by the teacher, as has been true in the past, the child's cultural identity is threatened, undermining the perception of their own worth and value (p.26).

Little more than a decade ago, the Supreme Court, in its decision in the case, Lau vs. Nichols, ruled that some provisions must be made for children entering the school systems in the country without the necessary skills in the English language. The case was initiated on behalf of some 2,000 Chinese-speaking children who received instruction solely in the English language. The Court, invoking section 601 of the Civil Rights Act of 1964, stated: "Under stated-imposed standards there is no equality of treatment merely by providing students with the same facilities, textbooks, teachers, and curriculum; for students who do not understand English are effectively foreclosed from any meaningful education" (in U.S. Commission on Civil Rights: 1975, p.563). The Court noted that school systems that make no provisions for those students severely limited in English are, in effect making a mockery of public education. The Court did not specify how the nation's school systems should meet the needs of those not proficient in English, only stating that some provision ought to be made.

Conceptualizing Cultural Differences

Michael Cole and Jerome Bruner, among others, have attempted to place the educational needs of the culturally different child in theoretical perspective (1975, p. 107). They note that the most persistent view of the sources of ethnic and social class differences in intellectual performance is one that might be termed the deficit hypothesis. According to this hypothesis, members of minority ethnic groups, who comprise a disproportionate share of the society's poor, are living in what are disorganized communities. When measured against the norms for the Anglo majority, members of these ethnic minorities exhibit various forms of behavioral deficits, including: less stimulating mother-child interactions, less positive, and more negative, reinforcement, less guidance in social seeking, less stimulating interaction with toys and other stimulating educational materials. In addition, these deficits in symbolic and linguistic environments of the minority-group child lead to the child's adoption of a restricted language or code. Cole and Bruner (1975) note that the deficit hypothesis stimulated programs of early intervention and education that would supply for these deficits before the child entered the classroom in kindergarten or first grade.

Cole and Bruner (1975) suggest that the deficit hypothesis is itself deficient, noting that linguists have shown that children, whatever their language, do not differ essentially in language development.

Invoking the work of Chomsky, the authors note: "We cannot attribute a cognitive capacity to people that is less than required to produce the complex, rule-governed activity called language" (p. 20). Cole and Bruner (1975), in a sum, argue for a cultural-difference hypothesis to explain differences in intellectual performance. They suggest that it is important, according to the cultural-differences hypothesis, to identify educational difficulties in terms of difference instead of deficit. Furthermore, it is important that educators cater to these cultural differences in the instructional process—giving the child instruction in his-her own language, for example—until such time as the child is able to transfer the skills acquired in his-her own language to command in written and spoken English.

Bilingual and bicultural programs have been introduced into the curriculum of the schools serving the Spanish-speaking and other sub-cultural language groups with the explicit rationale of the cultural-differences hypothesis (Guerra: 1970, p. 243). As Guerra points out, there is no one standardized method of educating the culturally different child in the classroom. Where a truly bilingual teacher is available, it is possible to use a concurrent method of communication, with the teacher alternating the use of Spanish and English within the same instructional unit. Some educators prefer to give instruction in the first years of education in the child's dominant language while concentrating too on oral language development in English.

The theory is that, if the child learns to read in Spanish while developing their oral mastery of English, they will be able to transfer reading skills from Spanish to English in the early elementary years. Attempting to teach reading before the child has an adequate command of the structure and lexicon of English, it is thought, is counterproductive and only serves to school the child in failure.

Often it is the case that bilingual teachers are not available in sufficient amounts to undertake bilingual instruction. In this case, it has become the practice to instruct the child via English-as-a-Second Language, and to use teaching aides who attempt to clear up any ambiguities surfacing in instruction in the child's own tongue. The Los Angeles Unified School District in search of remedies of this theory, went to Mexico and hired 25 of their very best instructors in all sorts of subjects to try and bridge the gap that had been created by not having enough bilingual and bi-cultural instructors. In addressing the problem in this way LAUSD is making a serious statement about how they will approach education in the future. They also, in a matter of speaking precluded the National Free Trade Agreement that just recently passed. Teacher preparation programs have still another area that is not addressed for in-coming teachers, once again leaving our students are left with insufficient instruction.

It is the general feeling that whatever the method of instruction used, it is possible to adopt a bi-cultural philosophy of education, one in which the teacher reinforces the child's sense of cultural identity, its value and worth, thus avoiding glaring instances where the child is punished for his early socialization in a language other than English. All educational eyes are upon the Los Angeles Unified School District they took the lead in this issue, although questions still exist at least some form of facilitating the bilingual-bicultural student. Maybe the issue will addressed in the classroom instead of just lip service at in-service conferences and teachers lounges. If the Mexican-American child is to be taught in this country we should be able to solve the majority of the problems after all this is AMERICA.

REFERENCES

Cole, M. & Bruner, J. ( ). Cultural differences and inferences about psychological process. In M. Maehr and W. Stallings, (eds.), Culture, child and school, pp. 107-123. Monterey: Brooks Publishing.

Guerra, M. (1970). Lanaguage instruction and intergroup relations. In H. Johnson and W. Hernanades, (Eds.), pp. 243-249. Educating and Mexican-American. Valley Forge: Judson Press.

Hernandez, L. (1979). The language of the Chicano. Los Angeles: California State University.

Olivas, M. A. (1988, May- June). Latino faculty at the Border: Increasing numbers key to more Hispanic access. Change, 20 (3), 6-9.

San-Miguel, G., Jr. (1987, Winter). The status of historical research on Chicano education. Review of Educational Research, 57 (4), 467-480.

San-Miguel, G., Jr. (1975). Status of historiography of Chicano education: A preliminary analysis. History of Education Quarterly, 26 (4), 523-536.

U.S. Commision on Civil Rights. (1975). A better chance to learn. Washington, D. C. Clearinghouse Publication 51.

Chapter 12

Multiculturalism in Our Schools: The School Administrator's Role

Dr. Tony J. Manson
Middle Tennessee State University
Murfreesboro, Tennessee

Dr. Joseph Jefferson
Texas Southern University
Houston, Texas

Overview

The school administrator is responsible for many aspects of the multicultural environment within a school. The principal's commitment and dedication to providing an education for all students affects the multicultural climate of the school. The administrator, who recognizes and supports the teachers as they integrate the many components of a multicultural curriculum into the content of all instruction, is working to provide the students with an education that promises success for their future. The effective school principal understands the value of parental involvement, how to build a relationship that bridges the school and community, and the importance of the parent's involvement for ensuring the students success. The administrator must also create a racially and culturally diverse staff to provide the students with a school environment that will prepare them to be successful in an increasingly diverse society.

The Multicultural Climate

The administrator must work to help create a school climate that recognizes the diversity of the cultures within the school and community. This requires a commitment to recreate the school to meet the needs of all the children from that community. The school must have a vision that represents the mission of the school and educational goals for the students." A major role of school leaders is to keep the purpose of the school visible, tangible and alive for everyone" (Morefield, 1998, p.12). This is achieved through a unity of purpose that demonstrates a set of core values that reflect the ideas, thoughts, and goals of the school and the community. The school is being built upon a foundation of cooperation and dedication to meet these goals.

Developing a multicultural school climate relies upon the ability of the principal and staff to "raise awareness about the needs of children and their parents who are not members of the mainstream culture, support the students who are members of diverse religious and cultural groups, and enhance sensitivity to cultural differences in the curriculum as well as in classroom instruction" (Kirmani and Laster, 1999, p.61). Educators must celebrate the diversity of the students. "Heritage months are opportunities to celebrate our achievements to date and to ensure that we will have a lot more to celebrate in the future" (Menkart, 1999, p.19). In addition to heritage celebration months, educators must integrate cultural diversity so that it becomes a "holistic and interdisciplinary approach" (Menkart, 1999, p.20) for all instructional areas within the school. "A multicultural curriculum is one that is part of the daily life at school, part of every subject and woven into the very fabric of the content of instruction" (Morefield, 1998, p.9). The teachers and principals must bridge the distance between the school and the parents of students from other cultures or religions to create a welcoming atmosphere. Students succeed in schools that are caring and nurturing where they are accepted, and encouraged by educators who can "foster warm and caring environments where children will blossom" (Morefield, 1998, p.5). The students, parents, and teachers should feel that the school belongs to them. "An empowering school culture and social structure is created when the culture and organization of the school are transformed in ways that enable students from diverse racial, ethnic, and gender groups to experience equality and equal status" (Banks, 1997, p.2). Administrators can influence and change the school climate to create a successful school for all children.

Multicultural Curriculum

One question addressed is to what extent is teaching being influenced by multiculturalism? In researching multicultural curriculum, I came across four models of multicultural teaching. The four are listed along with their different types of teaching. Gibson identifies five types of multi-cultural teaching for the culturally different to help students develop the necessary skills to become assimilated into the mainstream culture:

1. Education about cultural pluralism to promote cross-cultural understanding and respect for cultural difference;
2. Education for cultural pluralism to promote cross-cultural understanding and respect for cultural difference;
3. Bicultural education to help multicultural students acquire language and skills required in the mainstream culture and to support and maintain their specific culture; and
4. Multiculturalism as the normal human experience in which students are taught how to function in many cultural contexts in our multicultural society.

Sleeter and Grant also suggested five kinds of multicultural teaching:

1. Teaching the culturally different the skills and knowledge necessary to function in the mainstream culture;

2. Human relations teaching, in which prejudices and stereotypes are exposed to promote inter-group tolerance, respect, and harmony;

3. Studying single groups, whereby the class learns about a specific group's contributions, achievements, and culture;

4. Orienting the total school experience toward diversity issues; and

5. Multicultural education and social constructionist education to develop skills that help students confront and deal with social injustice and oppression.

Banks listed five multicultural teaching dimensions:

1. Content integration, in which teachers insert content about diversity into the curriculum by recognizing contributions of minority groups, adding units specifically treating multicultural topics, or using a trans-formative approach that changes the structure, assumptions, and perspectives of the curriculum so that the subject matter is viewed from the perspective and experiences of a range of groups;

2. Knowledge construction to reveal how scholars' perspectives in the various disciplines influence their conclusions;

3. Prejudice reduction and the development of positive attitudes toward minority groups;

4. Equitable pedagogy to improve academic achievement of multicultural students; and

5. Empowerment of the school culture and social structure so that students have equal access to all school experiences.

The Instructional changes Mehan proposed were distilled from ethnographic research. They are:

1. Academic rigor with social supports (having high expectations for academic success, focusing on understanding, presenting a demanding curriculum, and helping students learn);
2. Student centered classrooms and discourse organization, using small group instruction, cooperative learning, and student involvement;
3. Viewing the teacher as ethnographer, so that the teacher will have specific information about his or her students' actual lives rather than generalized knowledge about various ethnic groups;
4. Viewing student's knowledge as a resource to reinforce ethnic pride, to increase class participation, and to draw on when new topics are introduced; and
5. Adapting general principles to local circumstances.

In a study that was done in a culturally diverse middle school, there were ten teachers interviewed. Seven of the teachers were women, and three were men. Five taught English or reading, two taught social studies, one taught math, one taught education, and the other person taught music. All but one had participated in workshops or multicultural education. Their experience ranged from one to twenty nine years. The teachers were interviewed twice. On the first interview, they were asked to describe in depth a successful lesson they had recently taught. In the second interview, they were reminded of what had been said during the first interview, and asked if they would like to expand on their first interview.

Twenty six percent of the 800 students were non-white. The group consisted of 15% African American, 9% Hispanic, 1% Asian, and 1% Native American. Also the group consisted of 31% qualifying for free lunch, 15% from city's most affluent neighborhood, and 11% were special education students. There were four types of multicultural teachings that emerged from this study:

1. **Cultural Adjustment** – the goal is to have the students learn the established curriculum. The teacher presents the regular material but it is altered to fit the composition of the classroom.

2. **Cultural Embellishment** – the primary goal is to have the students learn the established curriculum and second to have them understand various aspects of different cultures for either assimilation or pluralism purposes. In other words content are added about important people, holidays, celebrations, foods, entertainment, and various topics from different cultures. Allows the student to work in cooperative groups they choose, and arranges assignments and appropriate materials.

3. **Cultural Integration** - The teacher has traditional goals, and multicultural goals, stressing pluralism. Fusing multicultural materials into the regular curriculum does this. The methods to infuse the topics are through group projects, problem solving tasks, and personal responses.

4. **Cultural analysis** - also integrates the regular curriculum and multiculturalism by helping students gain a deeper understanding of multicultural topics and acquire skills and attitudes necessary for creating a just society. Social, economic and political issues related to race, gender, and exceptionality are presented. Students are engaged in-group action problems and in voicing their viewpoints, proposals, and solutions.

It was found that although some of the teaching is influenced by the multicultural nature of the students, the influence is not uniform. There were some teachers that changed only the instructional methods, while others made instructional changes and changes in their curriculum.

The challenge for educators is how to build an inclusive multicultural community in the classroom. Four basic principles mentioned by Lucinda Katz are:

1. The practice of defining and validating the history, culture, and psychology of individuals within a community cannot be separated from the practice of encouraging each member of the community to accept, include and empathize with other.

2. Each school must devise its own plan for building a multicultural community.

3. Sophisticated skills are required to turn a diverse population into a multicultural community.

4. There are two important components to consider in the design of a multicultural curriculum: the sources of curriculum, and the methods of communication.

Multicultural Curriculum Implementation

Learning Styles VS Instructional Content

Dunn (1997) states that paying attention to the varied learning styles of all students will do more to accomplish the goals of multicultural education than misguided programs that often divide children. It is Dunn's continued belief that many practices schools promote make little sense in terms of how multicultural diverse students learn. Thus, we need to examine the data concerning how poor achievement has been reversed among culturally diverse students in many schools. Generally multicultural education has focused on two broad goals: increasing academic achievement and promoting greater sensitivity to cultural differences in an attempt to reduce bias. Drew, Dunn, and colleagues (1994) tested how well 138 Cajun students and 29 Louisiana Indian students, all poor achievers, could recall story content and vocabulary immediately and after a delay. Their recall differed significantly when they were instructed with (1) traditional versus multi-sensory instructional resources and (2) stories in which cultural relevance matched and mismatched students' identified cultural backgrounds. Each subject was presented with four story treatments (two culturally sensitive and two dominant American) and tested for recall immediately afterward and again one week later. The findings for Cajun subjects indicated significant differences between instructional treatments, with greater recall in each multi-sensory instructional condition - Cultural-Immediate, Cultural-Delayed, American-Immediate, American-Delayed. The main effect of instructional treatment for Louisiana Indian subjects was significant as well. Recall scores were even higher when they used multi-sensory materials for American stories. No significant main effect emerged for test interval with either group.

This study demonstrated that what determined whether students mastered the content was how the content was taught, not the content itself. The culturally sensitive curriculum did not produce significantly higher achievement for these two poorly achieving cultural groups; the methods that were used did.

Other studies of teaching methods revealed even more dramatic results. Before being taught with methods that responded to their learning styles, only 25% of special education high school students in a suburban New York school district had passed the required local examinations and state competency tests to receive diplomas. In the first year of the district's learning styles program (1987-1988) that number increased to 66%. During the second year, 91% of the district's special education students were successful, and in the third year, the results remained constant at 90%--with greater ratio of "handicapped" students passing state competency exams than regular education students (Brunner and

Majewski, 1990). Two North Carolina elementary principals reported similarly impressive gains as a result of their learning styles programs. In an impoverished, largely minority school, Andrews (1990) brought student scores that had consistently been in the 30th percentile on the California Achievement Test to the 83rd percentile over a three-year period by responding to students' learning styles. Shortly thereafter, Stone (1992) showed highly tactual, learning disabled (LD) elementary school students how to learn with Flip Chutes, Electro boards, Task Cards, and Pic-A-Holes while seated informally in rooms where levels of light matched their style preferences. The children were encouraged to study either alone, with a classmate or two, or with their teacher - based on their learning style strengths. Within four months, those youngsters had achieved four months' reading gains on a standardized achievement test-better than they ever had done previously and as well as would have been expected of children achieving at normal levels.

This research shows that there is no such thing as a cultural group style. There are cross-cultural and intra-cultural similarities and differences among all peoples. Those differences are enriching when understood and channeled positively. With this in mind, is it unwise for schools with limited budgets to support multicultural education in addition to - and apart from - regular education? Should schools focus on their instructional delivery systems and making them responsive to how diverse students learn?

Conversely, there is also quite convincing studies, which prove the instructional content, **NOT** the learning styles, are the source of awareness and change. Many classrooms today comprise children from diverse cultures, races, religions, socioeconomic groups, and family constellations. In addition, children with physical, mental, and learning disabilities, were once assigned to separate specialized classes, are now placed in grade-level classrooms. Even though these students share a common classroom, all their differences can easily work to isolate them from one another. Finding a way to prevent this from happening requires teachers to be knowledgeable about and sensitive to the wealth of variety around them, as well as to possess excellent observation, listening, and human relations skills.

At the C. W. Henry School, an urban, multiethnic idle school in Philadelphia, PA, Merri Rubin helps her students work with students from an upper-middle-class, white suburban school to compose, produce, and perform a musical on racial tolerance. This project not only features the content of interethnic understanding but also requires students from different racial, cultural, and economic backgrounds to work together.

Although the school's population is racially balanced, students initiated the task force to move beyond tolerance to acceptance, understanding, and celebration of racial and cultural differences. The task force meets weekly to share information that is sometimes controversial and difficult to talk about. Students build trust and empathy and gain experience in dealing with racial issues.

Currently, Clarksville/Montgomery County School System incorporates multicultural objectives within several subject areas to include:

In Music

Understand and explore the history and characteristics of the major theater dance forms, i.e. ballet, modern jazz, and tap, as well as ethnic dance forms.

Develop the ability to recognize dance as a form of individual and cultural expression.

Understanding music in relation to history and culture.

In Writing

Begin to develop an understanding of and respect for multicultural and ethnic diversity in language usage, patterns, and dialects.

Develop an understanding of and respect for multicultural and ethnic diversity in language.

In Math

Use, recognize, and value the varied roles of mathematics in their lives, culture and society.

In Science

Enable students to demonstrate ways of thinking and acting inherent in the practice of science; and to exhibit an awareness of the historical and cultural contributions to the enterprise of science.

All schools, even those with fairly homogeneous student populations, are finding they must address such issues of diversity as race, religion, gender, and socioeconomic stratification. We must take responsibility for preparing all students to live in a diverse society. We can enrich the lives of everyone in our community, by diligently and thoughtfully pursuing a policy of inclusion, instead of exclusion.

Core Knowledge

Core Knowledge is sometimes labeled as a multicultural curriculum. It is a curriculum that is designed to accommodate a variety of ethnic groups. It is an idea that for the sake of academic excellence, greater fairness, and higher literacy, elementary and middle schools need a solid, specific, shared core curriculum in order to help children establish strong foundations of knowledge. It is a school reform movement taking shape in hundreds of schools where educators have committed themselves to teaching important skills and the Core Knowledge content they share within grade levels, across districts, and with other Core Knowledge schools across the country. It is solid, sequenced, specific and shared (Core Knowledge Foundation, 1999). Even though it has multicultural aspects, it is more of a mono-cultural curriculum. "All students must have access to core knowledge if they are to be successful in school and in life," believes E.D. Hirsch, Jr., founder of Core Knowledge. Since his publication titled *Cultural Literacy: What Every American Needs to Know* in 1987, he has been the center of the debate surrounding what should constitute the school curriculum. He believes that it is not only possible but vitally important to specify the "core knowledge" that all students learn. (O'Neil, 1999). He thought that teachers needed more than just theory. They needed details of exactly what to teach and when it should be taught (Krantowit and Chideya, 1992).

The Core Knowledge sequences is the result of research into the content and structure of the highest performing elementary school systems around the world, as well as extensive consensus-building among diverse groups and interest, including parents, teachers, scientists, professional curriculum organizations and experts from the Core Knowledge Foundation's Advisory Board on Multicultural Traditions. It was implemented for a year at Three Oaks Elementary School in Ft. Myers, Florida. As more elementary schools adopt Core Knowledge, the foundation seeks their suggestions based on experience in order to update the sequence (Core Knowledge Foundation, 1999).

Schools must teach and share a body of knowledge grade by grade, to achieve excellence and fairness in education. Core Knowledge offers the guidelines needed to ensure that children are exposed to a variety of themes and ideas in all subjects and that each grade builds upon earlier work (Kantowitz and Chideya,

1992). Jeanne Storm, a teacher at Three Oaks Elementary school in Ft. Myers, Florida stated in her article that "Core Knowledge Curriculum has convinced me that teaching meaningful content is far more rewarding than teaching vague skills and ambiguous units. As E.D. Hirsch, Jr., has said: Children from every ethnic and economic background should have access to share core of knowledge that is necessary to reading, understanding, and communication."

The highest achieving schools systems in the world (such as those in Sweden, France, and Japan) teach their children a specific core of knowledge in each of the first six grades. American schools need to do this for the following reasons: commonly shared knowledge makes schooling more effective, commonly shared knowledge makes schooling more fair and democratic, and commonly shared knowledge helps create cooperation and solidarity in our schools and nation. (Hirsch, 1996). Today over 800 schools in our country have adopted a program based on Hirsch's concept (O'Neil, 1999).

Metropolitan Nashville Schools have adopted their own version of Core Knowledge. In the fall of 1997, Mayor Phil Bredesen approved Nashville's Core Curriculum. A panel of experts spent two to three weeks out of the summer to create a modified version to be implemented in Nashville schools. They had to incorporate the mathematics (MIP) and language (CCRP) skills that Tennessee had been implementing for many years. It was published and dispersed in all of Nashville's schools right before school began. As with most changes, there were a lot of conflicting opinions about this new curriculum. Teachers that had been teaching for ten or fifteen years did not like the idea of changing their methods. New teachers were pleased to have the whole year's worth of teaching laid out for them in the form of a core curriculum manual. Many teachers, though, had difficulty reading and understanding the manuals. Most of the in-service meetings in the fall of 1997 were spent explaining and discussing core curriculum. In the fall of 1998, core curriculum was updated and revised based on teacher recommendations and inserts were given to replace pages in the previous core curriculum manuals.

There have been positive and negative responses to Core Curriculum in Metro Nashville Schools. One positive reaction is that every teacher knows exactly what she must teach and when it must be taught. The manual gives detailed outlines explaining the content that must be taught each six weeks and most subjects are broken down into one to two week segments. It is sequenced in an orderly manner. Subjects are taught and expanded each year to increase memory .It is a "back to the basics" approach to teaching, since it focuses on teaching essential skills and facts. It provides a broad base of knowledge and a rich vocabulary that has been lacking in previous curricula. Parents are provided with a clear outline of what children are expected to learn each year in school. It is an effective tool for lesson planning and communication among teachers. It actually makes lesson plans easier, because a basic outline is provided. The teaching styles, procedure, and aids are the teacher's choice.

On the other hand, there have been some negative reactions to Core Curriculum. It seems to advance at a pace that is too fast for the students at times. It is also difficult for the teachers because they have to advance according to core's pace even if the students are not ready to advance. The resources are listed but not always provided for the teachers. They have to spend much of their time locating resources to use. Textbooks are used less because there is not a specific textbook that follows core's guidelines. There is more paperwork for the teachers. One goal of the Core Knowledge Foundation is to "provide all children, regardless of background, with the shared knowledge they need to be included in our national literate culture." The question becomes, is Core Knowledge really doing this? Here are a few suggestions to incorporate multicultural theories in the Core Curriculum classroom: (I) develop thematic lessons outside of the regulated curriculum that expands on the themes that should be taught (I.E. Kindergarteners are taught Christmas traditions, instead incorporate a lesson on Christmas around the world.), (2) decorate multi-culturally - welcome students of all cultures by decorating your class with pictures and decorations of a variety of cultures, (3) use manipulatives and aids that are pertinent to other cultures, (4) have positive expectations for children of all races, (5) encourage acceptance and appreciation for the cultural diversity in your classroom, and (6) create a learning environment that supports positive interracial contact (Bennett, 1999).

Culturally Responsive Curricula

Culturally Responsive Curricula (CRC) was developed by critics who claimed that multicultural education was divided and unorganized. Schools needed a curriculum that went beyond inclusion and focused on the students' backgrounds. CRC was developed with this focus in mind.

CRC is a fully integrated and interdisciplinary curriculum. It can be used in reading and science as well as in music and physical education. Secondly, CRC is authentic, child-centered and connected to the student's real life. Materials and resources are used to illustrate principles and concepts. Both of these concepts support the need for culturally responsive curriculum. CRC also incorporates current teaching practices. Culturally Responsive Curriculum develops critical thinking skills through cooperative learning and whole language instruction. These practices help to build self-esteem and recognize multiple intelligences and diverse learning styles.

Critics of CRC argue that it cannot be consistent across systems. Because the curriculum is based on student experiences, it must change not only from school to school but also within the classroom. Critics also believe that a curriculum that focuses on each child's background causes conflict between ethnic groups by separating each child. In addition, curriculum must also be covered that may not reflect a child's particular experience or background.

The question related to Culturally Responsive Curriculum is whether or not it brings multicultural education to all children. It is hard to see the positive outcome for all children with this curriculum. Every child needs to have a well-rounded education. Student experiences do affect how and what we teach but they shouldn't be the only factor.

Multicultural Curriculum

In combating racism, multicultural education is the primary curriculum reform. Administrators must advocate multicultural education programs, educate the community, provide professional development and planning time for teachers, evaluate the program's effectiveness and agree to continued improvement (Thomas & Collier, 1999). According to Parks (1999), the total educational program needs to be examined to minimize racism in school. Parks suggests the following steps to minimize racism by ensuring that:

- Curriculum promotes cultural competence and appreciates ethnic diversity;
- Instructional methods promote cooperation, interaction, and success for all students, regardless of the background, language proficiency, social class, or learning style;
- Assessment practices include alternative methods that allow for cultural differences and encourage community review to ensure an equitable appraisal of students' work;
- School culture of oneness supports growth of all students; and
- Public conversation and policymaking are sensitive to the perceptions and values of the total community, (p. 16).

Multicultural education needs to honor and embrace the cultures of the students and community. Bennett (1999) states:

Curriculum can be viewed as the experiences, both official and unofficial, that learners have under the auspices of the school. Following this definition, a multicultural curriculum is one that attends to the school's hidden curriculum-- for example, teachers' values and expectations, student cliques and peer groupings, and school regulations. It also attends to the values, cultural styles, knowledge, and perceptions that all students bring to the school. A multicultural curriculum, in its broadest sense, influences the total school environment, (p. 29).

Administrators have an important role in implementing a multicultural educational program. The components of a multicultural curriculum include: global education, critical thinking, antiviolence, service learning, emotional intelligence instruction, peer mediation and conflict resolution, peace education, moral education, and character education. Administrators must serve as role models and provide multiple opportunities for teacher and community workshops to promote support and implementation of the curriculum.

Parental Involvement

What Can I Do as Principal?

 1. *Analyze how well the school does or does not welcome parents.*

 2. *Set up a special parent lounge/center/resource room.*

 3. *Take school programs out into the community.*

4. *Create a handbook of guidelines and tips for parents.*

5. *Have a weekend or evening public information fair.*

6. *Award extra academic credit for parent involvement.*

7. *Sponsor an old fashioned family night at school.*

8. *Adopt a "Meet and Greet" Program.*

9. *Involve Senior Citizens.*

10. *Provide workshops for teachers on parental involvement.*

Some More Parental Involvement

The Administrator's Role

When children enter school, they bring their home and family with them. All of the experiences they have had up to this point are directly related to home and family life Wells (1992).

Twenty-five years ago, there were still family differences but the family structure was fairly consistent. Most families consisted of a father who went to work to earn a living, and a mother who stayed home with the children Wells (1992). The family of the ninety's is no longer a set structure.

Families now include boyfriends, girlfriends, just friends, and step parents. Many classrooms are filled with students from a variety of race, ethnic backgrounds, and cultures Aronson (1996). However, according to Aronson (1996) regardless of class, race, or educational background, all parents believe their children will benefit from their involvement with their children's school. All parents want to be involved. Low socioeconomic and minority parents report as much interest as other parents in wanting to help their children succeed in school Hollifield (1995). Schools need to involve all parents including the poor, minorities, and single parents -not just those who ordinarily seek out involvement Hollifield (1995).

If parents from different ethnic backgrounds feel their involvement within the school is important, why aren't more parents involved? According to Aronson, a growing number of parents do not speak or read English well enough to communicate with teachers and administrators (1996). Cross-cultural communication is a growing problem Quiroz, Greenfield, Altech (1999). Because of cultural differences, many parents are not familiar with the expectations of their children's school and don't understand how to go about getting involved, even if they want to Aronson (1996).

How can the school administrator promote parental involvement? According to Waler, no cow ever gave milk because a farmer sent her a letter. Principals, if they are truly serious about such improvement, need to "reach out and touch" parents and other citizens in personally meaningful ways (1998). Person-to-person is still the most effective means of establishing and maintaining that sense of "self" and identity that is absolutely essential to the success of everyone in and involved with the school organization Long (1997). The school administrator may establish a personable atmosphere by being open and truly caring, training teachers to welcome and use parent involvement effectively, and meeting parents where they are.

The school administrator must be open. Fostering a climate of hospitality and openness gives parents the information and confidence they need to become actively involved in school activities Waler (1998). A sense of humor, and a willingness to listen and hear what parents are trying to say will keep lines of communication open Long (1997). Parents feel honored when they sense that the school administrator respects their opinion Mapp (1997). The school administrator must accept that his or her own perceptions are not the only ones or even the better ones Quiroz, Greenfield, Altech (1999).

Inexperience may cause some teachers to feel threatened by the direct involvement of parents. To overcome this fear and distrust, the principal needs to share, model, and recognize creative ways in which teachers can effectively collaborate with parents Waler (1998). Parents are all experts in their field, they can answer questions and fascinate the children in ways the teacher cannot Brower (1997).

The key to improving communication with parents is meeting parents where they are Vandegrift & Green (1992). The success of any single parent involvement strategy depends on how well it matches up with an individual parent's needs. Administrators should not initially require high levels of commitment or participation. Something as simple as a friendly conversation can go a long way toward building parent support (Vandegrift & Green, 1992). Administrators should be down to earth. Phrases such as: "perceptual skills", "criterion-referenced testing", and "least restrictive environment" sound like double talk to many parents (NJEA Review, 1998).

Making parents feel comfortable is an important step toward improving parent involvement (Vandegrift & Greene, 1992). When recruiting parents, administrators should be sensitive to feelings of fear and intimidation about associating with school personnel and encourage parents who attempt to become involved with the school. Aronson (1996) states that creating a school atmosphere that welcomes visitors is an important start.

Coalition Building

Educational endeavors in any community will have potential adversaries and potential allies. People and groups who are positively engaged in the planning and implementing of education related efforts are more likely to become allies and less likely to become adversaries, according to Scott Thompson.

Why are teachers not using effective multicultural education practices in their classroom? Teachers are afraid of controversy or getting off the subject in their classrooms. Practically all teachers understand and believe we must value and respect cultural diversity, but many may fear multiculturalism is overly concerned with controversial issues. Many teachers already feel teaching is a precarious position, so they avoid controversy at all costs!

Using the tools of coalition building, "engagement" and "communications," we can diffuse potential adversaries and disengage controversy. Let's engage or involve teachers, staff, parents, and community in our efforts to integrate multiculturism into society. Let's use effective means of communication to present multiculturism to our school and community.
Coalition building can turn adversaries into allies.

Strategies for Multicultural Teaching, A - Z

A   *Assess* fairly in multiple ways

B   *Believe* in students

C   Appreciate *cultural* backgrounds of all

D   Understand language *development*

E   Provide *effective* feedback

F   Promote *family* participation

G   *Group* flexibly

H   *Help* develop social skills

I   Use *interactive* strategies

J   Teach *justice* and care

K   *Know* your students

L   Make *lessons* comprehensible

M   Promote *metacognition*

N   Have students *negotiate* meaning

O   Provide equal *opportunity* for access

P   Reduce *prejudice*. Understand *privilege*

Q   *Question* for high-level, critical thinking

R   *Read* multicultural literature

S   Elicit *student* goals and ideas

T   Align *texts* to children's needs

U   Promote *understanding* of others' ways

V   *View* the globe as our home

W   Provide a *win-win* situation

X   Hold high *expectations*

Y   Reflect upon *your* own culture

Z   Hold *zero* tolerance for put-downs

Creating a Supportive Environment Multiculturalism

Multicultural Education as defined by Banks (1993) is at least three things: An idea or concept, an educational reform movement, and a process because:

1. It incorporates the idea that all students--regardless of their gender and social class and their ethnic, racial, or cultural characteristics--should have an equal opportunity to learn in school some students may learn better with the students who shared their common characteristics.
2. A reform movement--change schools and other educational institutions so that students from all social class, gender, racial, and cultural groups will have an equal opportunity to learn.
3. A process ongoing goals is educational equality eliminate racism, sexism, and discrimination against people with disabilities.

Historical development

1. It grew out of the civil right movement of the 1960's.
2. African Americans started a quest for their rights that was unprecedented in the United States major goal of the movement was to eliminate discrimination in public accommodations, housing, employment, and education the consequences of this movement had a significant influence on educational institutions as ethnic groups demanded that schools and other educational institutions reform their curricula so that they would reflect their experiences, histories, cultures, and perspectives they also demanded that the schools hire more minority teachers and administrators so that children would have more successful role model.
3. The first responses of schools and educators in the 1960's were hurried courses/programs were developed without thought and careful planning needed to make them educationally sound holidays/special days/ethnic

celebrations/courses that focused on one ethnic group were the dominant characteristics of school reforms during the 1960s and early 1970s discrimination toward women in employment, income, and education was widespread and blatant.

4. Women's rights movement articulated and publicized how discrimination and institutionalized sexism limited the opportunities of women and adversely affected the nation leaders -Betty Friedan and Gloria Steinem major goals included:

- Equal pay for equal work
- Elimination of laws that discriminated against women
- Hiring more women in leadership positions
- Greater participation of men in household work and child rearing
- Demanded textbooks reflect women's contribution to history and women to be hired in administrative positions

5. Other victimized groups articulated their grievances and demanded that institutions be reformed.

Other definitions

Multicultural Education is an approach to teaching and learning based upon democratic values and beliefs, and affirms cultural pluralism within culturally diverse societies and an interdependent world.

It is comprised of:

1. The movement toward equity,
2. Curriculum reform,
3. Process of becoming inter-culturally competent, and

4. Commitment to combat prejudices and discrimination especially racism

Tiedt & Tiedt (1999) definition:

- It is an inclusive teaching/learning process that engages all students in
- Developing a strong sense of **self-esteem**
- Discovering **empathy** for persons of diverse cultural backgrounds
- Experiencing **equitable** opportunities to achieve to their fullest potential

Cultural Pluralism is a process of compromise characterized by mutual appreciation and respect between two or more cultural groups. In a cultural pluralistic society, members of different ethnic groups are permitted to retain many of their cultural traditions such as language, religion, and food preferences, so long as they conform to the practices deemed necessary for social harmony and survival of society as a whole. The terms: salad bowl and stain glass window are frequently associated with each part of a tapestry. Both being able to retain some of their uniqueness while mosaic contributing to beauty and strengths of the whole composition. A common misconception is that it is dangerous to society because it heightens ethnic group identity and leads to separation, polarization and inter-group antagonism. Examples include:

- The Amish community, school and tradition but expected to abide by the rules of the larger society
- Chasidic Jews who maintain their orthodox religion in a society that is highly secular and primarily Christian in religious outlook.
- Cherokee, Navajo, and Chippewa nations and other Indian tribes have territory rights to land, fishing rights and other special relationships with federal government.

Cultural Assimilation is a process in which people of diverse ethnic and racial backgrounds come to interact, free of constraints, in the life of the larger community.

- Between 1820-1970 more than 45 million immigrants, mostly from European nations entered the United States.
- Prevalent view was that newly arrived ethnic group would give up their unique cultural attributes and accept the Anglo-American way of life
- School was expected to play the major role in this forced assimilation term -melting pot.
- Concept of Race is a social construction used to group human according to observable traits – size, skin color, and hair texture physical characteristics
- Homo Sapiens (Latin for human being and wise) are groups that all humans belong to.

Culture is learned and can be modified over time.

- Prior to late 1950's, it was typically defined in terms of patterns of behavior and customs.
- Tylor 1871 defined it as "that complex whole which includes knowledge, belief art, morals, law, custom, and any other capabilities and habits acquired by man, a member of society."
- More recent it focus on shared knowledge and belief systems, or symbols and meanings rather than on habits and behavior.
- Geertz defined it as "an historically transmitted pattern of meanings employed in symbols.
- Spradley and McCurdy defined it as "the acquired knowledge that people use to interpret experience and to generate social behavior.

Until recently multicultural education focused primarily on ethnic groups within one society. Commitment is to combat racism, sexism, and all forms of prejudice and discrimination through the development of appropriate understandings, attitudes, and social action skills

Emphasis is on clearing up myths and stereotypes associated with gender and different races and ethnic groups, and stressing basic human similarities, and developing an awareness of the historical roots and current evidence of individual, institutional, and cultural racism and sexism in U.S. and elsewhere in the World.

Implementation of Multicultural Education

Why teachers are not using effective multicultural education practices?

Teachers are responsible for integrating multicultural education into every aspect of the curriculum because of the increasing diverse population in our schools. There has been much written about integrating effective strategies into the classroom. These strategies should ensure greater success for every student. Teachers are to translate educational theories into practice as they plan, select materials, facilitate instruction, assess, and interact with families. Interaction with students is a key in communicating attitudes and perceptions. Multicultural education touches all aspects of education. It is not inclusive.

A study was conducted to explore some of the reasons teachers were not practicing effective strategies in their classroom as it related to multicultural education. During the course of the study, graduate students enrolled in a multicultural education course concluded that all teachers are responsible for using effective practices to promote multicultural education just as they are responsible for using effective practices to teach other subjects in order to meet students' needs and interests. The findings of this study should help school personnel by making them aware of deficiencies and addressing concerns in their classrooms.

The graduate students involved in the study identified five major categories as reasons why teachers are not practicing effective multicultural education. These categories are that teachers do not know what multicultural education is; they do not know how to use effective multicultural practices; they are not motivated to learn effective multicultural education practices; they are resistant to learn effective multicultural education practices; and they do not realize their full responsibilities as educators for using effective multicultural education practices.

The reasons why multicultural teaching practices are not being used are not acceptable to schools, communities, and especially to children. As this study indicates, there is a definite need for reform in order to better implement multicultural education into the schools and the lives of our students.

Strategies for Incorporating Multiculturism

Many changes need to occur in order to provide a meaningful and beneficial multicultural program and consequently, atmosphere in public schools today." Administrators play a key role to guarantee equity in all education environments for students, families, and teachers (Gallavan)." Therefore, administrators, as well as teachers need to have substantial training in the area of multiculturism. It is my opinion that sample activities and lessons need to be identified, in order that the teachers and administrators fully understand the concept and the impact of such materials. Dr. Greta Nagel, a professor at California State University developed a set of guidelines/strategies that teachers can utilize to assess the progress and success of their individual multicultural teachings. I believe that these strategies are relevant to any classroom setting. To highlight a few of these will give you an understanding of the concept of multicultural attitudes.

B -*Believe* in students

Educators should believe that, given the opportunity, students would choose to do the right thing. Of course, this may not always happen with the very first incident. Other factors such as peer pressure must be taken into account. Given the proper atmosphere and guidance the student will come to the right conclusions. I believe that educators must give respect, be fair, and be compassionate and in turn the students will develop trust and respect for them.

C -Appreciate *cultural* backgrounds for all.

Not all students come from the same cultural or socioeconomic backgrounds. These are two areas that impact the students' outlook on life, which is directly related to school performance.

K -*Know* your students

Having an understanding of the type of environment that the student is going home to every day will provide significant information on the school performance and attitudes.

R -*Read* multicultural literature

Reading a variety of multicultural materials will allow the student to feel that their heritage is important. It will also give the other students exposure to other cultures besides their own.

I also believe that respect is a very important factor in multicultural education. "Recognize and value various culture and language differences." (Midobuche) If a parent comes into your classroom that speaks a different language, try to have someone available who speaks the same language. This may even be the student, if necessary.

W -Provide *win-win* situations

When students feel successful and accepted by the teacher and staff, it makes them feel more like contributing to their own education. Also, the diverse population in public schools today can help build a more meaningful multicultural program. f they feel that someone is actually interested in the cultural background from which they come, they will share a wealth of knowledge that the teacher can use for years to come.

Recruiting Minority Teachers

It is important for all teachers to have the knowledge, skills, and training to successfully teach the diverse student population of today. However, it is equally important for all students to have the opportunity to be taught by teachers who reflect their diversity. Minority educators enhance our students' understanding of the intellectual, social, political, and economic complexity of our democratic society (Futrell, 1999).

Today there are about fifty-two million school-age students in the United States. Approximately thirty-five percent of our school children are from linguistic or racial minority families and that figure is expected to increase forty percent in less than a decade (Futrell, 1999). Seventy percent of all public school students are white, sixteen percent are African American, and ten percent are Hispanic. When it comes to the teacher demographics of the United States, three out of every four teachers are female, eighty-nine percent are white, seven percent are African American, and two percent are Hispanic (Latham, 1999). By the year

2008 student enrollment is predicted to reach fifty-five million. In Addition one-third of the teaching population is fifty or older and twenty-five to thirty percent of new teachers leave teaching within the first five years of teaching. With this projected increase in size and diversity of the student population, an aging teaching profession, and high attrition rates there is a desperate need for new teachers, especially teachers that reflect the diversity of the United States culture (Futrell, 1999). The mismatch between the racial and ethnic profiles of teachers and their students reduces the likelihood that teachers will connect learning to all their students in a meaningful way (Latham, 1999).

In order to reach this goal of making the teaching profession reflect the cultural diversity of the United States, we must first look at why more minority groups do not choose teaching as a profession. According to Futrell there are three major reasons (1999).

The first of Futrell's reasons is the lack of academic preparation. African American students and Hispanics are less likely to be placed in gifted and talented programs in elementary schools or in advanced placement programs in high schools. These students are also more likely to be affected by the poverty of school programs and to be taught by poorly prepared or non-certified teachers. Therefore, the students from minority groups and economically disadvantaged backgrounds are not acquiring the academic background, skills, and knowledge that are prerequisites to succeeding in college.

Cost is the second of Futrell's reasons for minority students not choosing teaching as a profession. Many students, including those from racial minority groups, question the cost of preparing to become a teacher, particularly when the return benefits are considerable below those of other professions (1999).

Finally Futrell states that the lack of knowledge about the need for teachers is a reason more do not choose the teaching profession. He suggest that colleges and universities work more closely with local and state education agencies to identify critical areas of need and to prepare candidates, especially minority students, to meet these needs (1999).

Once these minority students become teachers, there are some recruitment strategies for the administrator to follow. Futrell refers to these strategies as career incentives He lists four career incentives that administrators should follow when recruiting teachers, especially minority teachers. These career incentives are: viewing teachers as professionals, help provide working conditions that support quality teaching and learning, provide teachers with the necessary preparation and training to successfully implement education reform initiatives, and to ensure professional compensation (1999).

Beverly Tatum, a professor in the Department of Psychology and Education, Mount Holyoke College, says that we should be working very hard to increase the diversity of the teaching pool, and many teacher education programs are trying to do that. Still, we need to recognize that it's going to be a long time before the teaching population reflects the classroom population. So it's really important for white teachers to recognize that it is possible for them to become culturally sensitive and to be pro-active in an anti-racist way (O'Neil1998).

156

REFERENCES

Bennett, C. (1999). Comprehensive multicultural education theory and practice. Boston. MA: Allyn and Bacon.

Futrell, N.H. (1999). Recruiting Minority Teachers. Educational Leadership, 56, 30-33.

Gallavan, N. (1998). Why aren't teachers using effective multicultural education practices? Equity & Excellence in Education, 31, 20-26.

Latham, A.S. (1999). The teacher-student mismatch. Educational Leadership, 56 [On-line], Available: http://www.ascd.org/pubs/ed/apr99/ extlatham.html.

Midobuche, E. (1999). Respect in the classroom: Reflections of a Mexican-American educator. Educational Leadership, 56, 80-82.

Nagel, G. Looking for multicultural education: What could be done and why it isn't. Education, 119, 253-262.

O'Neil, John. (1998). Why are all the Black kids sitting together? Educational Leadership, 55, 13-17.

Thompson. S. (1998). Moving from publicity to engagement. Educational Leadership, 54-58.

ADDITIONAL REFERENCES

Aronson, J. (1996). How schools can recruit hard-to-reach parents. Educational Leadership, 53 (7), 58- 60.

Brower, T. (1997). Recruiting parents and the community. Educational Leadership, 54 (5), 58- 60.

Hollifield, J. (1995). TIPS to involve middle school parents. Educational Digest, 61 (1), 50 -52.

Long, L. (1997). How to personalize the school environment. The National Association of Secondary School   Principals, 56 (2), 34 -35.

Mapp, K. (1997). Making family-school connections work. Educational Digest, 81 (1), 36 -39.

NJEA Review (1998). Making the most of meetings with family members. Educational Digest, 86 (1), 20-24.

Quiroz, B., Greenfield, P., & Altchech, M. (1999). Bridging cultures with a parent-teacher conference. Educational Leadership, 56 (7), 68- 70.

Vandegrift, J. & Green, A. (1992). Rethinking parent involvement. Educational Leadership, 50 (1), 57 -59.

Waler, J. (1998). How to promote parent and community involvement in school issues and activities. National Association of Secondary School Principals, 65 (2), 44 -45.

Wells, L. (1992). Getting parents involved in the classroom. Contemporary Education, 64 (1), 46 -50.

EXTENDED REFERENCES

Abdal-Hagg, I. (1994). Culturally responsive curriculum [Online]. Available: ERIC Clearinghouse on Teaching and Teacher Education, http:/ /www.ed.gov./databases/ERIC_Digests/ed370936.html.

Alaska standards for culturally responsive schools. [Online]. Available: Alaska Native Knowledge Network, http:/ /www.nerel.org/sdrs/areas/issues/students/leaming/lr1cre.htm.

Andrews, R.H. (1990). The Development of learning styles program in a low socioeconomic, underachieving North Carolina elementary school. Journal of Reading, Writing, and Learning Disabilities International, 63, 307-314.

Banks, J. (1998). Multicultural education: Goals and dimensions. Center for Multicultural Education, University of Washington, [On-line]. Available: http://depts.washington.edu/centerme/home.htm.

Banks, J .A. (1994). An introduction to multicultural education. Boston: Allyn and Bacon.

Bennett, C.I. (1999). Comprehensive multicultural education: Theory and practice. Boston: Allyn & Bacon.

Brunner, C.E., and W.S. Majewski (1990). Mildly handicapped students can succeed with learning styles. Educational Leadership, 48 (2), 21-23.

Culturally responsive education: Strategic teaching and reading project guidebook. [Online]. Available: http://www.ankn.uaf.edu/currstan.html.

Core knowledge foundation, 1999. [Online] Available: http://www.coreknowledge.org/Ckproto2/about/index.num.

Drew, M., Dunn, R., Quinn, P., Sinatra, R., and Spiradakis, J. (1994). Effects of matching and mismatching minority underachievers with culturally similar and dissimilar story content and learning style and traditional instructional practices. Applied Educational Research Journal 8 (2), 3-10.

Dunn, R. (1997, April). The goals and track record of multicultural education. Educational Leadership, 54 (7), 74.

Examination of Issues and Perspectives on Race in Mainstream Physical Education Journals. (   ).

Hirsch, E., Jr. (1996). What your kindergartener needs to know. New York: Dell Publishing.

Kantrowitz, B. & Farai C. (1992, November 2). What kids need to know. Newsweek, 120 (18), 80.

Katz, L. L. (1999, Winter). In pursuit of the multicultural curriculum. Independent School, 58 (2), 31.

Kirmani, M. & Laster B. (1999, April). Responding to religion and diversity in classrooms. Educational Leadership, 56 (7), 61-63.

Menkart, D. (1999, April). Deepening the meaning of heritage months. Educational Leadership, 56, (7), 19-21.

Morefield, J. (1998) Recreating schools for all children. New Horizons for Learning. [On-line]. Available: http://newhorizons.org.

O'Neil, J. (1999, March). Core knowledge and standards: A conversation with E.D. Hirsch, Jr. Educational Leadership Vl. 56 (6), 28-31.

Parks, S. (1999). Reducing the effects of racism in schools. Educational Leadership, 56 (7), 14-18.

Quinn, R. (1993). The New York state compact for learning and learning styles. Learning Styles Network Newsletter, 15 (I), 1-2.

Storm, J. (1993, May). Core knowledge: One teacher's experience. Educational Leadership, 50 (8), 26-27.

Stone, P. (1992). How we turned around a problem school. Principal 71, (2) 34-36.

Thomas, P., & Collier, V.P. (1999). Accelerated schooling for English language learners. Educational Leadership, 56 (7), 46-49.

Zahorik, J. A., & Novak, R. (1996, Nov/Dec). Multiculturalism: The range of teacher approaches. Clearing House, 70 (2), 5 and 85.

Chapter 13

Multicultural Education for Young Children: Racial and Ethnic Attitudes and Their Modification

Dr. Tony J. Manson
Middle Tennessee State University

Multicultural education as defined by James Banks is a process whose major aims are to help students from diverse ethnic groups attain equal educational opportunities and to help all students develop positive cross-cultural attitudes. There are three major approaches to multicultural education. Content approaches view multicultural education as a process that involves additions to or changes in the curriculum of content areas. The main goal of the achievement approach is to design the goals, theories, and strategies to enhance the achievement of the lower class students. Inter-group education aims to help all students develop positive attitudes toward all racial and cultural groups.

James Banks found that many teachers he has come across state that children are unable to see the racial and ethnic differences among themselves. There are many problems with the "color blind" approach. One major problem is that it is inconsistent with how children develop racial views. Research has found that over a 50 year period, young children are not only aware of racial and ethnic differences, but have internalized society's norms regarding the social stature of different groups (Goodman 1946; Horowitz, 1939; Katz, 1987; Lasker, 1929; Minard, 1932; Ramsey & Myers, 1990; and Spencer, 1982). Lasker's (1929) pioneering research indicated that young children are aware of racial differences.

Minard (1931) found that children's racial attitudes are formed during the earliest years of life. Kenneth and Mamie Clark (1939a, 1939b, 1940, 1947, and 1950) established a paradigm in racial attitude research that is still highly influential.

Kenneth and Mamie Clark (1947) studied racial preference, racial differences and racial self-identification. The Clarks used brown and white dolls with a sample of 253 African American children age 3-7 from Arkansas and Massachusetts. The Clarks found that:

- 94% chose the white doll when asked to give them the white doll;
- 93% chose the brown doll when asked to give the colored doll;
- 66% identified with the colored doll;
- 33% identified with the white doll;
- About 2/3 indicated they liked the white doll best and that they preferred to play with the white doll rather than the colored doll;
- 59% said the colored doll looked bad;
- 17% said the white doll looked bad;
- The preference for the white doll decreased in older children; and
- Southern children were less pronounced in their preference.

The Clarks concluded that youngsters have an accurate knowledge about racial differences arid that African American children often make incorrect racial self - identification expressing a preference for the white dolls.

There are many studies that support the Clark's findings. One such study was conducted by Radke and Trager (1950). Radke and Trager chose a sample of 242 K-2 students in the Philadelphia Public Schools. There was 90 African American and 152 white children chosen. The study used cut out figures of men and women, plywood clothes and plywood in the form of houses. The children were asked to dress the black and white figures and put them in houses. Radke and Trager found:

- 38% of white children assigned inferior roles to black dolls;
- 16% of black children assigned inferior roles to black dolls; and
- A majority gave the poor house to the black doll and the good house tom the white doll.

Since the pioneering research conducted by the Clarks and other researchers that have validated their findings, many social scientist have assumed that African American children have low self-esteem negative self-concepts and harbor self-hate because they internalize Euro centric racial attitudes. This hypothesis was popular from the 1940's through most of the 1970's. On the other hand some research has found weaknesses in the Clark's findings. Gregor and McPherson (1966a) conducted a study of 6 and 7 year-old children in the segregated South. They found that both white and African American students made own group preferences. The researchers used a variant of the doll test completed by the Clarks. Gregor and McPherson found that:

- White own group choices exceeded 79% of all preference request;
- African American children own group choices exceeded 50%;
- They hypothesized that the more minority group children are integrated into racially mixed settings, the more likely they are to express out-group preferences; and
- They believed that the African American children in their study made own group preferences because they lived in racially segregated communities and attended segregated schools.

A replication of the Clark's doll study conducted by Hraba and Grant (1970) found that both black and white children made own group preferences. The children between 4 and 8 attended interracial schools in Lincoln, Nebraska. They found that:

- A majority of black children of all ages preferred the black doll;
- Own group preferences increased with age; and
- 70% of black children had white friends and 55% of white children had black friends.

Today, there is still debate among researchers about young children's racial preference, attitude and identifications. However, researchers do agree that 1) preschool and kindergarten African Americans often make out group preferences on a variety of measures and 2) these out group preferences decrease with age but increase with interracial settings and situations. Recent research and theory indicates that personal identity and group identity are separate, and that young African American ch8ildren can express a bias toward whiteness and white people and yet have high self-esteem and positive self-concepts.

Modifications of Young Children's Racial Attitudes

Reinforcement Studies

Conducted by Williams and various colleagues in the late 1960's at Winston-Salem, North Carolina with 84 white preschool children. The goal was to modify attitudes and to determine if white bias toward objects and animals could be applied to people. This study used the pictures story technique involving for example a white and a black horse. Much like the one seen earlier. They also used pictures similar to those shown earlier of the two girls. Positive black statements were reinforced positively by giving candy to the student. Negative black or positive white were reinforced negatively by removing 2 pennies from a stack of 30 which belonged to the children. There were three experimental and one-control groups. Conclusions of the research indicated that reinforcement accounted for some gains that were statistically significant but the researchers called "not substantial".

Others conducted similar research that confirmed the Williams group studies. Spencer Horowitz "examined color perception of 24 African Americans and white children to modify their color connotations and racial attitudes. They found that black preschool children were as negative about the color black as were the white preschoolers. They also determined that the children generalized color concepts to racial concepts. There experiments showed that social and ~n reinforcement reduced white bias. The effects of the experiment were evident after a 2 week period and for some children over a 4 week period. There was no mention of a longer interval follow up.

Perceptual Differentiation Studies

Conducted by Katz and colleagues from 1973-1978. They examined the perceptual concomitants of facial attitudes. Katz's study in 1978 studied the effect of teaching children to differentiate minority-group faces and the effects of three interventions: (1) increased positive racial contact using a jigsaw puzzle, (2) vicarious interracial contact, and using stories of African American children who were heroes, and (3) reinforcement of the color black using positive reward of marbles. In the experiment, each treatment lasted for just 15 minutes. The results of '8 were: (1) each of the above had short-term reduction of prejudice on the combined attitude measures used in the study and (2) the most effective interventions (long term) were vicarious contact and perceptual differentiation conditions.

Curriculum interventions

Why does the educational inequality exist for ethnic minorities? James and Cherry Banks in there 1993, second edition of Multicultural education: Issues and perspectives, state their reasons on pages 181 through 183. They can be summed as follows:

1. Sameness of materials does not equate to equality;
2. Teachers graduate teacher colleges with little to no knowledge of diverse groups;
3. Most teacher training is Euro centered; and
4. School environments suit one ethnic group but not another.

Intervention comes in four methods:

(1) Teaching units and lessons,

(2) Multiethnic materials,

(3) Role playing, and

(4) Other kinds of simulations.

Studies have been ongoing from 1952 when a study by Trager and Yarrrow examined the effects of a democratic versus a no democratic method. Students and teachers performed better under democratic situation. Under the heading of Multi cultural materials one could place the popular young children's show Sesame Street. Bogatz and Ball studied the effects of Sesame Street in a 1971 longitudinal study. The show was determined to have a positive influence in racial attitudes of long-term viewers of the show.

Simulation was explored by a dividing a class into orange and green-banded children. The groups were selectively "discriminated" against only one day in two. Two weeks after the experience, children expressed less prejudiced beliefs and attitudes.

Finally, in this category , another study of 4 year-old black children exposed children to 3 types of curriculum:

1. Students read and discussed the materials,
2. Students read, discussed then took a related field trip, and
3. Students were exposed to traditional pre-school curriculum.

The findings indicated the first two approaches showed significant positive effects on the student's racial attitudes toward blacks and whites. The third had no effect-positive or negative.

Cooperative Learning and Interracial Contact

Cooperative learning works as a means of teaching multiculturalism only when everyone in the group is given an equal status. Students will, whether conscience or not, ascribed a higher level to whites than blacks. This was determined through two studies, Allport in 1954 and Cohen in 1974. In a related study by Cohen and Roper in 1972, black students were given the opportunity to be the "teacher" in a radio class. The researchers discovered the black students in this study received equal status treatment by all involved. It was noted that in all of the studies, there were positive academic effects for everyone involved.

Summary

The bottom line is that adults can change their attitudes. In order for this to occur, the approach to multiculturalism must be structured, well conceptualized, and executed well. Use of cooperative learning, vicarious examples, and simulation seem to work best to facilitate change or attitudes. Communication seems to be important in this and many other educational settings.

Implications for Research and Practice

A paradigm, as defined by Banks, is a set of beliefs, values, techniques, and research assumptions shared by the members of a specific scientific community. An interrelated set of postulates, principles, explanations, and theories constitutes a paradigm.

Research implications for a bicultural paradigm according to Banks:

- Assumes that be-group or biracial choices are both healthy and needed within a pluralistic society.

- Calls this new paradigm -biculturalism.

The 6-stage model to multiculturalism discussed as *"stages of ethnicity "* *compliments the bicultural* paradigm. Below is a brief discussion of these models.

- Cultural Psychological Captivity -These are institutionalized within the dominant society.
- Cultural expectation -Characterized by ethnic exclusiveness, strong in-group preferences, the recognition of out-groups, and ethnocentric beliefs and behaviors
- Cultural Identity Clarification -The individual is able to clarify his or her attitudes and ethnic identity and to develop clarified positive attitudes toward his or her ethnic group.
- Biculturalism -Also called biethinicity. These individuals have a healthy sense of ethnic identity and the psychological characteristics and skills needed to participate successfully within

their own ethnic culture, as well as within another ethnic culture. *This is critical: The individual has a strong desire and the knowledge, attitudes, and skills needed to function within, cultures-his or her own and one other.*

- Multiculturalism- The individual is able to function, at least beyond superficial levels, within several ethnic cultures in his or her nation. Individuals in this group have a strong commitment to their ethnic groups, an empathy and concern for other ethnic groups, and a strong reflective commitment and allegiance to the nation state and its idealized values, such as human dignity and justice.

- Globalism and global competency -The individual in Stage 6 has the ideal delicate balance of ethnic, national, and global identifications, commitment, literacy, and behaviors.

Implications for practice

There is a need for total school reform. The key word being total. A partial reform over of the school will not work. A total reform over part of the school will not work. The reform must encompass all of the school in total reform.

Curriculum Reform Approaches

There are several approaches to school reform. The following discusses these various approaches. The positive and negative attributes are those discussed by the James Banks.

1. Contributions approach – is frequently used by early childhood and kindergarten teachers to infuse ethnic content into the curriculum. It is characterized by the addition to the curriculum of ethnic heroes. It

leaves the mainstream curriculum unchanged in terms of its basic assumptions, goals, and salient characteristics.

2.   Heroes and holidays approach – a variant of the contributions approach. In this approach, ethnic content is limited primarily to special days, weeks, and months related to ethnic events and celebrations. Examples include: Cinco de Mayo, Martin Luther King's Birthday, and African American History Month. The problems with this approach include:

- Students study little about the ethnic group outside of the special event time me.
- It does not enable students to view ethnic groups as an integral part of U.S.society and culture.
- The ethnic group in question becomes viewed as an appendage.
- Many stereotypes are formed during such event-oriented times.

3.   Additive approach -the addition of ethnic content, concepts, themes, and perspectives he curriculum without changing its basic structure, purposes, and characteristics. It usually results in the teaching of ethnic content from the perspectives of mainstream writers, artists, storytellers, and historians. An example of the additive approach is the holiday of Thanksgiving. Native Americans are viewed from the perspective of the Pilgrims.

4.   Transformation approach -this approach changes the basic assumptions of the curriculum and enables students to view events, concepts, themes, issues, and problems from several ethnic perspectives. Using the Thanksgiving example, the students may be asked to assume the roles of both the Pilgrims and the Native Americans in role-play situations.

5. Personal, social, and civic action approach -includes elements of the transformation approach but adds components that require students to make decisions and to take actions related he concept, issue, or problem they have studied in a lesson or unit.

School reform

The Multicultural school environment figure 16-2 from the article: This figure describes characteristics of a Multicultural school environment that has been restructured and transformed. The total school environment is conceptualized as a system that consists of a number of identifiable factors as shown. In the restructured multicultural school, each of these variables has been changed and reflects ethnic, cultural, and social-class equality. Although any of these factors may be the focus of initial school reform, changes must take place in each of m to create and sustain a school environment in which students from diverse racial, ethnic, and cultural groups experience equality.

It is the teacher that will move the students from a contributions approach to the 4th stage of personal, social and civic action approach. Beginning at the lowest level is acceptable as long as the teacher moves from there. Teachers bring their own paradigm, values and beliefs into the classroom. These beliefs are converted into actions that directly affect the students and the students read the teacher and determine how the teachers' views the various ethnic groups within classroom. Teachers need to remember that their actions influence the actions of the students. If the teacher holds one ethnic group in higher esteem than another, the students are likely to follow that example, especially in early childhood education, teachers therefore become agents of social change.

172

Summary

There is a need for modification according to research findings. The need is perhaps not as great as perceived. The self-hate hypothesis has some merit but not as much as we have been lead to believe. The racial and ethnic attitudes of children can be modified through effective

is which include vicarious experiences and cooperative learning, The teacher plays a critical in this modification. Teacher educators should help classroom teachers attain the knowledge, attitudes, and skills they will need to function effectively in the Multi cultural classroom of the twenty-first century.

Cole, M. & Bruner, J. (   ). Cultural differences and inferences about psychological process. In Matin Maehr and William Stallings (Eds.), Culture, child and school (pp. 107-123). Monterey: Brooks Publishing.

Guerra, M. (1970). Language instruction and intergroup relations. In H. Johnson and W. Hernandez (Eds.), Educating the Mexican-American (pp. 243-249). Valley Forge: Judson Press.

Hernandez, L. (1979). The language of the Chicano. Los Angeles: California State University.

Olivas, M. A. (1988, May - June). Latino faculty at the border: Increasing numbers key to more Hispanic access. Change, 20 (3), 6-9.

San-Miguel, Jr. G. (1987, Winter). The status of historical research on Chicano education. Review of Educational Research, 57 (4), 467-480.

San-Miguel, Jr. G. (1986, Winter). Status of historiography of Chicano education: a preliminary analysis. History of Education Quarterly, 26 (4), 523-536.

U.S. Commission on Civil Rights. (1975). A better chance to learn. Washington, D. C.: Clearinghouse Publication 51.

Chapter 14

School Counselors Preparation for Diversity

Dr. Debra V. Bettis Britton

Texas Southern University

Houston, TX

School counselors in public education can be viewed as a catalyst for change in the 21st century. Along with the school board, superintendent, school principal and other staff, school counselors help to provide a safe school climate for all students regardless of cultural differences. A school Counselor's preparation for diversity begins with a thorough background in the behavioral sciences such as counseling, psychology, and or sociology adapted to a school setting (Gibson, Mitchell, and Basile, 1993). According to Edmund W. Gordon (1999), diversity refers to differences in status and function. In today's society, status defines a person's social hierarchy (social class, caste, gender, race, etc.) and access to material resources and rewards. In other words, you have 'the haves and the have nots'. Status can also influence one's worldview of him or herself. Gordon (1999) states that the functional characteristics of diversity include traits such as identity, culture, motivation, cognitive style, and temperament. Simply stated, function refers to the "how" of behavior. Why do people act the way they do?

As school counselors prepare for diversity on their campuses, they should consider three components: awareness, knowledge, and skills (Sue, Arredondo & McDavis, 1992). If school counselors are going to be effective change agents for diversity, they must examine their own worldview, biases, and values. Secondly, school counselors must have a comprehensive knowledge of family dynamics as it pertains to different groups. Lastly, school counselors must develop counseling skills that will use assessment and treatment to empower students and the learning community by being flexible and culturally sensitive to all students and staff.

Research by Pederson (1991b, p.7) found that not all persons of the same culture share the same experiences. Therefore, school counselors must develop skills to deal with a variety of differences among culturally diverse groups.

Not only do school counselors focus their work on meeting the needs of school children, they also interact with family and the community at large (Lee, 1995). *Counseling for Diversity: A Guide for School Counselors and Related Professionals (1995)* by Courtland Lee state that in today's society, it is not enough to work with the student and meet his or her needs; it is imperative to strengthen the entire family unit. As the family unit and the school will be strengthen with parental support.

Preparation for diversity is perpetual; it never ends. Locke and Parker (1994) believed that all school personnel not just school counselors must develop levels of awareness in order to be effective in meeting the needs of culturally different students.

Summarized Levels of Awareness by Locke and Parker (1994):

- *Self-awareness – Self-understanding of one's own thoughts and feelings regarding attitudes and cultural.*
- *Awareness of one's own culture- examines one's own name and its cultural significance.*
- *Awareness of racism, sexism, and poverty- personal prejudices, institutional prejudice, attitudes, and beliefs in the educator's school system.*
- *Awareness of individual differences- educators in general must become aware of individual differences before developing an awareness of cultural differences.*

- *Awareness of other cultures- previous levels of awareness creates the foundation for learning dynamics of other cultures. School personnel need to be sensitive to verbal and nonverbal behaviors unique to a particular culture.*

- *Awareness of diversity- to describe the goal of all cultures retaining their unique cultural identity, Locke and Parker (1994) uses the "salad bowl" as an example, rather than the melting pot.*

- *Skills/techniques- educators must have competent teaching skills along with awareness in order to relate learning theory to the developmental of psychological cultural factors.*

Along with awareness, Locke and Parker (1994) emphasized the need for all educational systems to become responsive to the values, visions, ideas, beliefs, dreams, and the hopes of all students.   Another way school counselors can prepare for diversity according to Zark VanZandt and Jo Hayslip (2001) is to bring diversity perspectives into the counseling curriculum.   In order to be effective with students, VanZandt and Hayslip (2001) suggest counselors to consider taking a diversity workshop or seminar. As a part of the curriculum they suggest that school counselors create lesson plans that will embrace diversity as apart of the guidance program.

The traditional educational system must pay more than verbal lip service to diversity. Greenman and Kimmel (1995) state that the road to Multicultural education is paved with good intentions, but rutted with potholes of resistance. In the infancy of the twenty first century, resistance to multicultural education and change is prevalent. Policies regarding multicultural education oftentimes reflect the worldview of the dominant culture.   According to Greenman, Kimmel, Bannan, and Radford-Curry (1992), resistance to diversity is generally embedded in institutional structures. Nearly three decades ago, the American Association of Colleges for Teacher Education (AACTE) declared that multicultural education rejected the view that schools should seek to melt away cultural differences (1973, p.264). As early pioneers of multicultural education, the American Association of Colleges for Teacher Education (AACTE) supported multiculturalism, equity, empowerment,, cultural and individual differences.

While preparation for diversity may be challenging for the school counselor, he, or she must keep in mind that preparation for diversity is not an overnight process. Not only must school counselors prepare for diversity, the entire learning community must be apart of the preparation. As trained Professional's school counselors have the skills to decompress resistance to programs and services (Thompson, 1992). The ultimate benefactor of diversity preparation is the student. As the learning community celebrates the cultural and individual differences of each child, it is creating a better school climate that is conducive to positive learning.

If school counselors are going to be effective change agents for diversity, there must be a paradigm shift in the school counselor's role and function in the public school (Allen, 1994). In preparation for diversity, and role change, counselors must be proactive and move out of their counseling offices and into the community. Allen (1994) viewed the counselor as a facilitator of team building, resource broker of services, information processor, nurturer, and a promoter of positive student outcomes. Through collaboration, the school counselor will unite students, faculty, staff and the community in a common vision and mission to prepare each student to be responsible and successful. Diversity is beautiful. Each student is unique and different. In the school setting, there are many diverse cultures, backgrounds and values. However, a prepared school counselor will value these differences and work to bring out the best in each child.

REFERENCES

Allen, J. (1994). Presidential perspective. The ASCA Counselor, 31.

Allen, J. (1994). School counselors collaborating for student success. ERIC Digest. ED377414.

American Association of Colleges for Teacher Education Commission on Multicultural Education. (1973). No one model. American Journal of Teacher Education,24(4), 264-265.

Gibson, R., Mitchell, M., & Basile, S. (1993). Counseling in the elementary school: A comprehensive approach. Boston: Allyn and Bacon.

Gordon, E. (1999). Education & justice: A view from the back of the bus. New York: Teachers College.

Greenman, N, Kimmel, E., & Radford-Curry, B. (1992). Institutional inertia to achieving diversity: Transforming resistance into celebration. Educational Foundations, 6(2), 89-111.

Holmgren, V. (1996). Elementary school counseling: An expanding role. Needham Heights: Allyn and Bacon.

Lee, C. (1995). Counseling for diversity: A guide for school counselors and related professionals. Needham Heights: Allyn and Bacon.

Locke, D. & Parker, L. (1994). Improving the multicultural competence of Educators. In P. Pederson & J. Carey (Eds.), Multicultural counseling in schools. Boston: Allyn and Bacon.

Pederson, P. (1991b). Multiculturalism as a generic approach to counseling. Journal of Counseling and Development, 70 (1), 6-12.

Sears, S. (1999). Transforming school counseling: Making a difference for students. NASSP Bulletin, 83 (603), 47-53.

Sue, D., Arredondo, P., & McDavis, R. (1992). Multicultural counseling competencies and standards: A call to the profession. Journal of Counseling and Development, 70 (2), 477-486.

Thompson, R. (1992). School counseling renewal: Strategies for the twenty-first century. Muncie: Accelerated Development.

VanZandt, Z., & Hayslip, J. (2001). Developing your school counseling program: A handbook for systematic planning. Belmont: Wadsworth.

Chapter 15

The Administrator's Role in Increasing Parental Involvement in a Culturally Diverse School Environment: Strategies and Techniques

Joyce Hendrick
Departmant of Defense

Introduction

As an educator for more than twenty-five years, I have recognized that a positive working relationship with parents is necessary for me to fulfill my commitment to their children. Yet, it has not been easy to accomplish. In my most recent and longest tenure in education, I worked for the Department of Defense Education Activity (DoDEA) and was a teacher and administrator in the Department of Defense Overseas School system. Our student population was comprised primarily of dependents of the military and civilian members assigned to duty overseas. Additionally, we had students whose parents were connected with the state department or private companies located overseas.

The composition of the schools was ethnically diverse with a minority population of approximately 43%, and nearly every state and territory in the United States represented in the schools. In addition to the diverse population's needs, there was a constant turn over of students, causing the make up of the schools and individual classes to change frequently. These factors made the task of getting parents involved in the schools and in their children's education even more challenging.

In recognizing the importance of parent participation and involvement in the schools, DoDEA included the National Educational Goal of "Parental

Participation" as part of its strategic plan for all of its schools. The goal was to promote partnerships that would increase parental involvement and participation in promoting the social, emotional, and academic growth of children (DoDEA, 2000). At the district and school level, parental participation/involvement was a part of the District Improvement Plan and the School Improvement Plans.

Living and working in a foreign country made finding current research and techniques on the topic of parental involvement more difficult. Hence, when I applied for a leave of absence in 1999, one of my goals was to learn more about techniques and methods for increasing parental involvement in schools. As I worked on this topic throughout the semester, I found that there is far more to getting parents involved than I had considered previously. My understanding and definition of parental involvement has expanded to encompass types of involvement that go far beyond the traditional thoughts of just getting parents into the school to participate in conferences, special programs, or volunteering in the classroom. The definition of parental involvement is more complex than merely participating in bake sales and field trips (Vopat, 1998).

Why is parental involvement important? What are some of the barriers to getting parents involved in their children's education? How can we, the teachers and school and district level administrators, encourage and increase parental involvement in the culturally diverse schools and in their children's education? These are the questions that are central to my research and ones that will be addressed in this paper.

Importance of Parental Involvement

Parental involvement in their children's education at all grade levels is critical and often extremely difficult to accomplish. Researchers, as well as educators' direct experience, emphasize the importance of parental involvement and the correlation between their involvement and student success in school (Brandt, 1989; Chavkin & Williams, 1988: Epstein, 1987, 1995; Hoover-Dempsey & Sandler, 1995, 1997; Lueder, 1998; Manning & Baruth, 2000; & Swap, 1987).

For more than two decades, major studies have been conducted on the topic of parental involvement in schools. The results of the studies indicate that parents are important educators of their children and that schools cannot do the job of educating children alone (Haynes, et al. 1996; & Rich, 1988). Furthermore, research shows that parents want their children to be successful in school and want to help. It also indicates that students are more successful when parents are involved (Epstein, 1995; Hoover-Dempsey & Sandler, 1997). Swap (1987) points out that parental involvement also benefits the school by parents bringing their own resources and talents to share with the students and to add to the school program.

Chavkin and Williams (1988) report that increased learning occurs when parents are involved with the schools their children attend. They cite the following advantages to parental involvement in their children's education and school and the positive impact, as well, on both:

* A rise in student achievement scores;

*An increase in student attendance;

*A reduction of student dropouts;

*An improvement of student motivation, self-esteem, and behavior; and

*More parent and community support of the school (p. 87).

What do we mean when we refer to parental involvement in their children's education? Rich (1988) writes that we can no longer define parental involvement as just involvement in children's schooling since many parents cannot go to the schools to be involved. She says that we need to redirect our efforts to involve families in the education of their children outside the school setting. Bermudez and Padron (1988) reinforce this idea and said "learning must not be associated only with school. Parents must be convinced that the whole family can foster learning at home" (p. 83).

Vopat (1998) makes a distinction between parent "participation" and parent "involvement" in school. He reports on the results of a 1997 survey conducted by Milwaukee's Public Policy Forum that asked parents, teachers, and school administrators to indicate what was most important to them in a school. The parents' most common response indicated that the school program was most important. Hence, he emphasizes that parents need to be given opportunities to be involved in meaningful ways rather than the traditional ways if the purpose of parental involvement is to help children do better in school.

According to Lueder (1998), the traditional parent involvement approach has been basically single-dimensional with parents providing their resources of time, money, and expertise "to support the school's curriculum, programs and activities" (p. 3). He writes that there is usually a small group of parents actively involved in the school in some capacity. Within this group, there is an even smaller group that is involved with practically all of the activities and programs. His concern is with the many parents or family members not taking an active part in the schools.

Barriers to Parental Involvement

Research shows that one of the main barriers to getting parents involved in their children's education and school is the change in families (Epstein, 1988; Frieman, 1998; Maeroff, 1992; & Swap, 1987). Not only are there more single parent families today but there are also weakened support structures of extended family members to provide assistance (Maeroff, 1992). Limited time for communication is another common barrier to parent involvement (Swap, 1987). More mothers are working and not easily available to speak with teachers. Many parents are so concerned with the demands of other aspects of their lives that they have little time for involvement in their children's education or school (Swap, 1987).

Another barrier, according to Swap (1987) is the type of parent-school contact. It is often seen as ineffective and limited by time restraints. Still, other parents have unpleasant memories of their own school experience and do not feel comfortable participating in school activities (Davies, 1997; Finders & Lewis, 1994). According to Lueder (1998), some parents experience the psychological barriers of fear and alienation while others lack the knowledge and skills needed to play a role in their children's education. He also points out that logistical barriers, such as transportation, childcare, work schedules which are inflexible, and time constraints, affect parents' ability to be involved.

As their children reach the upper elementary school grades and into middle and high school, parents often perceive that they are not needed as much in the schools and are receiving fewer ideas from teachers. They also feel less capable to assist their children with their homework at home (Epstein, 1987). In a study conducted by Dornbusch and Ritter (1988), they report that a high proportion of high school teachers indicate that they would like to have more contact with parents of students with learning problems or those making little effort in school.

Many teachers also want more contact with parents of students having disciplinary problems. According to the authors many of the teachers do not want more contact with parents who are actively involved in school activities, who have average or outstanding students, or who are interested in helping their children. Chavkin and Williams (1988) say that many teachers' perceptions of more contact with parents means more time and responsibilities on their part.

A lack of understanding of the diverse student and parent population in the public schools is yet another barrier to parental involvement. For more than a century, schools have been concerned with educating a student body that is diverse. Riehl (2000) reports from her research that of the students in the high school class of 2000 "40 percent could be classified as 'culturally different' from English-speaking, white European Americans, and 24 percent were born in poverty" (p. 56). She also writes that the African American and Hispanic, especially, populations are growing at a faster rate than the white population. Riehl says that the children from these groups have a greater likelihood of being poor.

Understanding and effectively educating students and working with the parents who are diverse, especially in terms of race and ethnicity, national origin, and native language, presents a challenge, as well as public pressure, for school administrators and teachers (Riehl, 2000). Language minority parents are unable to communicate easily and often do not understand the written or spoken communications from the schools (Bermudez & Padron, 1988; & Finders & Lewis, 1994). Families from different cultures may have a negative self-concept because of their differences and have difficulty feeling comfortable in the school environment (Phillips, 1988). Because of their culturally different backgrounds, they also may not understand the school's expectations (Manning & Baruth, 2000).

Critical to the issue of increasing parental involvement in children's education and the schools, as well as another barrier, is teacher training for parent involvement (Chavkin & Williams, 1988; Davies, 1996; Epstein, 1988; & Rich, 1988). In their article on this subject, Chavkin and Williams (1988) report that 86.6% of teachers surveyed said they needed training for working with parents, and 92.2% of the principals concurred. Rich (1988) avers that teachers need to be involved in training programs that provide research on families as educators so that teachers can develop strategies for reaching and working with adults.

Epstein (1995) reinforces the lack of and need for courses or classes for teachers and administrators. She says that, "Most principals and district leaders are not prepared to guide and lead their staffs in developing strong school and classroom practices that inform and involve families" (p. 710). Also, Comer (1980) points out "there are few in-service programs that prepare parents to work in schools. Few school systems have developed programs to help parents, administrators, and teachers blend agendas and work cooperatively" (p. 22).

Additionally, financial and technical supports are lacking even though there is ample evidence that parental involvement is necessary and positive (Nardine & Morris, 1991). Many states and school districts do not have policies for parental involvement programs, fiscal support, or necessary leadership and staffing for developing effective partnership programs (Epstein, 1995). On this issue, Epstein (1995) continues by saying, "Yet relatively small financial investments that support and assist the work of action teams could yield significant returns for all schools, teachers, families and students" (p. 711).

Strategies and Techniques for Increasing Parental Involvement

How can teachers and school level administrators encourage and increase parental involvement in the schools and in their children's education? Haynes', et al. (1996) research on reforming education reinforces the fact that school staff and parents not only want to increase the level of parental involvement in schools but also want to enhance the quality of their involvement. The question many school staffs and parents ask is "how do we do it?"

At the school level, the process begins with the administrator who must be willing to lead. Administrators are responsible for providing the necessary leadership to bring about change in their schools (Kowalski & Reitzug, 1993). Being an effective communicator is an important part of the leadership role in bringing about change. In the schools, administrators are the information link between teachers and other parties, such as parents, district and area administration, and other state and federal agencies. Communicating with others is often difficult and can cause problems for the administrator with staff and parents when it is not done effectively. Hence, it is important for the administrator to understand that communication is complex and involves various filters, such as past experiences, skill or educational level, age, sex, and physical environment, which can interfere with clear and effective communication. In order to communicate effectively, administrators need to know and understand their audiences whether they are teachers, parents, community, or other administrators (Kowalski & Reitzug, 1993). They need to be able to help their staff members, through education and training, understand the importance of being able to communicate effectively with the culturally diverse student and parent population. As Phillips (1988) points out, ...we must struggle to truly understand what culture means to a group of people, to understand how culture is a source of group power and strength, and to examine how to allow groups to retain their cultural integrity while they gain the skills to function in the larger society. This perhaps is the central struggle we face as   adults responsible for preparing today's children and tomorrow's leaders in a society that may devalue them by demanding that they give up their culture in order to achieve (p. 46).

Epstein (1987) writes that it is the administrator's role to coordinate activities that help the staff understand parent involvement and to lead the staff in developing, evaluating, and revising parental involvement programs. They are also responsible for creating or supporting policies to inform parents, community, teachers, and students about the school. Administrators can also influence and provide guidance to teachers so that they communicate with all parents in a more equitable and substantive manner (Epstein, 1987).

Haynes, et al. (1996) discussed strategies that they recommend for increasing enhanced parental involvement. The first step is to build trust and establish a climate that is open to ideas. They point out that parental involvement must be planned carefully and coordinated by school administrators and staff if it is to be successful and effective. Empowering parents by including them in planning and making decisions about the school program gives them a voice and encourages them to be an integral part of the school. The process needs to be consistently monitored, assessed, and modified, and the entire community needs to be involved.

Epstein (1995) reinforces this concept when discussing her model of a school, family, and community partnership. She says that the student is at the center of the partnership and that it is an inarguable fact "that students are the main actors in their education, development, and success in school" (p. 702). Students are also viewed as the "main conductors of the two-way communications between school and home" (Hidalgo, Bright, Siu, Swap, & Epstein, 1995, p. 499). Epstein (1995) proposes that through a partnership the educators create schools that are more family-like. These schools recognize each student as an individual and make each one feel included and special. In turn, she says that in a partnership parents make more school-like families in which the families stress the importance of school, homework, and activities that help students develop skills and feelings of success.

Davies (1996) writes that only one public school in ten has successfully developed true partnerships with parents and communities. According to Davies, in nine of the ten schools, the parents are held at arm's length by teachers and administrators and have a limited connection with the community. The traditional forms of parent involvement, such as open houses, conferences, and attendance at performances, are present but very few parents or community members are actively involved in the important decisions regarding curriculum, teaching, school rules, or policies for homework. He says that only in the tenth school is one apt to see a different way of doing doings. Davies says that collaboration between schools and family is dependent on the school principal wanting it and working hard to accomplish it.

Davies points out that principals need to lead and be willing to take risks if their schools are to be successful in the collaboration. He describes the tenth school as one that actively engages teachers in planning and following through with family and community partnerships. Teachers are also given training so they can acquire the necessary skills for working with parents.

The tenth school, according to Davies (1996), provides a variety of opportunities intended to address the diverse needs of its families and children, as well as the conditions of the school and district. What works best, says Davies, is a comprehensive plan that includes: education for parents and family support; volunteers from family and community members working in a variety of roles; multiple approaches, such as e-mail and Web pages, for home-school communication; methods for opportunities for children to learn at home or in the community setting; participation in decision making; and a variety of school-community exchanges (Davies, 1996, 1997).

Davies (1997) gives five recommendations for how to create successful partnerships with families and communities. He recommends communicating smarter by knowing the audiences to be reached and then finding ways to reach them. Next, he recommends making the school a welcoming place by having friendly signs and personnel. Having a family center located in some area of the school also helps in creating a successful partnership. His third suggestion is to reach out to parents who are reluctant to go to the school. Home visits are a good way, he says, to reach these parents. Enlisting families and community agencies in helping with the education of children provides another way of increasing children's success both academically and socially. Helping families get the support services they need is the fifth idea presented. Offering parent education is one aspect of this idea.

Nichols-Solomon (2000) stresses the importance of creating a school culture that actively involves parents and provides the following suggestions for school administrators:

1. Listen.
2. Support teacher leadership. Schools with collaborative leadership are more willing to partner with parents and other outside groups.
3. Invite parents to work with teachers and others to develop or refine clear and coherent educational goals.
   a. 4. Focus on curriculum and instruction. With a curriculum that is student-centered, parents, teachers, and students are natural allies.
   a. 5. Acknowledge differences and conflict. Use resources outside the school to help navigate the difficult terrain of race, culture, and class (p. 21).

Providing parents with ideas they can easily initiate fosters parental involvement starting when their children are young. Berger (1998) suggests involving parents by giving them ideas for things they can do at home and in school to help increase their children's literacy. Some of his suggestions include parents tutoring; using journals to communicate from home to school and vice-versa; developing a pen pal relationship between the teacher and students and then with the parents; reading with their children; making a literacy center at home so that children have books, writing materials, songs, and other creative materials to use; having children help prepare grocery lists; reading a variety of things, such as a menu, license plates, signs, while on an outing; and telling stories.

Additionally, Frieman (1998) discusses the important role early childhood professionals can play in helping divorced fathers be more involved in their children's lives. They can include them in all classroom activities and can act as consultants to help fathers become better caretakers. The author emphasizes that fathers need to be treated as competent parents and allowed to play an important role in their children's education.

Finders and Lewis (1994) report that parents are an important source for suggestions on how to promote active parental involvement. They write that the parents' views may differ from the role educators envision for parental involvement. The authors say that educators need to understand what parents believe can be done and provide the following parent suggestions:

> *Clarify how parents can help,
> *Encourage parents to be assertive,
> *Develop trust,
> *Build on home experiences, and
> *Use parent expertise (p. 53).

In the last suggestion, using parent expertise, the parents' suggestion includes developing lessons around a parent's expertise, such as "cooking ethnic foods with students, sharing information about multicultural heritage, and bringing in role models from the community" (p. 53).

Conclusion

The research clearly shows the importance of parental involvement in their children's education. This must be in place in order for parents to understand, value, and support what is being done in the classroom and school. Taking the first step to communicate with and help parents understand their vital role in their children's education is central to beginning a quality parental involvement program (Epstein, 1995).

Also, working and communicating with all parents in an effective manner is critical to student success and school improvement. We must address the interests and concerns of our diverse population and constantly work toward improving our methods of communicating with and involving the parents and families in a positive way. Hence, it is important for school administrators and teachers, in particular, to develop a partnership with parents that builds on trust and respect. How we respond to the parents, especially in times of conflict, will determine how they perceive us.

It is also important for administrators and teachers to study and try to understand the reasons parents are not more actively involved in their children's education and the schools. As the administrator and leader in the school, we need to evaluate how we are doing in building a climate within the school that is warm, inviting, and based on trust and understanding. In order to plan and implement an effective program to reach uninvolved parents, we must try to take away as many of the barriers as possible.

There are many suggestions for ways to develop parental involvement programs. Funding is essential to provide the staffing necessary for key personnel to research, study, plan, and coordinate a program that will work in a particular district or school. Technological support for developing a parental involvement program is also necessary and critical for successful implementation. Funding in this area needs to be made available for the districts and schools.

The district and school level administrators must provide the leadership to establish and support effective parental involvement programs. Without their willingness to take risks, to advocate for funding, and to provide the guidance needed, parental involvement programs will continue to be less effective or nonexistent. They not only need to advocate for parental involvement policies and programs, they must also work with higher education institutions to develop effective administrator and teacher training programs to help school administrators and teachers learn how to involve parents and families in their children's education and school.

Establishing an effective parental involvement program within the school takes strong leadership and support at all levels of administration. It requires commitment, training, funding, time, and a cooperative effort on the part of the district, school, parents, and community. The need for, and the benefits of, involving parents in their children's education and schools are worth the effort and is essential.

REFERENCES

Berger, E. H. (1998). Reaching parents through literacy. Early Childhood Education Journal, 25 (3), 211-215.

Bermudez, A. B., & Padron, Y. N. (1988). University-school collaboration that increases minority parent involvement. Educational Horizons, 66 (2), 83-86.

Brandt, R. (1989). On parents and schools: A conversation with Joyce Epstein. Educational Leadership, 47 (2), 24-27.

Chavkin, N. F., & Williams, D. L. (1988). Critical issues in teacher training for parent involvement. Educational Horizons, 66 (2), 87-89.

Comer, J. P. (1993). School power: Implications of an intervention project. New York: The Free Press.

Davies, D. (1996). The tenth school. Principal, 76 (2), 13-16.

Davies, D. (1997). Crossing boundaries: How to create successful partnership with families and communities. Early Childhood Education Journal, 25 (1), 73-76.

Department of Defense Education Activity (DoDEA). (2000). Community strategic planning research report. Available: www.odedodea.edu/2001_strategic_plan/ research_study/goal08.html.

Dornbusch, S. M., & Ritter, P. I. (1988). Parents of high school students: A neglected resource. Educational Horizons, 66 (2), 75-77.

Epstein, J. (1995). School/family/community partnerships: Caring for the children we share. Phi Delta Kappan, 76 (9), 701-712.

Epstein, J. L. (1988). How do we improve programs for parent involvement? Educational Horizons, 66, 58-59.

Epstein, J. L. (1987). Parent involvement: What research says to administrators. Education and Urban Society, 19, 119-136.

Finders, M. & Lewis, C. (1994). Why some parents don't come to school. Educational Leadership, 51 (8), 50-54.

Frieman, B. B. (1998). What early childhood educators need to know about divorced fathers. Early Childhood Education Journal, 25 (4), 239-241.

Haynes, N. M., Ben-Avie, M., Squires, D. A., Howley, J. P., Negron, E. N., & Corbin, J. N. (1996). It takes a whole village: The sdp school. In J. P Comer, N. M Haynes, E. T. Joyner, & M. Ben-Avie. (Eds.). Rallying the whole village: The comer process for reforming education. (pp. 42-70). New York: Teachers College Press.

Hidalgo, N. M., Bright, J. A., Siu, S. F., Swap, S. M., & Epstein, J. L. (1995). Research on families, schools, and communities: A multicultural perspective. In J. J. Banks & C. Banks (Eds.), Handbook of research on multicultural education (pp. 498-524). New York: Simon & Schuster MacMillan.

Hoover-Demsey, K. V., & Sandler, H. (1997). Why do parents become involved in their children's education? Review of Educational Research, 67 (1), 3-42.

Hoover-Dempsey, K. V., & Sandler. (1995). Parental involvement in children's education: Why does it make a difference. Teachers College Record, 97 (2), 310-329.

Kowalski, T. J. & Reitzug, U. C. (1993). Contemporary school administration: An introduction. New York: Longman.

Lueder, D. C. (1998). Creating partnerships with parents: An educator's guide. Lancaster, PA: Technomic Publishing Co.

Maeroff, G. I. (1992). Reform comes home: Policies to encourage parental involvement in children's education. In C. E. Finn, Jr., & T. Rebarber (Eds.), Education reform in the '90s (pp. 157-171). New York: Macmillan Publishing Company.

Manning, M. L., & Baruth, L. G. (2000). Multicultural education of children and adolescents (3rd ed.). Boston: Allyn and Bacon.

Nardine, F. E., & Morris, R.D. (1991). Parent involvement in the states: How firm is the commitment? Phi Delta Kappan, 72 (5), 363-366.

Nichols-Solomon, R. (2000). Conquering the fear of flying. Phi Delta Kappan, September, 19-21.

Phillips, C. B. (1988). Nurturing diversity for today's children and tomorrow's leaders. Young Children, 43, 42-47.

Rich, D. (1988). Bridging the parent gap in education reform. Educational Horizons, 66 (2), 90-92.

Riehl, C. J. (2000). The principal's role in creating inclusive schools for diverse students: A review of normative, empirical, and critical literature on the practice of educational administration. Review of Educational Research, 70 (1), 55-71.

Swap, S. M. (1987). Enhancing parent involvement in schools. New York: Teachers College Press.

Vopat, J. (1998). More than bake sales: The resource guide for family involvement in education. York, ME: Stenhouse Publishers.

SECONDARY SOURCES

Boyer, J. B. & Baptiste, H. P., Jr. (1996). Transforming the curriculum for multicultural understandings: A practioner's handbook. San Francisco, CA: Caddo Gap Press.

King, J. E., Hollins, E. R., & Hayman, W. C. (Eds.). (1997). Preparing teachers for cultural diversity. New York: Teachers College Press.

Nieto, S. (1992). Affirming diversity: The sociopolitical context of multicultural education. New York: Longman.

Ravitch, D. (1991). A culture in common. Educational Leadership, 49 (4), 8-11.

Sarason, S. B. (1995). Parental involvement and the political principle. San Francisco: Jossey-Bass Publishers.

Sleeter, C. E., & McLaren, P. L. (Eds.). (1995). Multicultural education, critical pedagogy, and the politics of difference. Albany: State University of New York Press.

Chapter 16

Bringing Tomorrow To Your Classroom Today: A Collaborative Effort

Dr. Tracey Ring

Middle Tennessee State University

Murfreesboro, TN

Since 1994 Tennessee has engaged in unprecedented spending for the improvement of our public schools (State Department of Education Report, 1999). There has also been an equally unprecedented rate of efforts on the part of local school districts to improve schools. Since 1994, over one billion dollars has been appropriated by the legislature which represents a 96% increase in spending. Yet, most of the success indicators unfortunately indicate that our achievement levels have not significantly increased. What have we learned from all of our improvement efforts? Numerous improvement efforts have focused on organizational changes, changes in standards and methodology or process changes (Mehlinger, 1996). If schools are to effectively serve Tennessee's elementary school children for success in the future then close examination should be given to the content presented in the classroom today. As stated at the Fifth Annual EFG Conference in Flagstaff, Arizona, "All of the innovative instructional practices, technology, and organizational strategies cannot make irrelevant content useful" (J.A. Barker, Personal Communication, January 1995).

If substantive improvement is to occur, we must not forget that it is the classroom teachers of Tennessee who are the keys. Changes that occur with large governmental entities such as the United States Office of Education or the Tennessee State Department of Education characteristically end with mixed or not necessarily long-lasting results. It is the elementary school classroom teacher at local school district levels who hold the real promise of change. We must provide our classroom teachers with a curriculum that has significant value. In far too many Tennessee elementary schools, the curriculum continues to be based on individual subjects, largely disconnected, featuring outdated textbooks with all students on the same page at the same time. A curriculum must have a longer lifespan and be connected to real-world issues than those typically found in too many elementary schools. In an effort to assist classroom teachers, Middle Tennessee State University provides a link from pre-service teachers to in-service teachers. This connection has proved to be valuable for the teachers in that they have added helpful assistance in their classrooms and the pre-service teachers have the opportunity for real life application.

A highly promising curriculum appearing in Tennessee has been the EFG National Curriculum Collaborative. Within the past seven years EFG programs have been initiated in Hamilton County (Chattanooga), the Murfreesboro City School District, and the Rutherford County School District. Teachers in these systems have had the opportunity to rethink the curriculum content in light of those skills which the 21st Century will demand for success.

Conceptual Framework

The original EFG design was created by Futurist Joel Barker in 1978. He was joined by Barbara Barnes in 1990 at which time the conceptual framework and content domains were developed. Barker had had experience working with Fortune 500 companies around the world while Barnes had been in the California public schools as an elementary school principal.
Both felt that a curriculum should stress the most relevant knowledge and skills needed by children for the 21st century. Accordingly, the EFG curriculum emphasizes issues surrounding our environment, the future and the world.

The first content domain represented by E, stands for Ecology. Since we only have one planet, students need to learn the importance of maintaining and improving the environment. An ecologically competent person defined as "one who has a working knowledge of the planet, understands his/her role within an ecosystem and the positive and negative effects he/she can have on it, and can use knowledge and skills to improve the environment" (Barnes, 1998). Eight broad competencies are identified ranging from students knowledge of the pollution of natural systems and how ecological balances are maintained to students identifying local environmental issues.

The next content domain represented by F, stands for the Future. A person prepared for the future is, "one who understands the relationships among the past, present, and future actions, has learned and can apply a broad range of futures thinking tools, accepts responsibility for thinking about long term implications of actions before applying them, and feels empowered to affect, adapt to, and respond to change" (Barnes). Competencies developed for this domain include providing experiences and projects in which the students explore their past, their present and how they might impact their own personal future.

The last content domain represented by G, stands for Global Education. A globally competent person is, "one who understands other cultures and languages of the world and accepts responsibility for helping establish global stability and peace" (Barnes). Broad competencies include the demonstration of knowledge of global interdependence and an understanding of the uniqueness and value of all world cultures.

An integral part of the EFG conceptual framework is the development of a set of core skills. These core skills are not unlike the traditional reading, writing, and math subject areas. However, they include skills such as information acquisition and management, project planning, problem-solving and teamwork proficiencies;

such skills are content irrelevant made relevant by content. Translated that means that the students learn a core skill and immediately apply it to a real world issue.

The unique feature of the EFG conceptual framework is that teachers can adapt the EFG units into projects that address local and community issues and needs. Furthermore, this process allows for the integration of all subject areas that are applicable.

Units of Study

The first school to implement the EFG Curriculum in Tennessee was in 1994 at the 21st Century Preparatory School, a public school in Chattanooga. It currently houses over 600 students in grades K-Competency. The school serves as a Professional Development School for the University of Tennessee-Chattanooga. Over 20 different multi-disciplinary units have been created for students since 1994, the first being "The Chattanooga Challenge" which allowed students to explore their community with regard to the past, the present and the future.

In the "Chattanooga Challenge" unit, students were engaged in researching such questions as:

- What can we do to make our community a more desirable place to live in the future?
- What were the economics of Chattanooga prior to and after the building of the Tennessee Aquarium?
- What possible scenarios would help the development of downtown?
- What social issues have changed over time in Chattanooga and what are they likely to be in the future?

Within these investigations, the students were using mathematical analyses when they were measuring garbage that was collected in the city each day, when they were developing charts that compared products made in Chattanooga. They were using other core skills when they were recording interviews with older family members, or when they were working with community leaders to identify public service projects, or when they were developing reports regarding the different jobs and occupations found within Chattanooga (Barnes, 1999).

Another Tennessee school that has implemented the curriculum is The Pittard Campus School, a K-6 elementary school, on the campus at Middle Tennessee State University. To date, teachers at Campus School have completed six units, one of which was "Water H2O". In this EFG unit, students were developing an understanding of the community's water sources, water quality and water use. Significantly, they were also investigating the need for responsible action to protect and preserve water as a limited resource both locally and globally. Within these projects, students were using core skills when they designed and created a small pond with fish, tadpoles, lily pads, water heater, thermometer etc. A butterfly garden and weather station were also included. These projects were located on a nature trail that extended around the school campus with flowers, trees and bushes that were indigenous to Tennessee. Through the development of these projects the children researched, analyzed findings, wrote or graphed information and subsequently presented their findings in small groups to invited visitors via a juried presentation.

Another school in the state that has initiated the EFG Curriculum is the newly built, year-round Siegel Elementary School in Murfreesboro. After one year of implementation the teachers in this school have studied various ecosystems. A life size animal food chain was created by kindergarten children as well as implemented a school wide recycling program. The second grade class planted and harvested a pumpkin patch and a group of first grade children studied 5 major land and water regions of the world. Concluding activities included a video tape written and produced by children. Pre-service teachers from the university assisted the teachers in a variety of ways including small group instruction and project development. The university students also played an instrumental part in the final assessment of a Juried Presentation. Specific people from the community were invited to the school to hear presentations given by the children followed by small group interviews. The invited guests would ask questions about the presentation, content learned and plans for what comes next with the project or unit of study.

Partnerships with Universities

A partnership between all levels of education provides a Cooperative method of identifying needs, sharing expertise and securing resources to address emerging issues in education specific to school renewal and increase learning. The partnership can be established with school districts, county offices of education, community colleges and local universities. The goals of these partnerships are to enhance:

*Student learning, preparation and performance
*Learning Lead recruitment and preparation
*The professional development of educators
*EFG curriculum review and department connections
*Educational research
*Validation of authentic assessments
*Redefinition or revision of the admission requirements

Higher Education Examples:

Universities, college and school districts provide college credit for participant Learning Leaders. Schools assist in recruitment by organizing training sessions. Work-study programs are made available to persons considering going into the teaching profession. Intern programs are implemented to facilitate new Learning Leaders entering the profession and to lower class size. Learning Leaders develop student teaching intern handbooks for their schools. Grade K-12 schools meet with higher education institutions regularly to ensure continuity of education programs. All levels work together to improve the professional development of educators. Research in curriculum and learning is shared between all levels of instruction. Competent students are allowed to take course work at colleges and universities. Assessment strategies are validated to meet admission criteria.

21st Century Preparatory School Chattanooga, Tennessee

At the start of the 1995- 1996 school year, 21st Century Preparatory School also joined in a partnership with the Education Department at the University of Tennessee at Chattanooga (UTC). A former Learning Leader assisted the UTC education faculty in developing the "Professional Development School" (PDS) program and now serves as the program's on-site coordinator at the 21st Century Prep. In return, UTC underwrote the salary of a first-year teacher to replace the coordinator in the classroom. The focus of the program is to provide "preserves" teachers with an accurate understanding of what teaching is really like. To this end, sophomore, junior and senior education majors spend an entire semester on the 21st Century Prep campus, participating two days a week on-site in classes taught by UTC professors and in one session per week with the coordinator.

Homer Pittard Campus School Murfreesboro, Tennessee

This K-6 laboratory school for the Elementary and Special Education Department of Middle Tennessee State University joined the Collaborative in 1995. They have implemented several EFG units including "Our Small World", "Romancing the Rainforest", "Your Land and My Land" and "Community Challenge". Throughout the year long study of "Water H2O", this group of teachers designed a Nature Trail around the school grounds. The trail features a pond, butterfly garden, weather station, cedar glades which were saved from development in the community, and a Greenhouse. With the help of university pre-service teachers participating in small group lessons as well as whole class teachings for their course work, this project was a huge success. Over the years of integrating real world projects with children in the classroom and maturing, pre-service teachers, the trail has grown and the students have accomplished a truly authentic hands-on experience. The university students were involved with actual teaching of the content with specific subject areas integrated within each lesson. The students also dug holes, spread mulch, planted trees etc. with parent volunteers. This added a whole new dimension for the university students. Along with bringing students to the school, this department from the university provides faculty support, weekly meetings, financial assistance and staff development.

Siegel Elementary School Murfreesboro, Tennessee

This K-6 elementary school began working with Middle Tennessee State University in the fall of 1999. One or more university classes integrate the course work required with the EFG program being implemented at the school. The pre-service teachers have assisted the teachers in a variety of ways including small group instruction and project development. This allows the pre-service teachers to have hands-on involvement in a real setting. The university students also play an instrumental part in the final assessment of a Juried Presentation.

This involves inviting specific people from the community to the school to hear presentations given by the children followed by small group interviews. The invited guests would ask questions about the presentation, content learned and plans for what comes next with the project unit of study.

The pre-service teachers help prepare the presentation with the children a well as assist with the teaching of the content that goes into the presentation. Depending upon the unit of study one or more subject areas are integrated within the project. This complete process proves to be a very comprehensive experience for the university students and the children.

Judson College Elgin, Illinois

A class of pre-service teachers wrote a new project called Global Celebrations for an elementary school close to the college. The students then went into the EFG classrooms and taught the unit of study. They also integrated the EFG website into the study as well. Again the in-service as well as the pre-service teachers benefited greatly from this experience.

Summary

One of the successes has been that EFG units of study are easily connected with state minimum basic skills. In addition to specific units of study being matched, the actual EFG competencies found under each domain have also been correlated to minimum basic skills for each grade level. Since the EFG curriculum is not an off-the-shelf, fixed curriculum, teachers have been empowered to use their own creative abilities to enhance the briefly defined units. In other words, teachers have the responsibility and legitimate power to develop the units according to the needs and developmental levels of the children in his/her classroom. Typically, teacher and student motivation is increased because of this flexibility and freedom. Perhaps more importantly, students are able to see a direct and meaningful connection between school and real life issues.

REFERENCES

Barker, J.A. Invitational Address at the Fifth Annual EFG Conference, Flagstaff, Arizona, 1995.

Barnes, Barbara. (1998). Learning architecture for the 21st century. Glendal, California: Griffin Publishing Company.

Barnes, Barbara. (1999). Schools transformed for the 21st century; the ABC's of EFG. Torrance, California: Griffin Publishing Company.

Mehlinger, H.D. (1996). School reform in the information age. Phi Delta Kappan, 77 (6), 400-407.

Tennessee State Department of Education. (1999). Annual report. Nashville, Tennessee: State Department of Education l.

Chapter 17

The Power to Empower: An Urban Teacher Communicates and Connects With Her Children's Families

Dr. Susan Kavney Meskos
LeMoyne College
Syracuse, NY

Dr.Patricia Ruggiano Schmidt
LeMoyne College
Syracuse, NY

Near the end of the year, in my first grade classroom, a mother screamed at me when she discovered that I had not taught her child to read. That scream shook me. I realized that she was a stranger to me. I had no words to explain and nothing to say.

It was at that moment that Susan, an educator from European American backgrounds, teaching in a lower socioeconomic, urban setting, understood that she needed to make changes in her communication with families. Susan had never lived or worked with people from minority backgrounds, and the city school's population was 80% African American, 14% Latino, and 6% European American. It also never occurred to her that the class monthly newsletters and parent conferences were not enough. As she explained, I believed my newsletters and conferences would encourage families to get involved in the school and my classroom. If they really cared about their children, I thought they would keep me informed about family information and help their children with reading and writing.

As part of her decision to make changes in communication between herself and families, she began studying the literature on home and school connections for her master's degree project.   She learned about the power relationships that exist between home and school, especially in urban settings (Nieto, 2000; Schmidt, 2000).   She recognized that these relationships often hindered the communication so necessary for children's literacy development (Diamond & Moore, 1995; Edwards, Pleasants, Franklin, 1999).   Therefore, she resolved to discover a way to communicate with her children's families.   The purpose of this chapter is to present Susan's successful use of the ABC's of Cultural Understanding and Communication (Schmidt, 1998b), a model that has helped teachers use their positions of power to reach out and empower children and families.   As a result of her implementation of the model, she connected and communicated with the parent of a child from African American origins in her classroom and began comfortably doing the same with the other families and children from minority backgrounds.

As Susan's advisor on the masters' project and the author of the ABC's model, I encouraged her to share what she had learned in this chapter with the idea that other teachers might benefit from the process.   Therefore, we planned and wrote together. This chapter first, presents literature on culture and power related to home and school connections and the model known as the ABC's of Cultural Understanding and Communication (Schmidt 1998b).   Then, through her own eyes, Susan takes the reader through the ABC's process.   Finally, Susan and I share a discussion of the process and implications for classroom practice.

European American Culture and Power

European American or white culture controls the education system and drives the content of the curricula as well as the structure, materials and methods. Consequently, students and families from minority backgrounds are often ignored in classrooms and schools at all educational levels (Cummins, 1986; Sleeter & Grant, 1991).

Furthermore, most educators, who are from white middle class backgrounds, have limited knowledge of minority populations, since their information is usually gained from media stereotypes, and few personal experiences (Pattnaik, 1997). Therefore, it is no surprise that this group of students often feels powerless and believes they have no control over their own learning. Consequently, school dropout rates for ethnic and cultural minorities are extremely high (Nieto, 2000).

In order to solve this national problem, it has been suggested that the teacher's responsibility is to make connections between home and school, since he or she has the power and position to reach out to students and families (Faltis, 1993; Edwards, et. al, 1999). Additionally, we know that teachers who implement the socio-cultural perspective, (Vygotsky, 1978; Heath, 1983; Trueba, Jacobs & Kirton, 1990; Au, 1993), a promising teaching/learning approach for students from minority as well European American backgrounds, have been effective in connecting home and school cultures to build classroom community for literacy development. However, many teachers are unaware of the socio-cultural perspective or do not have the information and practical experiences necessary for making connections between home and school (Kidder, 1989; Paley, 1989; Schmidt, 1998a). As a result, cultural conflict emerges as a key factor in the educational process and minority students and their families feel confusion, frustration, and disempowerment (Cummins, 1986;Trueba, Jacobs, & Kirton, 1990; Schmidt, 1998a).

Recently, a model known as the ABC's of Cultural Understanding and Communication (Schmidt, 1998b) based on the socio-cultural perspective and the premise, "Know thyself and understand others," is helping teachers use their positions of power to reach out and empower students and families (Schmidt, 1998c; 1999a). In the process, teachers gain a better understanding of diversity and successfully connect home and school for literacy learning.

Susan experienced the ABC's of Cultural Understanding and Communication and used the power gained from the process to empower the children and families in her classroom. Similar to Greene's (1995) notion of releasing teacher imaginations, she created opportunities for dialogue among and between students, families, and teachers to learn through multiple perspectives and build bridges for the celebration of human similarities and differences.

The ABC's of Cultural Understanding and Communication

The ABC's of Cultural Understanding and Communication (Schmidt, 1998b) was created and developed on the premise of, knowing oneself and understanding others. Its components include:

1. An autobiography is written, in detail, by the teacher and includes key life events related to education, family, religious tradition, recreation, victories, and defeats.
2. The biography of a person who is culturally different from the teacher is written from in depth unstructured interviews (Spradley, 1979) that include key life events.
3. Cross-cultural analysis of similarities and differences between the two life stories are charted (Spindler & Spindler, 1987).

4. Cultural differences are examined in writing and teachers are encouraged to explain personal discomforts and identify positive affect.

5. Classroom practice and communication plans are designed for literacy development and home/school connections based on the preceding process.

The ABC's model is based on a combination of findings from previous research that demonstrates the effectiveness of autobiography, biography, cultural analyses, and connections between home and school.

Autobiography

Research suggests (Noordhoff & Kleinfeld, 1993; Banks, 1994; Schmidt, 1998b) that the first step in developing culturally sensitive pedagogy is to discover one's own cultural identity in order to appreciate the similarities and differences that exist between self and others. Therefore, teachers begin with their own knowledge by thinking and writing about their family histories that include memorable life events. This helps them become aware of personal beliefs and attitudes that form the traditions and values of cultural autobiographies (Banks, 1994). Since it is well documented that writing is linked to the knowledge of self within a social context (Emig, 1971; Yinger, 1985), writing one's life story seems to construct connections with universal human tenets and serves to lessen negative notions about different groups of people (Progoff, 1975). As a result, teachers acquire an awareness of their own perceptions regarding race, class, gender and related social issues (Sjoberg & Kuhn, 1989; Banks, 1994). Finally, the process of writing an autobiography sets the stage for learning about another person's life story.

Biographies From Interviews to Discover Others

Through unstructured and semi-structured interviews, a teacher constructs the biography of another person from key events in that person's life (Spradley, 1972). Research suggests that when teachers meet with people who are different from themselves, the personal is accentuated and internalization of information is fostered. Additionally, interviewing to write life stories helps teachers become more culturally sensitive (Spindler & Spindler, 1987; Schmidt, 1998b, 1998c). Therefore, the interview process can serve as a means for sharing life stories and learning about similarities and differences for cross-cultural analysis (Spindler & Spindler, 1987).

Cross-Cultural Analysis

Teachers who have interviewed teachers or other people from different cultures and performed written, cross-cultural self-analyses, discover similarities and differences (Spindler & Spindler, 1987; Schmidt, 1998b) acquire insights about others and began to sense their own ethnocentricity. Similarly, comparing and contrasting similarities and differences is an interesting way to begin to develop an understanding and appreciation of diversity. When teachers have written autobiographies, cultural differences can be examined in a positive manner and can be related to their own personal histories (Britzman, 1986; Banks, 1994; Ladson-Billings, 1994). Traditionally, similarities among people have been celebrated and differences have been ignored (Cummins, 1986; Trueba, Jacobs, & Kirton, 1990). However, when differences are ignored in a learning community, a dis-empowering process occurs as a student's home knowledge is subtracted from the learning community (Cummins, 1986). It is empowering for students and families when differences are recognized, whether it be physical, academic, or cultural. That recognition is part of valuing each individual and his or her family and community (Paley, 1989; Derman-Sparks, 1992; McCaleb, 1994).

Classroom Practice and Communication Plans

Families are children's first teachers and have much to share in their literacy development. Therefore, teachers must be able to develop collaborative relationships with families in an atmosphere of mutual respect, so that students gain the most from their education (Goldenberg, 1987; Faltis, 1993; McCaleb, 1994). However, an imbalance of power exists between highly educated teachers and administrators and less educated, often lower-income minority parents. Additionally, educators may fear saying and doing the wrong things with people who are ethnically and culturally different. But, since teachers are in a power position, they are the logical ones to reach out to the families (Ogbu, 1983; Edwards, 1997).

After teachers complete the autobiography, biography, and cross-cultural analyses, they design plans for home and school connections for literacy development in classrooms and schools based on the first four steps of the ABC's model. This is the place where teachers can begin to connect with the children and families in their classrooms and school through methods and materials that are culturally responsive. It is also the time when they develop daily plans that inform their students of the diversity that exists locally, nationally and internationally. Susan's implementation of the ABC's model helped her begin to communicate with a mother of African American origins and thus develop strong home and school connections with the rest of her class. Susan's story follows with her explanation of procedure, excerpts from her autobiography, the biography of Ms. Jones, her cross-cultural analyses, and home/school connection plans. Susan's Procedure I began the ABC's process by creating a timeline of the 30 years of my life. I plotted important events that included religion, education, holidays and family traditions, and my successes and failures. I tried to remember as many details as I could about each event. I looked at my timeline and decided what events I would use for writing. As I was writing, I found that certain events were much more important to me than others. These events were the ones that changed my life. I broke my autobiography into three parts in order to help me organize it. Each time I sat down to write, I reread what I had written and I found myself reflecting on my life and experience much of the time. I thought about how my experiences had made me feel and how I felt about them now. I wrote about each experience, even though several were not pleasant, and at the time, it was difficult. The process of writing and reflecting on these situations helped me to deal with them and move on.

After completing my autobiography, I chose Quinton (pseudonym), a student in my class whose family member I would meet. He had been my student in first and second grade, since I am in the looping program and follow students for two years. I had met with his mother several times over the last year and a half, but felt that I didn't know her. Quinton was on a first-grade reading level and was considered at-risk. He was having speech and language problems and was extremely immature.

Interviewing a Parent

Mrs. Jones (pseudonym), a forty-five year old, African American female was born in a city located in the southeast but now lived in a central New York City. She had resided here for most of her life and was single with three children.

Mrs. Jones seemed older than the other parents and seemed very protective. Daily, she walked her son Quinton into the classroom, taking off and hanging up his coat. I allowed her to do this for several months until I knew Quinton was comfortable. Then I asked her to let him do it on his own. She appeared nervous at first, but went with my suggestion. Mrs. Jones also brought in extra money each Friday to the students in the class who do not have 50 cents for ice cream. Additionally, she helped Quinton with his homework.

I phoned Mrs. Jones and explained to her that I was working on a project for a college class on effective communication between home and school. I asked her if we could meet at least three times at mutually agreed upon locations for the purpose of interviewing her about school. Mrs. Jones asked if we could meet at her home. I went there and collected information by taking notes and audio taping our conversations. After our visits, I would review my notes, type them, and listen to the audiotapes.

The first time I phoned Mrs. Jones, the television volume was so high that we were yelling as we decided on a time to meet. Our first meeting occurred after school, 45 minutes before she was scheduled to leave for work. Quinton's home was a large, neat, light gray house with an empty lot next to it. He was playing outside when I arrived. The next house was some distance away that was unusual for this part of the city. I parked and Ms. Jones came out of the house to greet me. Quinton was riding a new bike with a little boy who he introduced as his brother. Mrs. Jones corrected him saying that the boy was Quinton's cousin. We walked up three steps to the front door and through a small porch into the living room. The day was unseasonably warm, so the door was left open. The living room was clean and tidy with an ell-shaped couch, area rug, child's desk, and a large TV and VCR. Mrs. Jones apologized for the mess and said they were painting. The dining room was filled with things that seemed to be moved from the living room during the painting. I brought eclairs, and was thanked by Mrs. Jones as she put them in the kitchen. We both seemed nervous, and the warm house seemed to aggravate these feelings. I explained my project, and she seemed to nod in understanding. Mrs. Jones signed the permission to be interviewed tape recorded.

Due to a death in the family, I rescheduled our next meeting. Mrs. Jones seemed somewhat flustered about the change, but agreed to the new time. Again, I arrived after school and approached the closed front doors of Quinton's home. The front doors were now nicely painted black and white. I rang the bell, and Mrs. Jones and Quinton came to the door to greet me. I took my shoes off and walked into the living room. The room was back together and the painting complete. Mrs. Jones shared that she was tired, so we sat on the couch and began our conversation. From the couch, I could see the dining room and framed family pictures covering the walls. Many pictures were of her children, but some were of parents and siblings. On the wall in the living room was a large print of a Native American women in traditional clothing and another print of two small African American boys with their arms around each other.

Mrs. Jones rescheduled our last meeting. The final meeting with Mrs. Jones was less formal and more like a social visit. I brought Mrs. Jones picture frames as gifts of thanks for her time. I also brought picture books, a writing pad, and markers for Quinton. He immediately sat on the floor and began reading the books, the only ones I saw in the home. For this meeting, I also shared picture of myself as a child and albums of my present family. The next day, Quinton carried to school one of the books I gave him, *Dr. Seuss Solar System*. He happily asked me to read it to the class. Of course, I did.

Excerpts From Susan's Autobiography

I lived in a nice three-bedroom home on a quiet street in a small village in upstate New York. We knew all of our neighbors, and all the moms stayed home while the dads went to work. I shared a room with my older sister; my older brother had his own room. My parents both grew up in the town and were married young. I think the earliest memory I have is Halloween 1974 at age four. I can remember getting our costumes ready with my mother and waiting for my father to come home from work. My older sister Jennifer was nine years old and was Cinderella for that Halloween. I can remember exactly what she was wearing. She had on a dress that my mother wore to a Christmas dance when she was in high school. The dress was an evergreen color, the top of the dress was the same color in velvet, and from the waist down there were layers of tulle. My sister had long, blond hair, and always looked beautiful. My older brother David was dressed as a bum. My costume was Raggedy Ann. I had a cheap store-bought, one-piece costume and a plastic mask to go with it. I couldn't breath in the mask, and I think I had a cold, because I had to keep taking it off to wipe my nose. We were fed sloppy-jo dinner, and then took our pillow case bags for trick-or-treating. My brother got the Charlie Brown pillowcase, and mine was plain white. We went out with my father to visit all of our neighbors. I don't actually remember ringing doorbells, but do remember dumping our candy in separate piles. We then catergorized it. My favorite pile was the chocolate candy bars. My brother always had the most, even though we went to the same houses. I then hid my candy in a safe spot and made it last until Easter, when my mother would find it and throw it out.

I can remember watching my brother and sister leave for school every day and being happy. I would watch Sesame Street and then play with my imaginary friends Nelsy, Kelsy, and Peanut Butter and Jelly Dog. We had wonderful fun playing school and house in the living room that was big and beautiful. We had a gold and green shag carpet to match the couch. The brown chair didn't really go, but it was comfortable, and it rocked. The green chair and ottoman was my favorite place to sit in our house. My mother would make the beds, dust and vacuum every day; our house was very clean. We would eat lunch together, and then I would play until Jen and Dave came home from school. I went to nursery school at the church down the street, and three afternoons a week my mom and I would walk there. I loved the playhouse area of my classroom. We had dress-up clothes; I don't remember playing with anything else. I played with my friends

Cory, Heather, Debbie and sometimes Tammy. Cory came over to play once and wet her pants on the green and gold living room couch; my mother was upset but didn't show it.

I started afternoon kindergarten the following year. My teacher was Mrs. Winn; she lived up the street from us and was very nice. I would walk to school with Caren, Debbie and Tammy; I took them on a short cut and Tammy fell in the mud. She cried and ran home; her mother didn't like me after that. I also broke a window at their house once, and their dad yelled at me; thank goodness they moved to Florida the year after that.

I spent many days in my childhood putting on shows and selling painted rocks. I also enjoyed picking flowers (other peoples) and selling them to them. We had a great group of kids in my neighborhood. One summer we organized a circus in my front lawn. We actually made money and all of our parents came. I guessed how many kernels of corn were in a jar and won a book of lifesavers; I gave everyone a roll.

When I was seven, my mother told us she was going to have a baby. I could not even imagine this, and kept asking if we were adopting my little cousin Amy. Two months before the due date, my mom told us at the dinner table she was having twins. I finished my hotdog and went out to tell my friends. I wasn't really sure what it meant, but it got a big reaction, so I felt important telling them the news. My parents then hired a contractor to put an addition on our house. It was remodeled to include a dining room, master bedroom and bath, a new bedroom for my brother and a remodeled bathroom for us. The project seemed to take forever, and we were always picking up wood to make piles. One day, as we were stacking wood, a bee flew up my bell bottom pants and stung me on the thigh. I started running around the yard screaming; Dave and Jen didn't know what to do. Finally my mom came out and brought me inside; she got the stinger out, and I have never piled wood since.

My Nana and Papa lived a block away from us. They owned and lived in Norris Funeral Home; the house is huge and filled with antiques. My Papa was the town's Mayor for twenty-seven years before he died. Nana and Papa loved to travel and quite often would take the three of us on trips with them. We went to Toronto and stayed at the Sheraton Hotel and loved the pool and hot tub. My grandparents did everything first class, and we had a ball. When we came home form the trip, the house remodeling as done. I was exciting to see the wallpapering and final touches. Jen and I got my parents old room. We had a new antique dresser that was gorgeous. The twins would have our old room. There were two cribs in it, a changing table, and baby stuff. I didn't like the baby room when the twins were born, we went to the hospital to see them and mom. My dad looked tired; I don't remember seeing my mom's face. I looked at the babies and instantly feel in love. They were my babies, and I couldn't wait to get them home. They had named one, Mary Elizabeth, but did not have another girl's name. I told them I liked the name Amanda, and they named the second twin, Amanda Lynn. Marybeth had dark hair that stood straight up; she weighed seven pounds. I remember the day they came home form the hospital. I told everyone at school. I ran all the way home and when I got there I found Mrs. Plumpton feeding Marybeth. Mrs. Plumpton was the old lady my mother hired to help her care for the babies. The twins were good; they would wake up in the night for a feeding which I would sometimes get up for too. My world had changed. I was now the middle child and the older sister of "THE TWINS." A baby always needed to be held or burped or changed and I loved helping. I would take the babies for a walk around the block and get a great deal of attention; I was proud.

The next few years of my life didn't really stand out. The good old days were over; the twins were here to stay. I can remember that my older sister won a scholarship to Manlius Pebble Hill School, a private school, when she was in the eighth grade. We were very proud of Jennifer, the genius of our family. She was twelve years old when the twins were born, and when they were about a year old, it seemed that she was always at my Nana and Papa's house. She didn't spend time with the babies or me. As for my brother, Dave, he seemed to like tormenting me. I used to think, "Why does he have to ruin everything."

My elementary school was a great place. I enjoyed it and always felt safe. In fifth grade, I went to the middle school and had a beautiful, new, young teacher named Ms. Cabral. She had long blond hair and wore great clothes. I never had a teacher like her. In fifth grade, the fifths from the other elementary school came to "our middle school" and that rocked my little world. I didn't like outsiders because I had a hard time making friends. Some of these new girls were nice, but I had a hard time mixing with them.

I was good at sports and I tried out for the girl's soccer team in 7th grade. It was a sport taken very seriously in our community. I never really enjoyed it, but I liked the attention.

A significant event happened one day when I was finishing soccer practice. M y sister Jen went by in her friend's car and yelled to me "get home fast!" I thought she was being a wacko, so basically ignored her call. When I arrived home, I discovered that Papa was dead of a heart attack at age seventy-two; he died alone. My family was devastated. We went to Uncle Hugh's house to make plans. I just remember watching TV, but not really watching it. The funeral service was long and tiring. My sister Jen stayed nights with my Nana, so she wouldn't be alone. The soccer coach told me not to worry since I made the team.

I was good at volleyball and softball. I easily made the teams and loved playing much more than soccer. My family also joined the Country Club when I was in 7th grade and I took golf lessons and joined the synchronized swimming team. I did not do well at either one. I felt like a small fish in a huge pond. I had no confidence there, but really wanted to belong.

In the fall of 1983, I was thirteen years old, and my father was transferred to a small city about 50 miles away. Our house went on the market and sold fast. We found a new huge beautiful and planned to move in January. I got mononucleosis and was sick during Christmas. I did not want to move to a new place and make new friends. My brother was in high school, and he refused to move. He was going to finish school living with my Nana. Jennifer was at college and didn't care. The twins were in Kindergarten and had each other. I started school in the new place and had to ride the bus. I had nowhere to sit, and didn't look like the kids on the bus. The school was incredible: big money. The kids that went to the school were well dressed, confident and had incredible amounts of money. I was picked on for the first time in my life. I was buddied up with the biggest nerds in the school; they knew I didn't belong with the cool kids. My clothes were a joke here. I needed a makeover and a friend. I hated school, so I ate. I put on forty pounds. I was already at the ugly age of fourteen so it really didn't help. On the other hand, the twins did great and had lots of friends in the neighborhood. My parents had many friends and acted like teenagers. I was so unhappy. I spent the summer back in my small town with my friends and even found a boyfriend.

Back in the new school, I went through several sets of friends that weren't right for me. In tenth grade, I finally made it into the right group. My best friends enjoyed a lot of the same things that I did. They were from different backgrounds and I loved it. Mary Jean's family was Italian American and they were great. She had an older brother Frank (who I was in love with) and a younger brother Joey. My other best friend was Julia who was Korean American. Julia's dad was a surgeon and they also had a ton of money. She didn't care; she was one of the funniest, smartest people I have ever met. We played volleyball together and really became close. The three of us did everything together. It felt as though I belonged now. I had a place, and people were interested in me. I began to take more of an interest in how I looked and was more confident, but on the inside I was very insecure and shy. Sometimes people mistake that shyness for being "stuck up."

My parents were very busy with their new life, and the twins had many friends also. I am not sure how it all started, but at some point I stopped eating. I started throwing up my meals, and my body seemed to change overnight. I lost weight fast and no one knew what I was doing; it was a shameful secret. I loved all the new attention I was getting. Everyone commented on how great I looked. I continued to lose weight this way, and my life was again out of control. I became very thin, and my parents finally confronted me when we were visiting my Nana one weekend. They had heard me getting sick and were shocked. They demanded that I stop and yelled at me. They had no idea what to do, and made it worse. They started watching me closely, and I guess I didn't want to disappoint them, so I really cut back on getting sick and only ate in private. Instead of purging three times a day, I would not eat for two days and then in private, binge and purge. I kept this up for a while. I wasn't going out much because I needed to be home alone. My parents had me join a health club that I liked. I worked out everyday after school and would eat only popcorn for dinner. Then I would work out in my room. I kept the weight off and was very thin. I looked terrible and felt worse. I started to see a therapist and hated it. It seemed like punishment, and my parents didn't want to talk about it. I was on my own, and they were disappointed in me. I had the feeling that the family had divorced me. The twins were the center of the attention.

That same year I went to what was the former Soviet Union with my Russian class. My parents threatened that I couldn't go if I didn't eat. I ate; I don't know what changed. It wasn't the goofy therapist or the threats. Mary Jean, my best friend, went on the trip, and her parents chaperoned. I had the time of my life. We saw everything. We drank a lot of vodka and had a ball. I met my first real boyfriend, Mike. He was nice, funny, tall and thin, a year younger than me and from a good family.

When I came back from that trip, I felt different. I was wiser and stronger and gradually began to eat again. However, I also started to smoke and drink. My father smoked, so it was easy to steal cigarettes from him. I don't know why I smoked. None of my friends did, I guess I wanted to be big. We went to parties every weekend, and I was usually in charge of bringing the beer or vodka. I bought it at a little market in the area. It was exciting without being too dangerous. When I drank I had the confidence I longed for when I was sober. I was funny and could flirt with boys. I had broken up with Mike because I didn't know how to have a relationship with another person. I acted as if I didn't care, but didn't know how to express myself. He didn't seem to fit in with the party people. I think I also got bored. I needed drama in my life. I always had a wild car to drive, minimally graduated from high school, and barely made it into college.

College was another wild scene with wealthy friends and over indulgence. Depression landed me in the arms of another therapist who actually helped me. She knew when I was acting and lying. I finished the first year of college and came home. I lived with my parents, worked at a day care and took classes at a community college at night.

I met George in a sociology class. There was something about him I could not ignore. He had gone to school in the area and was attending community college for the first two years of a degree. We talked often before and after class; one day I called him. He called back and we began to date.

It was very hard to get to know George; he did not share much information. He was a year younger than me and lived in the area his whole life. He worked long hours at his family's bakery. His family was Greek and very proud of it. This was a world I did not know or understand. George lived at home with his mom and his older sisters. His brother was at Colgate. His sister ran the bakery with his mom. After dating for a while, he told me his father had died when he was fourteen. I had never known anyone who had such strong family values. I really enjoyed spending time with George. I was finally able to come to his house and meet his family; I was very uncomfortable. I thought his mother's attitude as cold and rude, and I felt she completely controlled George. This house was the opposite of my own. My family made everyone welcome and would go out of their way for friends. George's family was private and outsiders were not welcome. This enraged me, and made me want to belong even more.

We continued to date, and struggled with the cultural differences, but I knew George and I were soul mates. We graduated from the community college and went to a State College together. George loved his family's bakery, and I learned to hate it. The bakery was always open and George was the one that had to work the times when no one else would. I saw the State College as a place we could go to without his family and the bakery. We spent two years there and realized we could never live too far from our families.

Without my knowledge, George asked my father for my hand in marriage. During my student teaching experience, he proposed and gave me a beautiful ring. I said yes and the celebration began. George's family treated me like a princess from that day on. When I finished student teaching, I moved in with my Nana. She was eighty years old and liked the company. I could not find a teaching job, so I went to work for NEC, the company I worked for two summers. I liked my job and the money was good.

I spent a lot of time planning the wedding. We had many arguments about our cultural differences and what should and should not be part of the wedding. We had the wedding at Bellevue C.C. and it was beautiful. The service was at St. Sophia's Greek Orthodox Church. I was Christmated into the orthodox religion about a month before the wedding because we have the same religious beliefs. The church community was very strong, and everyone knew each other. The closeness and sense of community in the church drew me. We wanted our future family to be raised in this church. Father Costa was our wonderful Priest at the time. George and I lived in an apartment on Tipperary Hill when we got married. I finally had a home. It was rough at first, because I am very difficult to live with. I am as hard on other people as I am on myself. I demanded a lot from George. Also George's mother sold the bakery and George seemed lost. He missed it a great deal and didn't know how to work in an office. He tried very hard and did a great job, but after a year in the city, we moved to a house my nana owned in my hometown. At last, I began a real teaching job at an elementary school in a city school district.

I began as a teaching assistant and found that I had to prove myself. I cried many nights and worked hard cleaning up messes, and doing the jobs no one else wanted. After three months, I was offered a first grade job. The first year was a struggle, but I was ready to return the following year.

I became pregnant with our first child in January of that year. My sister had three ectopic pregnancies and was unable to have children. I always had the thought that this could also happen to me, so I yearned to have a baby. The day I told George I was pregnant was the day he quit his job in the insurance field and bought a restaurant in the city. It was a scary time but we were young and had no idea what life was going to bring. My pregnancy went well, and during the summer I worked at a day camp in the morning and helped at the deli in the afternoon. We had a good time and everything was going well. We started looking for a house.

I went back to school to teach second grade for three weeks and then went out on maternity leave. Evan was born, and we closed on our house five days later. We moved when Evan was a week old. This was hard on me, and I think I was too busy to see how hard it was on George. George was born with a congenital heart defect and was seeing a cardiologist about once a year. I really did not know the facts about his condition, and we didn't discuss it much. When Evan was eight weeks old, I went back to work and we tried to keep an impossible pace. Evan went to an excellent daycare, and I picked him up and dropped him off. George worked from 6am-6pm and Evan kept us up all night. We also worked on the house in our spare time. This life took its toll and George came down pneumonia on top of his heart problems. As Evan and I were leaving the doctor's office, shortly after the diagnosis, our doctor came running out of the office and looking as white as a ghost, he shouted, "Mrs. Meskos you need to get to the hospital right away. Your husband is very sick!"

I called my mother and told her to meet me at my house. I drove home with Evan screaming in the back seat and left him with my mother. I didn't understand what was going on. I got to the emergency room and they ran me in and found my mother-in-law looking very upset. The doctor took us out in the hall and said that George was in heart failure and might not make it. I went into shock and just stared. My father then showed up and took over asking for the team of cardiologists and more information. George was moved to intensive care with a calm smile on his face. We stayed until about ten then I came home to Evan. I was in total shock over the whole thing and that is the day I became a different person.

George made it out of ICU and was put into a crowded cardiac unit. I was there all day and I could see he was not getting any rest. When I got home that night, I called George's doctor and demanded that George be moved to a private room with better care. The doctor called the hospital and took care of it.

Due to our family situation, I had to request a leave from my job. I then had to figure out how to run the deli for George. Our mothers began working there full time. I spent most of my time at the hospital and taking care of Evan. I also did research into George's rare condition and informed the doctors. The cardiac team at our hospital did a cauterization when George was stabilized. The team told tell us that George's heart was greatly damaged and there was nothing we could do except keep him comfortable and be sure that he had no stress. After many tears and a long walk, I went to see George and pretended everything was great.

At this point, everything in my life changed, my goals, my plans, and my dreams. Every ounce of energy I had went to surviving. My family and their role in my life changed. I really needed them to be there for me, and they were. I also had to do many things alone and be very assertive. I told the doctors to find a doctor who could do something. I used all the contacts we had, and ended up at The Children's Hospital in Boston. We had a wonderful doctor who gave us hope. He sent us to Columbia Hospital in NYC to one of the best specialists in the world for the problem. That doctor knew her stuff and treated us well. George went through tests and we tried medication. He needed to rest, first.

We sold the deli several months later as a successful business for three times what we paid. It was his dream and he never complained. I went back to work and Evan went to daycare. My parents bought a beautiful camp on a nearby lake and we spent many hours there. In August of that year, we were called to Columbia Hospital for the installation of a permanent IV pump that would hopefully help with his pulmonary hypertension. He came home with a temporary pump that went into his arm 24/7. A nurse came each day and taught me how to flush out and care for it. Soon after we became pregnant again and were very happy. I was scared, but would manage.

For three months the pump worked and then George returned for more catherization and other tests. George and his mother flew to New York and I was going to come down two days later. The pump had been in long enough; I think it was three months. George was going to have a catherization and other tests that would tell us what to do next. The doctors thought he would be a candidate for a permanent pump of medication that would take some pressure off his heart. The other option mentioned was a heart-lung transplant. I didn't want either; I felt so selfish, but I didn't want to deal with the pump for the rest of our lives. The outcome for heart-lung transplants is not very good. I flew down to join them, and I prayed the whole way. I got to the hospital and George was in the most beautiful hospital wing and room I had ever seen. It was comforting to know he was being treated well, but it also frightening to know that his case was so special. He went into surgery and the doctors were wonderful. He was no longer a candidate for the pump, and nothing major needed to be done. The doctors decided to adjust his medications. I was very happy and thanked God.

I really tried to finish my master courses at night. I took two classes each semester, and between working and caring for Evan and George, I don't remember much. I was tired from being pregnant and getting lost. Maxwell Gary was born on April 21 (two weeks early). I worked on Monday and he was born on Tuesday morning. I delivered him the same as Evan without drugs and quickly. I felt great after he was born and had so much energy. I went back to work after five weeks, because I ran out of sick time.

Summer was wonderful. I lost the weight for Max so fast no one could believe it. I wasn't feeling great, but I thought I was just tired. I went water-skiing one afternoon on the lake, and thought I was going to die. I went to the doctor, and was told that I had a hyperactive thyroid. I started seeing a specialist and was put on medication.

The next year was the worst year of my professional life. I had many days that if I could have quit my job I would have. I had the worst class and no support. I made it through, but I went on several interviews.

I will be turning thirty this year; and am looking forward to the new millenium. I hope it can bring peace to my life. I have become a spiritual person who tries to enjoy the simple treasures that I have been given. I know what is important now although sometimes I let my day-to-day life get me stressed out. I am a strong, intelligent, caring women.

Writing my autobiography was a great learning experience. I thought I knew who I was and why I was that person. I found this to be a growing experience that forced me to face every part of my life and take ownership of it. I think it was also a great exercise to do the year I am turning thirty. I was forced to reflect on what I have done, it helped me deal with where I am in my life, and it has helped me deal with where I want to be. It also gave me the courage to talk with the parents of the children in my class and begin sharing my life story with them.

Biography

Mrs. Jones was born in Birmingham, Alabama in 1954. She lived there with her family until she was four years old. Mrs. Jones is a woman from African American backgrounds; she is the oldest child in her family. Her mother, father, two sisters and three brothers moved to Central New York in April of 1959. The family packed up and came by train. Mrs. Jones remembers it was a long and difficult ride, because the children were all about eighteen months apart. The Jones family came to Syracuse to be close to a grandmother, aunts, and uncles, and also, because of the Civil Rights Movement.

Mrs. Jones' father worked for the post office and her mother worked cleaning houses. Her grandmother took care of Mrs. Jones while her parents were at work. She was the oldest girl in the family, and because of that, she helped a great deal with the other children and the housework

Mrs. Jones also attended school. She would not talk in great detail about her school experiences, but did share that she went to elementary and junior high schools in the city. She then had to take a test to see if she could go to a special school; she padded the test and went to a technical high school and graduated in 1972. Mrs. Jones believes she had good teachers, friends, and experiences in school. She believes that if she had stayed in the south, she would have had a better education because they had schools for black children. She went on to explain that here the teachers just pushed the Black kids through without caring if they learn or not. She has a strong belief in education due to her strict and hardworking father.

Mrs. Jones had just started school when Black History was introduced. She remembers teachers being scared and people had attitudes. She recalls Black Power and White Power being talked about often, and the school seemed militant. Black students and white students did not mix at school; groups stayed separate. Mrs. Jones believes the struggle was greater in Central New York because the South had the Black schools with Black teachers. Her teachers here were all White through grade school; she remembers her first Black teacher, Mrs. Perry. Mrs. Jones does not remember too much about Mrs. Perry except that she was nice.

After graduating from high school, she got a job cleaning an office. When she was twenty years old, she had her first son, and when she was twenty -five, she had her second son. Mrs. Jones loves being a mother; her children are very important to her. She took many pictures of the boys and devoted hours to them. She played with them and took them to visit family members. When Mrs. Jones was thirty- eight she had Quinton. Quinton's father worked for General Motors and was transferred to Michigan when Quinton was very young. Mrs. Jones decided to stay in Central New York with her three boys; the long distance relationship with Quinton's father did not work out. He now lives in Syracuse, but they do not see him very often. Quinton has never mentioned his father, and Mrs. Jones did not give me much information about him.

Mrs. Jones' mother still cares for Quinton each night while she is at work. She has a sister who is mentally retarded due to lead poisoning, and she also lives with her mother. Mrs. Jones helped care for her sister all her life and has learned to be very patient and caring. Mrs. Jones' grandmother was Native American and her large framed photo hangs on the wall of the living room. She is proud of her heritage and has a large print of a Native American woman in traditional clothing hanging on the wall of the dining room. Mrs. Jones' grandmother was an important influence in her life. "The lady took care of everyone and was always there when they needed her." Mrs. Jones also takes care of many people in the family and is always willing to help a family member

Mrs. Jones' oldest son was an extremely bright child in school, and she is very proud of how well he did in school. She saved everything from the school, as well as his scrapbook. When he got older, he got into drugs and is now mentally ill. He lives at home and, she cares for him. Her second son is in jail; she visits him to make sure he is all right. Mrs. Jones keeps a scrapbook of all the things her boys have done, both good and bad. She loves her sons very much and will always take care of them. She is not sure what the future holds for Quinton, but she takes one day at a time.

Mrs. Jones has not traveled and does not have much free time for recreational activities. She loves putting her family photographs in frames and displays them in her house. Mrs. Jones feels that she is working hard in order to survive. She is sometimes a private person who gets emotional. Her feelings can get easily hurt, so she often keeps to herself and family.

Mrs. Jones met with me three times. We also spoke on the phone twice and wrote to each other. I feel honored that Mrs. Jones opened up and shared private information with me about her life. Even after our first meeting, I felt as though I was a better teacher, and knew Quinton better. Each morning after I began the visits to Quinton's house, he would come into the classroom and ask me if I could come to his house today. He enjoyed my visits at least as much as I did.

Cross-Cultural Analyses

After using the information from the autobiography and biography, many differences between Mrs. Jones and myself were found. These differences along with similarities are summarized in Table1. It shows how we compare and contrast.

Table 1.

Similarities	Differences
Close Family	Ethnic and Cultural
Celebrations	Religion
Large Family	Economics/Career
Grandparent Help	Education
Work Hard	Role of Men in the Family
Working Mothers	Working Mothers
	Age
	Travel
	Food
	Recreation

I will next analyze the differences I discovered between Mrs. Jones' life and my life. I will explain the differences I admire as well as the one's that make me feel uncomfortable.

Ethnic and Cultural Differences

I was the most uncomfortable the first day while driving to Mrs. Jones' home for our first meeting. I had never gone on a home visit by myself, and this was considered a dangerous street. I was relieved the minute I drove up and found them waiting for me outside. It is difficult to go to a place where you have heard so many negative things. Fear seems almost natural. When Mrs. Jones told me about her two older sons, I was shocked. When she told me about her older son and the drugs and brain damage, I was sick. I saw her tears and wanted to hug her. When Mrs. Jones took her scrap book out and showed me her son's arrest record and told me about jail, I was trying very hard to look like I had experienced conversations like this before, and it was alright. This information made me the most uncomfortable, and also made me admire her the most. She has such unconditional love for her sons, and she cares for them so unselfishly.

Mrs. Jones told me about her experiences with racism in school. She told me that Black students were pushed through. I had the feeling that Mrs. Jones was holding back. I felt that she had many stories to share about being discriminated against, but she would not. Maybe she thought she would offend me or maybe she didn't think I would understand. She might not have trusted me enough or felt like I was interested. I wanted to hear the whole story with all her emotions. I am not judgmental, and wanted her trust, but we will continue to try and build trust.

Religion

Religion was a difference in our lives. I grew up attending a Presbyterian Church, and religion was part of my life. When I married my husband, I decided to become Greek Orthodox so that our children would have a strong sense of religion and our family would attend one church. Our Greek Orthodox Church allows us to see and be social with my husband's family who all attend it. It also teaches our children about tradition and their past. Mrs. Jones indicated that she does not attend church because Sunday is her day off. When I asked her about religion, I did not want to imply that she should go to church, or make her think I feel I am better because I go to church. She almost apologized to me for not going to church, and this made me feel uncomfortable and seemed to build up the power relationship. I wanted to express how much I needed spirituality in my life, but I did not want to make her feel worse.

Economics/Career

The next difference that emerged had to do with economics. When I was growing up, I was fortunate enough to have money. My father worked hard, and my parents started out with very little. Having five children also put a strain on finances. We had a nice house and cars, and as I grew older, we had more. I also grew up in the 80's, which was a flashy decade. Now I am older and my little family is middle class. I work very hard to support my family. We don't have a great deal, but what we have is nice. Mrs. Jones also provides for her family, but the difference is I could always get money if I needed to. Mrs. Jones worries about money for survival. I worry about money for luxuries. At first, I felt guilty for having this lifestyle, and then realized that I provide for my family. I should not feel guilty. I then admired her for providing for her family, and that seemed to change our relationship. We have a mutual respect for each other; we both take care of our families to the best of our abilities using what resources we were given. Tied to economics is also the career choice. I never realized that I had the choice (and still do) to be anything I want to be. Mrs. Jones really did not have a choice, and the choices she had were not nearly as good as mine. When we talked about her night time cleaning job, I found myself tuning her out and thinking how I can get her a better paying, daytime job. I remember thinking that she is so wonderful; she could work in many places. I did not even bother to ask her if she liked her job and the hours. Thinking about working at night is unimaginable to me, and I had a tough time really understanding this. This made me uncomfortable when we were talking about this, because she does not have many choices. I also admire Mrs. Jones a great deal; she is a single mother who works very hard. She could easily go on public assistance, and if I was in her position, I am not sure what I would do. She had her mother help by babysitting Quinton at night while she goes to work. She has figured out a way to work and have quality care for Quinton. This is a difficult choice mothers have to make.

Working Mothers

Mrs. Jones' mother worked outside the home when she was growing up, and my mother did not. I feel lucky that my mother could stay home with us, and I thought all moms stayed home when I was growing up. I need to work and the fact that my husband stays home makes this a little easier to take, but it is still difficult. As a mother, my heart is telling me to stay with my babies, but it is not a choice. Mrs. Jones does not have a choice either. She also must go to work as her mother did. I admired Mrs. Jones for being such a help to her family when she was growing up. With her mother working, she helped a great deal in the house. Due to the fact that Mrs. Jones' mother worked, she was cared for daily by her grandmother. My mother did not work, but we would visit my grandmother. My grandmother did not baby-sit us, but my grandparents took us out to dinner and on trips when we were older.

Role of Men in the Family

The role of men in our families is very different. In my family when growing up, my father provided the money, and my mother stayed home with the children and supported my father's career. My father did do many things around the house, all the things my mother could not. My parents also worked together in redecorating and remodeling. In my family now, due to my husband's illness, I have the career, and he stays home with the children. This has been very difficult for me because the society I live in does not accept that. My husband does the cleaning, shopping, and laundry. Quite often, when people ask George what he does, and he tells them, they say ignorant things such as, "Wow, what a great setup." This used to brother me, but now I think how bad that person would feel if they knew what George has been through.

Mrs. Jones expressed to me that while growing up her brothers were not expected to do anything. She also stated that her own three boys do not help around the house and they are not employed. When she was telling me this, it was making my blood pressure go up. I cannot imagine having grown men who are not expected to do anything. This really made me uncomfortable, and I had trouble dealing with it.

Education

Our next difference examined was education. I went to suburban schools that were mainly White middle to upper class. I attended college and graduate school. Mrs. Jones went to a city school that had just been desegregated. She graduated from high school. When we were talking about education, I felt uneasy. After we started talking about her school, I was uneasy about her experiences and lack of choices. She explained that African American kids were just pushed through and not valued. She also stated that Blacks and Whites were separated and fights broke out often.

Age

The difference in our age is fifteen years. This does not seem like a big difference, but because of the time she grew up, it is significant. She was maturing during the Civil Rights Movement. I could only read about it in textbooks and that gave little information. I never knew there were race riots in Central New York. My family was not affected by racial tension since we lived in a small sheltered community of middle class White people. We never talked about it. I admire Mrs. Jones for what she has gone through. She never seemed bitter or angry for what has happened. She had to go to school in a hostile setting where people were separate and did not value her.

Travel

Our travel experiences have also been very different, and when we discussed this, I had an eye opening experience. I have taken for granted that people travel and have vacations away form their day-to-day life. I have been on many trips with my family and as a student in high school and college. Mrs. Jones told me they did not really go on vacations, and she doesn't plan on any. She continued to say that they would be unable to attend her family reunion due to finances. I really got frustrated with this. I wanted to say to her that she has to go for a better quality of life for Quinton. He needs to see his family and also have more chances in his life.

Food

We talked about the foods our families ate at holiday and special occasions. I can remember thinking I have never even seen collard greens. Mrs. Jones talked about her Christmas celebration and told me they ate sweet potato pie, prune cake, potato salad, chitlins, turkey, ham, and pork. I strongly believe that food is a major part of a culture. I grew up without a strong cultural influence and any special foods. When we moved to the small city, I developed friendships with Italian Americans. I found that I loved the culture and the family gathering that seemed to focus on food. When I married my husband, I learned about the Greek culture and their foods. Mrs. Jones did not seem to know about Greek foods. After our conversations, I felt that I wanted to have a meal that included the foods Mrs. Jones' family traditionally enjoyed.

Recreation

Recreation is a large part of my life, and since I have had children, our ways of enjoying the days have changed somewhat, but we still make time for it. I enjoy shopping, reading, skiing, walking, watching television, movies, restaurants, day trips, spending the summer on the lake, and going to the zoo. Mrs. Jones did not seem to have forms of recreation besides some shopping and watching television. This made me think about her life and how time and money limit her recreation. I did feel guilty and sorry for her.

Summary

After completing the analysis, I sat and looked at how different we were and thought, "How can this work." Then I realized that it does work! We need to understand how and why we are different and celebrate that. We can teach each other why we act certain ways due to our experiences. Through our conversations, I became more at ease with Mrs. Jones. I found that I did not have to act overly nice to get her to like me. She opened up more and would give me more information when I asked a question. We learned to share our lives and questions and laugh. We developed a sense of trust and the power relationship between teacher and parent seemed to disappear. She felt comfortable and I did too. This allowed us to begin talking about her child's program and how we could help him with his literacy development. Now that I have gone through this experience, it will be much easier for me to do the same with other parents in my class. My initial fear of home visits is gone. The information I gained will help all the families and children in my classroom. Many of the ideas that follow came from the discussions that Mrs. Jones and I had during the home visits.

Plan for Future Practice

My discussions with Mrs. Jones, helped me make a plan for future practice, a plan that will connect home and school for real conversations that will benefit the children and help develop a learning community that facilitates reading, writing, listening, speaking, and viewing. I am planning on getting to know all of my students' families.

I will begin in the month of August by sending a postcard to each student to welcome him or her to our class. I will also decorate the classroom with inviting pictures that are representative of the students in the class. These will include bulletin boarders with multicultural children on them, books displayed that represent all cultures, and posters with African American children on them. I will have the students names posted several times around the room and be sure each child has a special space of his or her own.

September will be kicked off with a family newsletter before school begins, telling families what students will need for school and general information. Once school begins, I will send home a survey for families to fill out, giving me information about their children. I will then follow up this survey with a home visit, and talk about the information on the survey; families who do not return the survey will be able to answer the questions with me through conversations at home and on the phone. This information will help me get to know the child and the family and what their goals and concerns are for their children. The students and I will use interactive writing to produce a quick "weekly news" report from our classroom that will go home each Friday. I will send home a monthly calendar of events for families to mark on their own calendars. Our new reading series has a family involvement activities book that I intend to use once contact has been made. I am also going to have "Pride" newspaper written by the urban community delivered to our classroom so students will be able to read about and discuss their neighborhoods.

Our open house in October will be different. I will invite questions from the whole group of parents, something I never thought to do before. I will have sign-up sheets for field trips and classroom events. After the open house, I will reflect on the conversations I had and keep notes on families.

During the third week in October, the children in the class will begin to collect information by interviewing each other. Students will report on each other by writing and speaking. We will save this information in our autobiographical portfolios compiled during the entire year.

I will start the "students of the month club" and model a report on myself featuring a poster with information about my life. I will bring in items from my home to share with the students. On the day I present information about me, I will have my husband and sons come to school, and will introduce them to the class. Students will be given materials and general directions to create a poster about themselves. Families will be encouraged to help students with this project. Finally, students will bring in artifacts from home that are important to them and use them in their presentation. When the poster is completed, a family member or members will be invited into the class to help the student share the information I will call families at the beginning of the month and explain what we are doing; we will schedule a day and be sure transportation is not a problem. I will send home a note the day before and make a quick call to be sure they are able to visit.

During November, we will have days of thanks where students write about what they are thankful for and why. This information will be part of the autobiographical portfolio that will be complied through out the year.

In December, we will celebrate holidays around the world by inviting family members to share family traditions that focus on a holiday. This could include reading a story, presenting pictures and/or craft, and preparing a special recipe. I think this will only be successful if I have built strong relationships with families thus far. I will also work with families to provide materials and transportation.

During January, I plan to have a weeklong multicultural reading celebration. We will have been reading stories all year, so students can share one that is special to them. I hope to invite parents and family members to read aloud a book or tell a story that reflects their cultural heritage. If parents are hesitant, I can help them select a book or if desired, they can tell a story. This will really let me get to know more about families and their backgrounds.

February and March will be the months that we focus on the famous African Americans that we have been learning about all year. Even though we have been celebrating diversity all along, I will schedule to create something from our information we have accessed. We will make a time line of famous people's lives, read biographies and autobiographies and compare and contrast differences and similarities. Also, during March, I will hold family conferences. Our district does not have formal conferences after the fall conference, but I would like to meet again. We will know each other very well by then and can reevaluate the goals set for their children.

In the past, I have had students write about themselves in September without any organization; it has fail miserably. I will now have the students write about themselves in April, using the information compiled in their autobiography portfolio. Additionally, I will encourage them to be creative when they present their stories to the whole class.

May is the month that our school prepares to celebrate the multicultural festival. We usually pick a country or theme and learn about that culture. My class will take it a step further. We will compare and contrast the culture we learned about with our own. We will examine what we like about the differences and what we don't like and talk about why we like and dislike certain things about a culture. We will celebrate those differences in a variety of ways.

In June, we will wrap up our year with our "celebrate me portfolio party". We will invite families and have a party with food and drinks to celebrate our hard work and what we have learned. I will then give parents another survey asking them about to evaluate their children's year in my classroom.

Final Word

I am making a commitment to myself to take the time to reflect on my own life on an ongoing basis. I will add to the autobiography I have started. I plan to keep a journal, which will include contacts with families, ideas for conversations and goals for positive communication.

I know I could never have gained the knowledge about home and school communication from books alone. I needed to get out of the school and classroom and get to know for myself. As a result, I discovered that I needed to consider the lives and experiences of each student. Once I get to know students and their families, I then can try to make sure they feel valued and a part of their school community. I want the students and their families to feel empowered and have a positive school experience. I want my students to learn about understand, and appreciate human differences

Discussion

Since educators are in positions of power and have the power to empower, they have the responsibility to develop learning communities that connect home and school for reading, writing, listening, and speaking (Faltis, 1993; Edwards, et.al. 1999). The ABC's of Cultural Understanding and Communication is a model that appears to empower teachers to do just that (Schmidt, 1998 c; 1999a; 2000; 2001).

The ABC's assignments had a profound effect on Susan. Writing the autobiography, recording and reporting the interview, and analyzing the cultures allowed her to design plans for connecting home and school.

Hopefully, Susan's experiences will convince other teachers and teacher educators to systematically attempt to connect home and school by experiencing models such as the ABC's of Cultural Understanding and Communication. However, there are specific aspects of the model that must be considered before implementing it.

ABC's Model for Teacher Education: Commendations and Cautions

Since 1993, I have used the ABC's model in the multicultural literacy courses for those in graduate and undergraduate, teacher education programs. They have added statements on course evaluations, such as:

- "This is the most significant education course I have taken."
- "This should be a required course for everybody in the college."
- "The ABC's of Cultural Understanding and Communication was a wakeup call."
- "I am actually sharing with parents. We are really talking to each other."
- "I can't believe the changes in my classroom."

These are significant statements, but there are cautionary notes related to the ABC's of Cultural Understanding and Communication. First, the ABC's assignments should be cleared through the Human Subjects Board of the college to prevent any possible abuses related to coursework and research. I always assure those in the course that the autobiography is confidential. I explain that the assignment is meant to be rigorous, but should not make one miserable or uncomfortable. But, I make clear that life stories, with the greatest detail, are the most helpful for cultural analysis assignments. I also emphasize that no one's life will be graded and that the autobiographies may actually be the beginnings of family histories. Finally, I share excerpts from my own life story, and with permission, autobiographies from previous classes.

Most life stories, from the last seven years, have included intimate details, human tragedies, and traumas. 90% of those enrolled in the colleges' teacher education program are white, middle class women, and when I read their stories, I am overwhelmed by the courage and resiliency portrayed.

The biographies are also remarkable in their descriptions. Teachers, after writing their autobiographies, seem to gain the confidence needed to share portions of their own stories with interviewees. This stimulates the interviewees to share in kind. Because pseudonyms are used and the tapes returned to interviewees, they also trust the interviewer. Generally, interviewers meet more than three times with their interviewees; they become fascinated with the people and their stories. As each pair spends time together, much is revealed. Confidences are divulged, and friendships take shape. Interviews occur almost anywhere-homes, restaurants, schools, libraries, taverns, markets, recreation centers, automobiles, synagogues, churches, and mosques. Participants have often described the experience as "wonderful listening and learning "

Similarly, when Susan and Mrs. Jones went through the ABC's process, their relationship developed through authentic conversations. They discovered similarities and differences, but more importantly, they discovered real communication. From the visits with Mrs. Jones, Susan created a plan for connecting home and school to build a classroom community. In the classroom community students would have daily opportunities to read, write, listen, and speak about similarities and differences related to themselves, thus, promoting home and school connections for literacy learning and the appreciation and celebration of differences.

The Power to Empower

The stories from a teacher and a parent in this chapter support the idea that teacher education programs must prepare teachers for responsive and relevant pedagogy through experiences and assignments similar to the ABC's of Cultural Understanding and Communication.

When Susan wrote her autobiography, she became aware of her own struggles and triumphs. She realized that her family had traditions. She recognized human similarities and differences as she interviewed and analyzed Mrs. Jones' family culture. When teachers share their lives with families and permit questions and comments, families return, in kind, with their stories. Similarly, Edwards (1997), in her parent interviews, found that families have a wealth of knowledge to share that helps the teacher motivate and promote the child's reading, writing, listening, and speaking. When a teacher knows the family and /or community values, and also values what the family and /or community knows, the boundaries between home and school become blurred in an atmosphere of learning and collaboration (Schmidt, 1999).

REFERENCES

Au, K. (1993). Literacy instruction in multicultural settings. New York: Harcourt, Brace Javanovich College Publishers.

Banks, J. A. (1994). An introduction to multicultural education. Boston, MA: Allyn and Bacon.

Britzman, D. (1986). Cultural myths in the making of a teacher: Biography and social structure in teacher education. Harvard Educational Review, 56, 442-456.

Cummins, J. (1986). Empowering minority students: A framework for intervention. Harvard Educational Review, 56 (1), 18-36.

Diamond, B. & Moore, M. (1995). Multicultural literacy: Mirroring the reality of the classroom. White Plains, NY: Longman Publishing Co.

Derman-Sparks, l. (1992). Anti-bias curriculum: Tools for empowering young children. Sacramento, CA: California State Department of Education.

Edwards, P. (1997, May). Examining dialogues used in facilitating parental understanding of first graders' reading and writing development. Paper presented at the annual meeting of the International Reading Association, Atlanta, GA.

Edwards, P., Pleasants,H., & Franklin, B. (1999). A path to follow: Learning to listen to parents. Portsmouth, NH: Heinemann.

254

Emig, J. (1971). Writing as a mode of learning. College Composition and Communication, 28, 122-128.

Faltis, C. J. (1993). Joinfostering: Adapting teaching strategies for the multilingual classroom. New York: Maxwell Macmillan International.

Goldenberg, C. N. (1987). Low-income Hispanic parents' contributions to their first- grade children's word-recognition skills. Anthropology and EducationQuarterly, 18, 149-179.

Greene, M. (1995). Releasing the imagination. SanFrancisco: Jossey Bass Publishers

Heath, S. B. (1983). Ways with words: Language life and work in communities and classrooms. Cambridge, UK: Cambridge University Press.

Ladson-Billings, G. (1995). Culturally relevant teaching. Research Journal, 32 (3), 465-491.

McCaleb, S. P. (1994). Building communities of learners. New York: St. Martin's Press.

Nieto, S. (2000). Affirming diversity: The sociopolitical context of multicultural education (3rd Ed.). New York: Longman.

Noordhoff, K., & Kleinfield, J. (1993). Preparing teachers for multicultural classrooms. Teaching and Teacher Education, 9 (1), 27-39.

Ogbu, J. (1983). Minority status and schooling in plural societies. Comparative Educational Review, 27 (2), 168-190.

Paley, V. G. (1989). White teacher. Cambridge, MA: Harvard University Press.

Pattnaik, J. (1997). Cultural stereotypes and pre-service education: Moving beyond our biases. Equity and Excellence in Education, 30 (3), 40-50.

Progoff, I. (1975). At a journal workshop: The basic text and guide for using the intensive journal. New York: Dialogue House Library.

Schmidt, P. R. (1998a). Cultural conflict and struggle: Literacy learning in a kindergarten program. New York: Peter Lang

Schmidt, P. R. (1998b). The ABC's of Cultural Understanding and Communication. Equity and Excellence in Education, 31 (2).

Schmidt, P. R. (1998c). The ABC's Model: Teachers connect home and school. In press. In T. Shanahan and F.V. Rodriguez-Brown, (Eds.), National reading conference yearbook 47. National Reading Conference.

Schmidt, P. R. (1999). Focus on research: Know thyself and understand others. Language Arts, 76 (4), 332-340.

Schmidt, P. R. (2000). Teachers Connecting and Communicating With Families for Literacy Development. In T. Shanahan and F.V. Rodriguez-Brown, (Eds.), National reading conference yearbook 49. National Reading Conference.

Schmidt, P.R. & Mosenthal, P. (2001). Reconceptualizing literacy in the new age of multiculturalism and pluralism. New York: Ablex.

Sjoberg, G., & Kuhn, K. (1989). Autobiography and organizations: Theoretical and methodological issues. The Journal of Applied Behavioral Science, 25 (4), 309-326.

Sleeter, C. & Grant, C. (1991). Race, class, gender, and disability in current textbooks. In M.W. Apple and L.K. Christian-Smith, The politics of the textbook, New York: Routledge & Chapel Hall.

Spindler, G., & Spindler, L. (1987). The interpretive ethnography of education: At home and abroad. Hillsdale, NJ: Lawrence Erlbaum Associates.

Spradley, J. (1979). The ethnographic interview. New York: Holt, Rinehart & Winston.

Trueba, H. T., Jacobs, L. & Kirton, E. (1990). Cultural conflict and adaptation: The case of the Hmong children in American society. New York: The Falmer Press.

Vygotsky, L. S. (1978). Mind in society: The development of higher mental process. Cambridge, MA: Harvard University Press.

*Yinger, R. (1985). Journal writing as a learning tool. Volga-Review, 87 (5), 21-33.

Chapter 18

Instructional Design Variables to Enhance Cultural Diversity: Instructional Design, Technology, and Cultural Diversity Variables to Consider to Improve Learning

Dr. Doreen Barrett

Kansas State University

Manhattan, KS

Demographics

Designing instruction with the challenge of equity and excellence, is to provide all students with equal opportunity to learn. Demographic projections indicate that an increasingly diverse group of students will populate public schools well into the 21st century. These demographic changes indicate a need for new kinds of instructional environments that are consistent with today's diverse society. This will take into consideration the physical environment, the classroom culture, the instructional materials, the instructor or coach, the students and the instructional strategies. Changes in school population demand some changes in educational theory, curriculum, teaching strategies, and most importantly the designing of instruction. Materials must utilize a design process that allows for and promotes diversity inclusion.

Given the changing demographics, there is a need to develop instruction that is responsive to the varied racial and cultural backgrounds of the learners for whom it is designed. Information that provides a focus on the development of curricula, instructional treatments, instructional strategies, and instructional materials should be used to promote an acceptance and appreciation of racial and cultural diversity.

With the changing demographics and student population, it becomes more evident that a variety of different teaching strategies and techniques are needed to enhance the learning of a diverse population.

Culture

Culture involves style, ethos and values. Culture has a lot to do with the way people give and receive information. In short, it has everything to do with the way people learn. Much of our thinking, including the conceptual categories used to organize ideas, values, relationships, and so forth, is rooted deeply in the symbolic processes and patterns of our cultural group.

The importance of culture on learning outcome warrant looking at culture as an important educational issue. Instructional design teams, members of the academy and corporate developers must be cognizant of the many principles or heuristics for designing instruction that take into account learner cultural diversity. The following are components of cultural diversity: ethnicity, race, gender, religious affiliation, socioeconomic level, social class, language, exceptionality, and age (Boyer, 1992).

This knowledge could allow individuals to incorporate a variety of strategies into their instructional design process. It is important to expand the knowledge base of how cultural diversity can be addressed systematically within the process of developing instruction. The cultural background of individuals has been found to influence learning style preferences. The more that is known about the history, language, values, nonverbal behavior, and learning styles of the learners, the better the instruction can suit their needs.

We need to understand how culture influences cognition. Culture is understood to mean one's system for perceiving, evaluating, believing, and acting. We need to go beyond individual difference variables to an understanding of the concepts that give rise to learning styles' theory. Many approaches to learning have been rational, logical, symbolic and analytic. By comparison, a broad spectrum of learners are more likely to learn through spatial, analogic, holistic and intuitive thought processes. There is emerging evidence that learners possess different learning styles based on cultural characteristics (Samovar & Porter, 1994). Students learn not only for different reasons, but they learn in different ways.

Affective Domain:

The way students approach, interact, and persevere with an instructional program is directly related to how they perceive the task and the situation. This perception is influenced by their particular learning style and their level of motivation. Both factors can ultimately increase or decrease achievement, time-on-task, selection options, attitude. We can establish relationships between learning styles, motivation and instructional programs .

The division of learning objectives into separate domains has been largely accepted by educators since the landmark effort by Benjamin Bloom (1956) established categories of educational objectives, which they called affective, cognitive, and psychomotor. The cognitive and psychomotor domains are widely used and promoted. The affective domain has been much more difficult to pin down as it relates to instructional strategies. More instructional development will have to include strategies and content for the affective domain.

A type of learning to consider is affective learning: attitudes and values, morals and ethics and social development. The affective domain is a central component for consideration in the designing of instruction for a diverse student population. Individuals have sought to neutralize rather than amplify the effects of individual differences in the affective domain. The goal of instruction has a focus on identifying optimal methods that work well "on the average" Instructional design models and practices have focused primarily on the acquisition of knowledge and psychomotor skills. Concern for the affective domain has been limited.. At best, the issue of individualization is mentioned.

Individual differences

Because we know that individual difference variables impact the learning process, we need to become cognizant of its impact on designing and developing instructional materials. Personality variables in the affective domain are one of the individual difference variables. The personality difference that most affects learning is motivation. In many instances, motivation is the strongest predictor of learning after attitude Motivation can be used as a partial explanation for why some individuals soar to positions of prominence while others, with similar endowments, never rise above mediocrity. Motivation becomes an important criterion for making changes when developing instruction that will incorporate cultural diversity. John Keller' created the ARCS model (Keller, 1988), which gives theoretical background for the inclusion of motivational strategies in the design of instruction. Keller has an acronym for the four sets of conditions that must be met to have a motivated learner:

A for attention,

R for relevance,

C for confidence, and

S for satisfaction.

These conditions mesh well with the needs of many culturally diverse students. Each condition is an aspect shown to be necessary to enhance cultural diversity.

Clearly individuals who are responsible for designing, producing and implementing instructional materials must provide evidence of its quality in content, methodology, presentation, diversity inclusion. The information of what variables to incorporate or expand upon within the design of instruction, that are conducive to the diversity of the client population, is of great importance. Changes in school population require some changes in educational theory, curriculum, pedagogy, teaching strategies, and most importantly the design of specific instruction.

Individuals with diverse backgrounds bring cultural values, goals, and expectations to the learning environment that affect how they interact with others and how they learn. Three specific strategies fall under this category. First, identify cultural backgrounds. Obtaining accurate information about the cultural background of each learner is essential. Second, identify individuals' preferred learning styles. And third, find out more about the culture represented by the learners. The more that is known about the history, language, values, nonverbal behavior, and learning styles of the learners, the better the instruction can suit their needs

Many of the instructional design models seem to incorporate a number of unexamined traditions of thought that reproduce in the present the misconceptions of the past, particularly about how knowledge is represented Therefore, it is important to examine current instructional design models for evidence of attention to culture and authenticity of content. It is important to expand the knowledge base of how cultural diversity can be addressed systematically within the instructional design process.

Instructional design work extends beyond the packaging of facts and devising new and efficient information management systems, Instructional design is important because it can create efficient and effective instructional programs based on analysis of learners, content, and the learning environment.

Instructional design models do take into account individual differences. However, the only principle that has consistently guided attempts to individualize instruction is that learners be allowed to work at their own pace (Jia, 1994). Two important individual differences are learning style dimensions and attitude dimensions.

Culturally Influenced Learning Styles

With the changing demographics and student population, it becomes more evident that a variety of different teaching strategies and techniques are needed to enhance the learning of a diverse population. There are various styles of learning and attention to each is important. Learning styles are the various methods individuals have for perceiving and processing information while reacting to their environment. Matching learning styles with the design of instruction is important for both achievement and positive attitudes.

Learning styles are evident in the ways students exhibit what they learn and how much they have learned. The traditional educational setting rewards students who exhibit the following characteristics: an attentional style that focuses on tasks and verbal instructions rather than on the people in the environment; an informational processing approach that is

logical, linear, sequential, and analytical; the ability to sit for long periods and attend to one idea, event, or task; the desire to be independent, self-starting, and competitive; the ability to deal with ideas and concepts without concrete replication of them; a perceptual style that helps in the differentiation of relevant from irrelevant information (field independence).

Students from culturally different backgrounds are often more field dependent process information in nonlinear ways instructional strategies such as cooperative learning provide a more appropriate cultural match between instructional styles and learning style for some culturally diverse students and result in improved learning. One of the most important distinctions in learning style seems to be that of the field dependent learner and the field independent learner. These two categories are like the color spectrum. There is not only one shade of blue but rather a range going from one extreme to another.

Field dependent students are best described as people who need to learn in a context that is connected to their lives in a real way. Learning is facilitated by cooperative groups and helping others learn. They are affected by the feelings and opinions of others, in general, and by the teacher, in particular. Thus, for this learner, concepts are best presented when objectives are clearly explained and are related to personal interests and experiences. These learners need to know the why of something and what the results of an action will be.

At the other end of the spectrum is the field independent student who does not rely on context to make the learning meaningful. The field independent person prefers to work alone, is energized by competition, and is task-oriented. They are not concerned about their social environment during the learning process. These students do not seek the attention of the teacher; their interaction with the teacher is "on-task." These issues are important because individuals who are responsible for the design of instruction, need to be aware of the underlying thought processes used to learn specific information. Students who are aware of their thought processes can modify how they approach tasks so as to choose the approach best suited to the discipline.

A basic cultural mismatch occurs as students from diverse cultural backgrounds come to school valuing intuitive learning and prizing nonverbal behavior more highly than institutional norms that assume that all students will think in a linear, analytical manner. The situation is magnified when it is determined that other styles demonstrate less excellence.

Learning styles information is based on the theory that individuals respond to learning situations with consistent patterns of behavior. When this knowledge is applied to culturally diverse students, it has sometimes been used to explain why children of the same culture and ethnicity often employ similar strategies for learning.

Learning styles instruments, which attempt to operationalize the theoretical variables, have been moderately successful in distinguishing many of these styles. The beginning point in designing appropriate instruction for culturally diverse students is to understand some of the characteristics of the various learning styles.

How Cultural Variables Affect Learning

Differences in cognitive styles (e.g. analytical and relational) do not imply a superiority or inferiority relationship between cultural groups. Educators, developers and designers of educational software would do well to remember some basic assumptions from Hilliard (1989) who suggested these criteria:

1. A behavioral style is a framework from which a person views the world.

2. Several styles can be described. At one example is the analytical and at the other extreme is the relational, other possible styles are on the continuum between.

3. A person may change one's basic style by learning aspects of other styles.

4. Since styles are the framework from which one views the world, the style can be observed in all areas of one expression, such as through one's world view, language, music, religion, art, work, dance, problem solving, sports, writing, or any other area of human expression.

5. Some relationship exists between style and socioeconomic level.

6. A strong relationship exists between style and cultural or ethnic group membership, especially when a given ethnic group is located at a traditional point in the socioeconomic scale.

7. No evidence exists of a relationship between basic intelligence and style. Able people are found to be the same degree among style users.

8. Every style is necessary and useful in human experience if society is to function fully.

9. A "gifted" person is one who has integrated and harmonized style

Learning styles are evident in the ways students exhibit what they learn and how much they have learned. Replication of them; a perceptual style that helps in the differentiation of relevant from irrelevant information (field independence).

What is apparent is that new instructional models need to be developed or existing models need to be adapted to better meet the needs of today's teachers and students. New models should be in contrast to other design models, which usually address instruction intended for homogeneous grouping. School-based design models can be developed to accommodate learning that is more relevant and learner driven. These models need to provide for students with diverse needs

These design models all incorporate the five steps included in the instructional systems design process. The five steps are: analysis, design, development, implementation, and evaluation. Different models are applicable to different situations. Therefore, individuals designing instruction must adapt an existing model or develop one to meet their needs. Models are visual or verbal representations of a process.

Individualized Instruction vs. Cultural Diversity

Although it has been promoted and practiced in various forms, there is little consensus regarding exactly what constitutes individualized instruction. Terms such as individualized, personalized, and adaptive instruction abound in the educational and psychological literature, suggesting that most educators agree with the premise that individuals differ in ways that effect learning. If and how educators should respond to these differences is unclear however. Perhaps as a consequence of this uncertainty, the only principle that consistently has guided attempts to individualize instruction or accommodate individual differences is that learners be allowed to work at their own pace.

To manage the task of development and delivery, educators and technologists must work together to understand and integrate the communication process, learning theories, teaching methods, and media productions into a systems approach to instruction. The task of setting standards for the development of quality instructional software for school use is difficult. There are a multitude of opinions about what should be included and what constitutes effective software.

There are a variety of opinions because of the differences in instructional theories and pedagogy. Instructional theories and pedagogy give rise to the instructional design of any given curriculum within the software design. Individuals who are developing curriculum gather information and make decisions about the approaches based upon different theoretical frameworks (Gustafson, & Branch, 1998). This will create different presentation methods, and instructional approaches. The development and presentation of instructional strategies vary depending upon the instructional goals and outcomes.

An individual's perception of the educational process and it's relationship to the rest of their lives depends largely on values, attitudes and behaviors of those within their cultural group. These perspectives are shaped by their primary group interactions as well as mediated experiences. In a media-dominated society, those with limited exposure and interactions with culturally diverse populations tend to perceive the reality of these groups through mediated descriptions.

Whenever communication is constricted, exactness in representing those ideas is limited. This impacts the effectiveness of instructional designers as they attempt to communicate concepts, higher order rules, problem solving and analytical skills to their targeted learner (Powell, 1993). Represented ideas and strategies could take on a one-sided perspective, if exposure and interaction are not included.

Classrooms of this century will experience great changes due to emerging technologies. As the hardware and software capabilities have grown, so have the advances in development.

The design of instruction for technology-based instructional systems is more complicated than the design of traditional instruction, because the instruction itself must anticipate student behaviors and understandings. The beginning of the process starts with courseware development. The visual aspect of courseware design is an important variable to enhance content.

Although culture is recognized as an important aspect of communication, culture is virtually ignored as a variable in the design and implementation of interactive multimedia. An individual's perception of the educational process and it's relationship to the rest of their lives depends largely on values, attitudes and behaviors of those within their cultural group. In a media dominated society, those with limited exposure and interaction with culturally diverse populations tend to perceive the reality of groups through mediated descriptions. Whenever communication is constricted, exactness in representing those ideas will be limited.

Technology

Infusing technology into instructional strategies can have positive effects if used appropriately. Technology is constantly changing. These changes can have an impact on the designing of instruction. A trend that is pervasive is the on going battle between software priorities and hardware capabilities.

In looking at software and the use of technology there are existing formats that can unequally benefit certain domains (Barrett, 1996).

    a. The images in the form of ethnic group representation are shown more in a ratio for balance than images of substance. Even looking at the ethnic balance, you do not see representation from the variety of cultures that exist within the school population. Some cultures are still almost non-existent.

    b. Language is handled in a very isolated way. There are some courses in reading and math that have the same content with the language changed to Spanish. There is no development of courses to teach various languages to English speaking students.

c. Utilizing the capabilities of the technology (ex; Hypermedia), the courses could allow for students to access and experience different perspectives.

  c1. Hypermedia can be strongly motivating if the elements that stimulate challenge and curiosity are used to increase emotional involvement.

  c2. The tools we use with hypermedia can allow us to capture the senses and then have interaction. Video ,audio graphic, computer interaction, direct manipulation, proper interface design, culturally inclusive and cognitively varied metaphor and instructional strategies are some of the important tools for learning.

  c3. Hypermedia is an enabling rather than directive environment.

  c4. A recent trend in the authoring of hypermedia is the emphasis of visuals. Appropriate inclusion of various ethnic representation in all aspects of the curriculum is very applicable to hypermedia.

  c5. Hypermedia/hypertext can be used to allow a learner to incorporate individual information, access, interact and interrelate ideas to make learning more culturally meaningful.

The use of technology is a potential vehicle for leveling the playing field toward educational excellence. Technology use can enhance the opportunity for students of various learning styles and abilities to gather, synthesize, and process information. The use of technology allows a wide variety of instructional strategies and techniques, while also being able to facilitate various responses. The wider the opportunities the more level the playing field.

Multimedia technology allows the integration of print, voice, visuals, recordings, and interactive video. Environments are created in which informational presentations can successfully and efficiently be transferred into knowledge by a diverse and ever changing population of learners. Multimedia technology offers education a window to augment traditional methods, materials, and strategies for teaching and learning .

A preliminary analysis of educational software illustrates it can still retain many of the misconceptions and omissions found in textbooks (Powell, 1993). Many programs include "artistic flair" rather than systematic objectives of the learning task to be accomplished.

The quality control criteria curriculum developers and individuals developing instruction instructional designers typically use to monitor their processes take on new meanings that have pluralistic dimensions to them when used to assess the appropriateness of curriculum for students who are ethnically and culturally different. The "test" for *balance* is no longer merely checking to see if objectives, content, activities, and evaluation have attended to each of the three domains of learning- the affective, cognitive, and psychomotor- or whether there is a blend of students interests and societal needs. Now individuals developing instruction also need to know if these elements of the curriculum include information representative of a wide variety of socially and culturally different groups.

Routine checks for *internal consistency* of the curriculum elements are broaden to look for agreement or congruity between students' learning styles and the kinds of learning activities proposed, and comparability of experiences suggested for different cultural and ethnic groups of students. *Learner verification* of the instructional plans is no longer established by merely determining how well content and activities designed for the traditional average, low, and high ability students do indeed work for them.

It now has to extend to ascertain whether the courseware design works for a variety of students who are female, from urban or rural areas, have various handicapping conditions, and are Asian American, Hispanic, African-American, and Native-American. Assessments for *relevance* ascertain whether ethnic or socially diverse students find the materials, methods of instruction, and media personally meaningful (Gay, 1994).

An individual's perception of the educational process and it's relationship to the rest of their lives depends largely on values, attitudes and behaviors of those within their cultural group. These perspectives are shaped by their primary group interactions as well as mediated experiences. In a media dominated society, those with limited exposure and interaction with culturally diverse populations tend to perceive the reality of these groups through mediated descriptions. Whenever communication is constricted, exactness in representing those ideas will be limited.

Individuals are motivated for different reasons and by different stimuli.
What may cause one individual or group to become highly motivated to achieve may have no observable influence on another.

Having a range of navigational tools to aid the variety of learning styles is essential. Accurate content, positive and inclusive visual images impact the outcome of the instruction. For meanings to remain relatively constant across sources and receivers, the message itself should change, since the interpretation of the message is sure to change. Interactive multimedia can assist in conveying a variety of messages across cultures.

Although culture is recognized as an important aspect of communication, it needs to be recognized more and incorporated as a variable in the design and implementation instruction. Given a need to develop curricula, instructional treatments, instructional strategies, and instructional materials which promotes an acceptance and appreciation of racial and cultural diversity, and understanding of the cultural attributes of how people give and receive information, some changes must be made to existing design models.

There are specific variables which need to be included in an instructional design model to enhance cultural diversity . These variables are:

a. Relevance

b. Prior knowledge

c. Various perspectives

d. Authentic content

e. Various instructional strategies

f. Language

g. Collaborative and cooperative learning environments

h. Preferred assessment methods

i. Open-ended courseware

Use of these variables in designing instruction will enhance the overall pedagogical effectiveness (Barrett, 1996). The three steps in a systems approach to instructional design are:

Instructional treatments

Instructional strategies

Instructional materials

There is one step in this approach that promotes an acceptance and appreciation of racial and cultural diversity, and understanding of the cultural attributes of how people give and receive information. This step is instructional strategies. This particular step is conducive to the design changes needed.

The components of an instructional strategy are pre-instructional activities, informational presentation, student participation, testing, and follow-through. The following examples show how the *nine variables* mentioned above can be incorporated.

Pre-instructional activities- motivation (attitude)

This is where the ARCS model (Keller, 1988) can enhance the instruction. Relevance, which is one of the points in the ARCS model, is motivational when prior knowledge of the student is a part of the design. When various perspectives are incorporated into the design, this is also motivational.

Information presentation- (examples)

Authentic content should be used in the development and design of the instruction. Various instructional strategies (simulation, discovery) allow for different learning styles. Language translations and capabilities for a wide range of ethnic groups are important components.

Student participation

Instruction can be designed for the courseware to use more collaborative and cooperative learning environments.

Testing

Identification of assessment methods and techniques for a variety of student preferences and styles. Open-ended courseware will give students an opportunity to show their ability without the constraints of timed instruction.

Standardized testing and assessments that focus on logical, analytical, competitive, and timed methods are not inclusive of all cultural groups.

Follow through

Including these variables within the design of the instruction will allow students to work with confidence and satisfaction which are the CS in Keller's ARCS model.

Within the five components is the ability to make changes and add strategies that allow for diversity. When individuals are at the step of developing instructional strategy within the instructional design process, the nine variables mentioned above can be discussed and incorporated. Utilizing these variables will enhance the opportunity for a more culturally diverse instructional program.

REFERENCES

Barrett, Doreen. (1996). *Analysis of the instructional design variables within selected integrated learning systems (ILS): Implications for design changes to enhance cultural diversity*. Unpublished doctoral dissertation, Kansas State University, Manhattan.

Bloom, B. S. (1956). *Taxonomy of educational objectives: The classification of educational goals, handbook 1: Cognitive domain*. New York: McKay.

Boyer, J. (1992). Multicultural concerns in educational research. *Mid-Western Educational Researcher, 5* (2), 7-8.

Gay, G. (1994). *At the essence of learning: Multicultural education* (1st ed.). New York: Longman.

Gustafson, K., Branch, Robert (1998). *Survey of instructional development models*. Syracuse: ERIC Clearinghouse of Information Resources

Hilliard, A. G. (1989). Teaching and cultural styles in a pluralistic society. *National Education Association, 7* (6), 65-69.

Jia, C. (1994). *The relationship of student learning styles, computer attitudes, and learning outcomes in a mathematics course using a CAI lab*. Unpublished doctoral dissertation, Kansas State University, Manhattan.

Keller, J. M. (1988). Development and use of the ARCS model of instructional design. *Journal of Instructional Development, 10* (3), 2-10.

Powell, G. C. (1993). *Incorporating learner cultural diversity into instructional systems design. An investigation of faculty awareness and teaching practices*. Unpublished doctoral dissertation, University of Georgia, .

Samovar, L. S., & Porter, R. E. (1994). *Intercultural communication: A reader*. Belmont, C.A: Wadsworth.

Thompson, J., & Branch, R. (1995). *Prescriptives for incorporating culture into instruction*. Paper presented at the meeting of the Association of Educational Communications and Technology, Anaheim, CA.

Chapter 19

School Staff Development Cultural Diversity: Multicultural Curriculum Programming (School Staff Development Workshop)

Bonita Manson, Ph.D.
Middle Tennessee State University

Tony J. Manson, Ph.D.
Middle Tennessee State University

SCHOOL STAFF DEVELOPMENT WORKSHOP OBJECT ON CULTURAL DIVERSITY

Objective:

Participants will have a heightened awareness of both their personal cultural lenses and the impact of those lenses on individuals from other cultural groups.

What is diversity?

The term "diversity is very broad in scope. When diversity training was new, the term "diversity" basically meant "race". "Diversity training" was just a buzz phrase for racial awareness and sensitivity training.

What many people in the field began to see fairly early on, however, is that while race is a very important part of diversity, and not to be minimized in any way, it is only one aspect of diversity. They began to realize that if we are really going to live and work successfully in our very diverse country, we're going to have to learn about, understand and hopefully value our diversity in all its manifestations and how these different categories are the same, or that they impact our lives in the same way. Racism may, for example, impact the life of an African American woman quite differently, and to a different extent, than sexism. The point is not that all of these differences are the same. It is just when we think of the word, "diversity" it is important to be mindful of the many ways that we are diverse from each other and the importance of understanding those differences.

Iceberg exercise:

The objective of this exercise is where the majority of the writing is on the iceberg. It is below the water. What we want to learn is to interact with people based on more of the information below the line, become aware of when we are judging people based on superficial information and in time, hopefully, stop making judgements.

What is cultural diversity work?

The nature of diversity work may best be explained by considering what it is and what it is not. To do that, it is helpful to use what is sometimes called, "The Head, Hand and Heart Model".

The **Head Work** is the cognitive part of the work, the part that asks the questions.

The **Hand Work** is comprised of the legal nuts and bolts.

The **Heart** focuses on how we interact with each other in the workplace.

The model is designed to improve the answers to the following kinds of questions: What are the interpersonal and inter-group relationships like across cultural lines? Do people truly trust each other across culture lines? Can people work together in effective cross-cultural teams? Are culturally inappropriate/offensive remarks and jokes tolerated in the work place? Is there any power sharing at the highest ranks with women, men of color, people with physical and mental impairments, elders, etc.?

History of diversity

In the 1960's the Congress and the President attempted to end historical discrimination to put a stop to the practice of excluding some people from educational, employment, housing use of public facilities and services and other opportunities based on race, color, national origin, religion and gender. This was an attempt to eradicate widespread legal discrimination.

In the 1970's Affirmative Action occurred. Affirmative Action, as a concept, is not based in statues or legislation. The objective was to make the employer's workforce more representative of the general population in its geographic area.

In the 1980's, improvements in the representation of previously underrepresented groups in some areas of employment. Two phenomena accompanied the new presence of minorities: (1) the revolving door, those individuals were not staying with employers very long; (2) the minorities were not being fully integrated into the workforce. There were few professional relationships that crossed race, gender and other cultural lines. People were neither working well together, nor trusting each other across cultural lines.

Even though there was progress shown from Equal Employment Opportunity to Affirmative Action to Diversity work, we must continue to be aware of discrimination and we should pay close attention to the numbers of underrepresented individuals in different areas of the workplace or we will repeat the mistakes of the past.

The process :

The objective of the exercise Getting off of automatic requires making a conscious choice of paths as they begin with life experiences. The main point is that no one is totally on one path or the other. We usually go back and forth between paths throughout our lives.

Stereotyping: What is it and why do we do it?

Stereotyping is a shortcut version of perception. When we stereotype, we place the person in a particular mental file, not based on information gained through knowledge about or personal experience of the particular person. We assign the person a mental file based upon what we believe about a general group to which the person belongs (either consciously or unconsciously). Freeing ourselves of the emotional baggage of stereotyping people allows us to work more positively and effectively with people who are culturally different from ourselves.

Gender, sexual harassment and sexual orientation issues in the workplace (lecture):

It is important that we look at the fact that society's rules are changing with regards to gender, sexual harassment and sexual orientation. Behaviors that were acceptable a few years ago, are no longer. The challenge is to know what the new parameters are acceptable and unacceptable. Many men feel that they have to walk on eggshells for fear of being accused of sexual harassing someone. Sexual harassment is wrong no matter who engages in it. Some women do harass men, it is just as wrong and just as illegal in situations in which a woman harasses a man. However, 90% of harassment is male to female, and one significant difference between a man's experience of sexual harassment and that of a woman is that for women, there is often the additional fear that the harassment may result in sexual assault.

Closing of the workshop:

All the things talked about here today are things we all should be aware of during our workday. We should really dedicate ourselves to make changes within ourselves to make this organization the best it can be. I would like to thank all of you for being so attentive and cooperative during the presentations and we welcome any questions you may have after the session, again thank you for your time.

Iceberg analogy

Fine arts
Drama * cooking
Literature * games
Folk dancing * dress
Classical/popular music
Ideals governing child raising
Arrangement of physical space
Notions of modesty * rules of descent
Pattern of superior/subordinate relations
Conversational patterns * eye behavior
Relationship to animals * conception of beauty
Definition of sin * dating practices * conception of justice
Incentives to work * notions of leadership * tempo of work
Patterns of decision-making * conception of cleanliness
Attitudes toward the dependent * conception of status mobility
Roles in relation to status by age, gender, class, occupation, kinship

Conception of past and future * definition of insanity
Nature of friendship * ordering of time * social interaction rate
Notions about logic * emotions * facial expressions * body language

AND MUCH MORE

Just a nine-tenths of an iceberg is out of sight (below the water line), so is nine-tenths of culture out of conscious awareness. The out-of-awareness part of culture has been termed "deep culture."

Behaviors – beliefs – attitudes – values – most unconscious
"FAMOUS" STEREOTYPES

Afro-Americans: the happy-go-lucky Sambo eating watermelon; the fat, old eye-rolling mammy.

Chicanos: the sombrero-wearing peon, sleeping under a cactus; the fiesta-loving macho bandito with a fat wife and lots of children.

Native Americans: the naked savage who scalps white people; the crafty hunter; the primitive craftsman and his squaw.

Asian Americans: the sly, inscrutable, slant-eyed "oriental"; the ever-smiling, hard-working, uncomplaining laundry man and pig-tailed wife.

Puerto Ricans: the docile, friendly little family speaking broken English; the strident switchblade-toting teenager spoiling for a fight.

Women of all races: the mother who is only portrayed in domestic situations; the little girl in a spotless dress playing with dolls and standing on the sidelines as boys do all the fun things; the helpless Princess rescued by Prince Charming; the wicked stepmother.

From *Bulletin,* C.I.B.C., Volume 5
Number 3, 1974.

REFERENCES

Banks, J.B. (1991/92). Multicultural education: For freedom's sake. Educational Leadership, 32-36.

Banks, J.B. (1998, Spring). Approaches to multicultural curriculum reform. Multicultural Leader, 1 (2), 1-2.

Brown, T.J. (1986). Teaching minorities more effectively a model for educators. Lanham, MD: University Press of America, Inc.

Bruner, H. (1981). Developing positive multiethnic/multicultural learning environments. In W.E. Sims & B.B. de Martinez (Eds.), Perspective in multicultural education (pp. 139-159), Washington, DC: University Press of America, Inc.

Eskenaski, M. & Gallen, D. (1992). Sexual harassment know your right! New York, NY: Carroll & Graf Publisher, Inc.

Garcia, E. (1994). Understanding and meeting the challenge of student cultural diversity. Boston, MA: Houghton Mifflin Co.

Gay, G. (1990, September). Desegration, racial attitudes, and intergroup contact: A discussion of change. Phi Delta Kappan, 25-32.

Hostile, H. (1993). The AAUW educational foundation survey. The AAUW survey on sexual harassment in America's schools.

284

Jones, J.E. & Pfeiffer, J.W. (1979). The 1979 annual handbook for group facilitators. La Jolla, CA: University Association, Inc.

Lightle, J. & Doucet, B. (1992). A guide for prevention. Los Altos, CA: Crisp Publications, Inc.

Lynch, E.E. & Hanson, M.J. (1992). Steps in the right direction. Developing cross-cultural competence a guide for working with young children and their families. Paul H. Brooks Publishing Co.

Lockwood, A.T. (1992, Summer). Approaches to multicultural curriculum reform. Multicultural Leader, 1 (2), 1-2.

Morris, B., Terpstra, J., Croninger, B. & Linn, E. (1985). Tune in to your rights a guide for teenagers about turning off sexual harassment. (Regents of the University of Michigan).

Schniedewind, N. & Davidson, E. (1983). Open minds to equality a sourcebook of learning activities to promote race, sex, class, and age equity. Allyn and Bacon.

Shoop, R.L. & Hayhow, Jr., J.W. (1994). Sexual harassment in our schools what parents and teachers need to know to spot it and stop it! Needham Heights, MA: Allyn and Bacon.

Sleeter, C.E. (1990, September). Staff development for desegregated schooling. Phi Delta Kappan, 34-40.

Secrets in Public. (1993). A joint project of NOW legal defense and education fund and Wellesley college center for research on women

Chapter 20

Politics in American Education: Is There A Place?

Tony J. Manson, Ph.D.
Middle Tennessee State University

"In addressing problems and issues related to the secondary student, it is almost impossible to escape the taint of politiczation that has infected the entire educational process."(K. Ferrel, 1992, p.8). This statement sets the tone of the American educational system, to which this discussion will be confined. Having just emerged from an era in which the self-described education president, George Bush, could baldly twist the issue of public versus private school funding into a campaign sound bite, it is difficult to approach any element concerning secondary education without maintaining a wary eye on the electoral process.

Yet taking in to account the political atmosphere is now such an integral part of the American educational system that it **must** be considered at all levels of educational practice, reform and philosophy. The politiczation of U.S. schools did not begin recently. Indeed, the very founding of such institutions as Harvard and Yale were as much in political protest of their contemporary **status quo** as they were affirmations of particular theoretical suasion. The late 1800's saw "separate but equal" politics divide our school systems into black and white, while the 1950's and 60's saw that institutional division dismantled (in theory- this matter to be discussed later). Still, when President Jimmy Carter persuaded Congress to raise the Department of Education to Cabinet-level status in the late 1970's, the organizational foundation of the educational establishment-as-a-political entity was made complete. Theory be damned, as a major player in the Administration, as a competitor for a piece of the federal budget pie, the Secretary of Education was politician first, an educator second.

Carter's successor to the presidency, Ronald Reagan, recognized that fact immediately and placed Republican political pro William Bennett in the Secretary of Education's chair, with the mandate to use his position as a bully pulpit to explain federal cutbacks in education and related social welfare programs. (G.C. Winston, 1992, p. 22). Rather than step forward as an aggressive advocate of improving the educational process, Bennett was soon spearheading the nebulous rallying cry of conservative factions-Back to Basics!- meanwhile presiding over a demoralized Education Department that found itself forced to issue directives on the base level of deciding that catsup should be considered a vegetable in federally-subsidized school lunch programs (since it was made from tomatoes).

It can thus be seen that, at least since 1980, one of the most serious problems facing the secondary school student has been the lack of serious federal government commitment to that student's education. Politically naïve though they may be, high school students are sensitively aware of the low opinion the adult establishment holds of them: it is a demoralizing situation, one that does not encourage a pro-education stance from the vast, insecure majority of teenagers.

How could it? The messages a secondary student receives today are decidedly mixed. The Back to Basis movement, (E. Van den Haag, 1992, p. 35) such as it was, received much attention for its slim premise: American students are unable to compete with Europeans and Asians because they are falling behind in simple reading and arithmetic skills. The problem with this premise and its accompanying hoopla has been that it is essentially beside the point. Statistics may provide the facts to back up this argument-another politicized issue- but fail to elaborate on the more pressing issue: **simple** reading and arithmetic skills are inadequate for the complex, high-tech world of the U.S. is a part. Indeed, it was the education president who first brought up this matter, drawing a contrast with his predecessor-sponsor, only to drop the ball in the face of right-wing, conservative opposition to progressive theories of education that might address American students' lack of fundamental skills in more innovative, **effective** ways than their nostalgia-driven Back to Basics agenda called for (i.e. rote learning). It has taken a new presidency to (verbally at least) pick up the issue of education standards in today's world and keep it rolling in the direction its implications point. That there has been so little alarm sounded from the public indicates that the right-wing noise of a few years back was just that-more noise than substance.

Which is not to say that every conservative issue affecting the educational process for secondary students is fading away under a centrist Democratic administration. The very foundation of public versus private school funding came into doubt with the campaign proposal of George Bush advocating a voucher system (recently defeated vote in California) whereby federal monies earmarked for public education could be used by parents sending their children to private institutions (C.J. Sykes, 1992, p. 35). Once again, the high school student receives a mixed message from the adult community; the school voucher proposal attacks the core premise of the student(s) public education on two fronts: economically and (intangibly) value-wise. Financially, if a voucher system is enacted, it is not impossible to foresee a future wherein public schools are unable to function competitively with private institutions because of the drain-off of federal funds. For middle-class students, this is a cause for concern, with the only alternative switching to private secondary schools hoping that their parents' additional payments will bridge the gap. For students below the middle-class it is a cause for alarm: by definition, **their** parents will not have the money to compensate for reduced federal funding of the American education. For students at an economic level where education is already not considered an important part of their lives, this could be the final blow to the concept of opportunity through education as a part of the American Dream. (I have already stated previously the voucher has been defeated through popular vote in the November, 1993 California election)

Ironically, should the ghetto-ized public school population organize and resist the down sliding inclination a school voucher system would inspire, class and race divisions in the United States could grow to crisis proportions. Such organized resistance, in the form of mass enrollments in public schools, parental participation, aggressive lobbying for every funded dollar available would inevitably create (**require**) a class-and-race-based political movement. This is something the U.S. political system has generally avoided to its benefit. Painting a prettier picture, should the school voucher system be enacted someday, and the public schools somehow maintain and/or improve standards, look to the advocates of private schools to push for further reductions in federal funds to the public schools "so that our children can keep up with the **government-aided** (read: undeserving) welfare programs." This argument is not a speculation, as it is the exact argument being put forth now in support of federal vouchers.

Still, whatever the inevitable decision on the school voucher system, the immediate effect on the secondary school population is felt at once: for the past year, the adult community has been telling its children that "the schools you are in don't work, you're not working in them, it's all a failure." If motivation is considered the prime force in education, our students are certainly deprived of it when hearing dialogue such as this.

As implied in the speculations above, inevitably the problems of race and prejudice enter the picture when discussing issues pertinent to secondary education. The easy race issues are still with us, of course, leftovers from the segregation laws of the Jim Crow era and the **de facto** separation of minorities from the white populace developed in our cities' urban expansion periods. Does bussing work? The issue is still not resolved. Should something be done? Yes, but is **something** sometimes worse than the problem itself? Does full integration mean submersion of cultural identity? Which identity?

Multiculturalism is the new catchword for addressing issues of racial and cultural prejudice in the secondary curriculum, a dropdown from the university debates of the past decade, where the issue has yet to be settled, but can more easily be papered over by the offering of a few classes that interested parties may attended while the vast majority remain unaffected by the change. This is a facile dismissal: given budget cutbacks at the university level, every course offered means another has been dropped from the curriculum. Still, universities have more opportunities to avoid the issue head-on than secondary schools. Multiculturalism as a secondary school issue is not yet nationwide: cosmopolitan, urban states such as California and New York are forced by necessity to confront the identity of their student populace in the cultural literature of their curriculums; the largely rural, more homogenous populations of Iowa or Kansas and like other regions have leisure to observe our fits and starts in handling the issue. Or so they believe (Brookhiser, 1992, p. 74).

Multicultural curriculum development has its roots in the civil rights movement of the late 1960's, when Black leaders rightly noted that the Black contribution to American society had been conveniently erased from all official school texts. In the 1970's, this error by omission strategy of cultural domination was attacked by women's groups, Native American activists and Hispanic cultural organizations. By the 1980's, the results of the efforts, at least in terms of acknowledgement by the educational establishment, were an accepted recognition that U.S. curricula should reflect the multicultural influences of the population comprising American culture.

The recognition displayed in token Black History Months and Latino Day special events (Cinco de Mayo) was to collide head-on with the white, European-oriented conservative-based backlash of the Reagan-Bennett Education Department of the 1980's. A proponent of multicultural curricula would be labeled as being politically correct and all legitimate debates ceased from that point on. Politically correct became, on all levels of the educational establishment; the sarcastic designation for one whose ideology is so blundered by liberal philosophy as to render that person's opinion anathema to open-mindedness.

And yet, politics aside, the concept of what constructs a multicultural society's curriculum should be built on remains a valid point of debate. Eliminating the backlash voices of protest, it s recognized by most interested parties that American society is founded on a Western European cultural base. If that is accepted, the next question becomes, should that Western European cultural foundation be perpetuated? Historically, until the 1960's the American melting pot ideal put questions such as this at rest; everyone is expected to meld into the mainstream so, of course, that tradition should be perpetuated.

As technology has shrunk communications with the rest of the world, however, such cultural chauvinism has clashed head-on with the reality of needing to understand other cultures on a daily basis. This need has coincided with the emergence of racial and ethnic demands for cultural recognition within the American cultural mainstream. Hence, even if the Western European cultural base is deliberately decided to be the direction American education will pursue, there is still the need to accommodate the multicultural factors influencing U.S. culture. Hence, the next legitimate point of debate is:

- To what degree?
- Tilted in whose favor?

The fact remains that, far from the simple matter of throwing in a Martin Luther King Day, recognizing the accomplishments of Madame Curie and reading

Don Quixote (abridged) as if they were bones tossed to their respective constituencies, high school students today are more than likely to share a classroom with Asian, African and Middle Eastern immigrants, people whose impact on the American lifestyle fluctuates with the region, and whose cultural identity is far removed from Western European assumptions. Moreover, each racial and ethnic group is competing for cultural attention in the classroom, if not aggressively, at the minimum in terms of a fair-play demand for equal time. It should also be noted that, with the breakdown of the Cold War, there is also increasing Eastern European influx into American society that has been reared on Communist ideals for the past three generations. Far from assuming Western European cultural norms in total, their identity must be accounted for as well. Development of a curriculum that addresses the cultural needs of future society in light of current identity is a ticklish issue for the secondary school educator.

Perhaps even more pressing, though, is the hidden matter of sexual discrimination that currently divides American classrooms from the elementary through university levels, finding its peak in secondary schools, where the individual's social patterns for adulthood are generally hashed out, experimented with, and set. Again, this is not a new issue, as recognized in various discussions above, but it has reached a point where the simple solutions have all been used. Now the subtle forms of discrimination need to be addressed, and this requires a change in the way both educators and students think and behave.

Typical of the subtlety involved is that of mathematics education. Research data, passed on to education majors in the universities, indicates that females tend to learn mathematical concepts faster than males during the elementary school years, then are caught up to and fall behind males in the middle/high school period. To date, this has been accepted as the primary reason why males predominate in mathematics and science-based professions. Recent studies, however, indicate that the dominance of males in these fields is as much a product of end fulfillment as it is sexual differentiation. (A. Eisenberg, 1992, p. 122). That is: in the secondary school years, male students are expected to prepare for careers in technical fields, women are not; pressure and attention are put on males to succeed, while female students are left to their own resources and drive. (Glamour, 1992, p. 157). In essence, then, while the '70's and '80's have seen the demise of "women are only meant to be homemakers" in the everyday world, the secondary school educational establishment is still operating in a closed environment offering **de facto** males-only opportunities.

Related to that, it will be interesting to see how the new administration of Bill Clinton handles the issue of sex education on the secondary school level. Reagan-Bush policies had attempted to push back the clock as compared to the responsibility of making such teenage identity issues as conception, contraception and abortion invisible within the federal government's concept of education. Clinton's recent executive order vacating the previous administration's ban on federally-funded health clinics disseminating birth control information indicates a reversal of federal policy on the same information being provided in high schools as well. Nevertheless, as abortion continues to rage as an emotional issue throughout the country, secondary students are buffeted by the demands of a conflict that refuses to address one of the key elements of the matter: men must treat women as equals, deserving of respect as equals.

It may be too much to ask of male high school students until male high school **teachers** recognize their responsibility to set the example. **Sexual harassment** in the classroom, and as part of the institutional make-up of secondary school organization, appears to be a problem only recently being considered important enough to address in the public forum. Pedophilia has long been the bane of educators, a temptation and perversion giving the profession an unsavory shading since its inception in the days of the Greek philosophers, but the sexual harassment indicated as a problem here goes beyond the occasional teacher making moves on any particular female student. As recent lawsuits indicate, within the context of some secondary school environments, such wholesome institutions as the cheerleading team and booster squad have been considered as little more than sexual payoff organizations for male high school athletes. (Gleick, 1992, p. 126). Those are the obvious programs under scrutiny. Equally destructive are those classrooms where the daily environment promotes male sexual aggression as an undertone to the regular lessons. (Atkins, 1992, p. 32). Often there is a difficult distinction for the male teacher to recognize: the need to communicate with one's students on a level they can understand can easily degenerate into an apparent endorsement of the students' immature sexual attitudes. It is likely then, given the serious implications involved, that male awareness training in sexual harassment behavior will have to be incorporated into education courses for the secondary school teacher. The **time** has come for **BIG CHANGE!**

BIBLIOGRAPHY

Atkins, A. (1992, August). Sexual harassment in school. Better Homes and Gardens, 32.

Brookhiser, R. (1992, August). We can all share American culture. Time, 31, 74.

Conant, J. B. (1964). Shaping educational policy, New York: McGraw-Hill, 123-124.

Eisenberg, A. (1992, July). Women and the discourse of science. Scientific American, 122.

Ferrel, K. (1992, June). Some direction for our schools: Our politicians educational priorities are out of touch with students. Omni, 8.

Gay, G. (1993, May). Building cultural bridges: A bold proposal for teacher education. Education and Urban Society, 25 (3), 285-299.

Gleick, E. (1992, November). The boys on the bus: S. Mutziger files sexual harassment case against Eden Prarie, Minn. school system on behalf of daughter C. Hentz. People Weekly, 30, 125-126.

Multiculturalism: On the importance of being tribal. (1992, July/August). Utne Reader, 67-95.

Sykes, C.J. (1992, August). Opening up the public school gulag. National Review, 3, 17-18.

Van den Haag, E. (1992, August). Why do American kids learn so little? National Review, 3, 34-36.

Were any of your teachers biased against females? A survey. (1992, August). Glamour, 157.

Winston, G. C. (1992, July/August). Hostility, maximization and the public trust: Economics and higher education. Change, 20-27.

Additional Readings:

Baldwin, J. (1963). The fire next time. My dungeon shook: Letter to my nephew on the one hundredth anniversary of the emancipation. New York: Dial Press, p. 24.

Brown v. Board of Education of Topeka et al., 347 U.S. 483 (1954).

Didham, C. K. (1993, February 13-17). In fusing a multicultural perspective in teacher education through cooperative learning. Paper presented at the annual meeting of the Association of Teacher Educators 73rd, Los Angeles, CA.

Chapter 21

Against All Odds: The Plight of African-American Males to Acquire Knowledge from American Educational Institutions

Michael A. McMorris, Ph.D.

Ferris State University

Big Rapids, MI

INTRODUCTION

From the first day that Africans were brought to America in chains, their quest for knowledge has been a difficult one. As they attempted to develop into intelligent, intellectual beings, their efforts have, and continue to be thwarted, by the Anglo-American status quo. No perpetrator has played a more villainous role in maintaining the (Anglo-American) status quo than the American Educational Institutions.

Through its policies, employees, and unethical (and sometimes criminal) practices, America's Educational Institutions, have perpetrated a long-lasting fraud on African Americans...especially African-American males. The fraud I speak of is that of convincing African Americans that they are intellectually inferior to their white counterparts. Aiding, subsidizing, and perpetuating this practice of instilling intellectual inferiority into African Americans is, none other than, the United States Government.

Clearly, when she first set out to establish herself, America felt the need, if not the responsibility and duty, to insure herself total superiority, over people of color, by reducing to print her interpretation, and assessment of Africans (slaves). This was accomplished in one of her most celebrated documents, to date...The United States Constitution. Article One, Section Two, Paragraph Three of this famous document intended to cement the status of African Americans as, "less than human" when it referred to them as "three-fifths" of a human being, for taxation purposes (Remy, Elowittz & Berlin, 1984). This classification of being less than human has had a lasting effect on African Americans, that has not been overcome, to this date. Ironically, the negative impact, and backlash perpetuated by this kind of mindset also victimizes Anglo- Americans. Specifically, the mere thought that a person of dark skin is not fully developed, intellectually, or otherwise, leads to a false sense of superiority among some Anglo-Americans, and unfortunately an unwarranted, yet psychologically devastating inferiority complex among some African Americans. For the most part, this sense of being intellectually inferior has claimed perhaps hundreds of thousands, if not millions, of African American males, as they struggle to develop intellectually, in a country that has never accepted them as intellectual equals. Difficult as their plight may be, African American males have, and will continue to develop into intellectual giants, with the aid of, or in spite of America's Educational Institutions.

Throughout America's history, Blacks (African-Americans) who have come to her shores, (as the only nonimmigrant group in American) have been mistreated by a system of hostility, indifference, injustice, and inequality. For the millions of African slaves who came, unwillingly (in shackles) to America, as well as the more than thirty-five million descendants of slaves, who possess American citizenship today, obtaining an education (formal or informal) has not been an easy task, to say the least. It has meant enduring the most vicious tortures, fighting the most powerful of enemies, and maintaining courageous calm, in the face of what many have considered insurmountable odds. For some, even death was the price paid, when they attempted to gain knowledge through America's Educational Institutions.

This chapter attempts to investigate and discuss some of the problems that African American males continue to have, in their plight to develop intellectually, in America's Educational Institutions.

Human Development in Primitive Societies

According to Good and Teller (1969) modern education began in about 1800, when European States established public school systems, not in the "The Renaissance." However, they do point out that movable type and paper were joined together, to produce printed books, in about 1450. Thus, we know that education, in some form had to have taken place prior to that.

It is clear that reading, writing (communicating) in itself, is evidence of some sort of education. Good and Teller provide the following to illustrate this point:

Early man was ignorant, but his ability to learn, not his ignorance, was his

most important characteristic. Man is pre-eminently a learning animal.

However, in the beginning what he learned died with him, unless and until

he was able to communicate it, which was possible only through language

or gesture in direct or friendly contact with others. When men came

together in groups, and after centuries in settlements, communication

became easier: it became in fact, a form of unsystematic self-instruction-

the earliest example of adult education. The young were inquisitive and

we shall assume, convinced that they could improve on the ways of their

elders (1969, p. 3).

According to Atkinson and Maleaska (1965) in primitive societies,
education was

considered completed when the individual finally reached the group standard.
The

training itself, included ways and means of satisfying basic physical needs. The

educational pursuits of boys were hunting, fishing, and fighting. While girls were

taught to cook, make clothes, care for children and perform similar domestic

tasks.

Good and Teller (1969) also offed the following discussion on early forms

of education:

...as more stable groups developed, traditions began and became man's

earliest effort to preserve his history. While this information was an oral record, repeated around campfires, it was also subject to distortions.

Consequently, written reports were needed so that experiences could be

accessed, and recovered, at will. Inevitably, the need was met by the

evolution of writing, and later libraries, museums, galleries, and other

collections. Schools to teach writing and libraries to preserve what's been

written, were the earliest efforts to fund knowledge (p.3).

The idea espoused by some, that writing is an art-form, is certainly not

new.

According to Good and Teller (1969, p.17) in Ancient Greece, writing was a

custom (an art) to choose and to make improvements. The Phoenicians developed

a kind of alphabet, with characters obtained in Egypt and developed in South

Canaan. The Greeks added signs for the vowels and changed the direction of

writing, to go from left to right. Before 700 B.C. it was used over much of the

Greek world; in time, it was borrowed by the entire West. Consequently, writing

became an invaluable tool in one's own mental development. Therefore, its

invention has become one of the great achievements in the history of education.

With the Western ideas and tools, Greeks formed and polished a Western

language (Greek)which has been a great influence on modern languages. It is

both a cause and a means in the development of Western Civilization (Good and

Teller, 1969 p.18).

Education in Colonial America

As previously discussed, Western Civilization and its development is

directly associated with the development of its citizens, relative to reading, writing and understanding languages. The influence that education played on

Western Civilization did not stop with France, Switzerland, Germany, or even

England. Through many centuries, it evolved throughout all of Western

Civilization, and eventually landed on the banks of The James River, in 1607,

with a band of 105 colonists. Initially, times were very difficult for the colonists.

Starvation and disease killed off most of them within six months. However, after

years of trying their hands at planting various crops, the Virginia Colonists

discovered the profitable crop of tobacco (Good & Teller, 1969, p.432).

With the discovery, and inevitable profitability of tobacco, also came the

need for cheap and unskilled labor. Initially, England transported its prisoners,

those persons who were in debt, children from poorhouses, and persons

kidnapped in London's alleys, to Virginia to work in the tobacco fields.

However, in 1619, the first ship of slaves, from Africa landed in Virginia, and

provided a never-ending pool of unpaid workers (Good & Teller, 1969, p. 432).

It was with this introduction to Colonial America's shores, that Africans

(Black Americans) later would learn true heartache, in their plight to gain

knowledge, in a new world, miles away from a land where many had served as

kings, tribal elders, and community leaders.

Once the tobacco planters were firmly installed as the upper class, in

Virginia, the working class, which consisted of slaves or redemptioners was

doomed to occupy the lower class, until their debts were paid and they were

released. Of course, being set free was not an option for the African slave. Once

freed, education was not unattainable.

According to Good and Teller (1969, p. 432) the planters were refined and their homes were furnished with books, musical instruments, and English furniture. For the most part, their children were educated by the clergy, or in schools maintained on the plantations. There were a few Latin Schools (grammar) and some of the boys form wealthy homes were sent to English Schools. For the poor, neighborhood or "old field" schools were established, in which itinerant teachers taught, on occasion. The system of apprenticeship provided opportunity for vocational training. Many children received little or no schooling.

Transplanting Educational Institutions

According to Good and Teller (1969, p. 437) four main types of educational endeavors characterized the 17th Century: 1) apprenticeship to the manual vocations; 2) reading and religious instruction directed by the churches and missionary societies, or obtained in dame schools, otherwise; 3) the formal secondary and higher education of the Latin schools and colleges, although near the end of the period Harvard was the only college; and 4) practical schooling in mathematics and applications to accounting, navigation, and surveying together with supplementary work in English. Only the first of these was transplanted and the last was mainly a native development. Each of these four types of education was found in the Colonial regions: New England, the Middle Colonies; and the South.

The apprenticeship training was the most widespread form of education. It was written in English Legislation and strictly followed. Its rules and regulations were spelled out in the document called an "indenture." This document spelled out all of the duties, responsibilities, and privileges of the master and apprentice (Good & Teller, 1969, p. 438).

Overall, the foundations were laid for our public and private school systems, and for public policy that permits private schools to compete with public education. With the formation of a new nation, education to overcome sectionalism and to promote citizenship became important needs. Moreover, education was to help with the constant rise of industry, and the increasing immigration. As mentioned earlier, before the adoption of the Constitution, land was granted for the support of elementary schools; and the encouragement of schools by the government was demanded by the Northwest Ordinance.

What about Educating the Large Population of Slaves?

As time passed, the population of slaves continued to grow through the 1600's and 1700's. Clearly, their education was a concern to many. Not necessarily their academic education but the education that they must learn, understand and internalize…the principles of master and slave, and all of the rules and customs that accompanied that very special relationship. This education was the most important one to both slave and master. Important to the slave because if he/she didn't fully comprehend and follow the tenants of this education, whippings, and even death could result; important to the master because a slave whom wasn't properly educated in the knowledge of being a slave, could start to develop ideas and begin to question his plight, consequently the master's crops and plantation could suffer. No, this was an education that had to be taught. It was truly a matter of life or death. Although it was important for the slaves to understand their "place" in Colonial America, some citizens felt the urge to teach the slaves how to do more than utter simple phrases like, "Yessir, Massa," "Nosir, Massa." These citizens didn't realize that by entertaining themselves with thoughts of their slaves abilities to write alphabets, they were actually paving the way to freedom, for the slaves. The damage that would be done to the ideal way of life, in white America, would be irreversible.

Early Advocates to Educating Blacks in America

As previously mentioned the education of slaves probably started out as merely entertainment for the sons and daughters of slave owners. However, there were individuals and groups of people who were very serious about not only educating slaves, but also seeing the institution of slavery abolished.

In 1784, Anthony Benezet, a teacher of the Free School for the Black

People in

Philadelphia made sure that schools would be provided for Blacks, as he made special provisions and instructions to his Executors in his Will, relative to the education of Blacks. He wanted it understood that after he passed and after the passing of his wife, that the Executors of his Will "....hire and employ a religious minded person or persons to teach a number of Negro, Mullatto, or Indian Children to read and write, Arithmetic, plain Accounts, Needlework &c (University of Philadelphia Press, 1937)."

In 1789, Benjamin Franklin made a proposal for Educating Negroes that came as part of a meeting of The Society for promoting the Abolition of

Slavery and the Relief of Free Blacks:

> The business relative to free blacks shall be transacted by a committee of
>
> twenty-four persons, annually elected by ballot, at the meeting of this
>
> society, in the month called April; and, in order to perform the different
>
> services with expedition, regularity, and energy, this committee shall
>
> resolve into the following sub-committees, viz.

> III.　"A Committee of Education, who shall superintend the
>
> school instruction of the children and youth of free blacks.
>
> They may either influence them to attend regularly the
>
> schools already established in this city, or form others with
>
> this view; they shall, in either case, provide, that the pupils
>
> may receive such learning as is necessary for their future
>
> situation in life, and especially a deep impression of the
>
> most important and generally acknowledged moral and
>
> religious principles. They shall also procure and preserve a
>
> regular record of the marriages, births, and manumissions
>
> of all free blacks (Sparks, 1836, pp. 513-514)."

Additional Efforts Made to Educate Slaves and Free Blacks in Early America

According to Woodson (1919) the history of education of the Antebellum

Negroes falls into two periods. The first extends from the time of the introduction

of slavery to the climax of the insurrectionary movement, about 1835, when the majority of people in America answered in the affirmative the question whether or not to educate their slaves. The second period was when the Industrial Revolution changed slavery to an economic institution, and when intelligent Negroes, encouraged by abolitionists, made so many attempts to organize servile insurrections that the pendulum began to swing the other way. Woodson (1919, pp. 2-3) further asserted that there were three classes of people who were advocates of educating Negroes: 1) masters who desired to increase the economic efficiency of their labor supply; 2) sympathetic persons who wished to help the oppressed; and 3) zealot missionaries who, believing that the message of divine love came equally to all, taught slaves the English language that they might learn the principles of Christianity. It was through the kindness of the first class, that slaves had their best chance for mental improvement. Each slaveholder dealt with the situation to suit himself, regardless of public opinion. Later, when measures were passed to prohibit the education of slaves, some masters continued to teach their slaves, in defiance of the hostile legislation. The second class of sympathetic persons weren't able to accomplish much because they were usually reformers, who did not own slaves, but dealt in practically free settlements far from the plantation on which the bondmen lived (Woodson, 1919).

The first settlers to offer the Negroes the same educational and religious privileges that they offered to their own people were the Quakers. This third class of religious missionaries believed in the brotherhood of man, and the fatherhood of God. They taught people of color to read their own "instruction in the book of the law, that they might be wise unto salvation (Woodson, 1919, pp. 4-5)."

After 1760, the general movement to educate slaves began to arouse the development of the coming age of a social doctrine among American Colonists, such as Patrick Henry, and James Otis, who demanded liberty for themselves and conceded that slaves were entitled at least to freedom of body. There were soon frequent acts of manumission and emancipation, which followed this change in attitude toward persons of color. As a result, schools, missions, and churches were established to enlighten these "freedmen". The co-laborers included the Baptists, and Methodists, who were allowed access to the Negroes, bond, and free (Woodson, 1919, pp. 5-6).

Of course with the new opportunities to learn available to Negroes, they quickly developed mentally. They also proved themselves as faithful servants, laborers, artisans, and many of them displayed administrative abilities adequate enough to manage business establishments and large plantations. Some of them learned to appreciate and write poetry, as well as calculate mathematics, science, and philosophy (Woodson, 1919, pp. 5-6). The mental development of the Negroes was so rapid that certain Southerners, who had not objected to their being given an education, began to advocate that the Negroes who were going to be educated be colonized. This was interesting, since some of the whites who supported the colonization of the educated Negroes, were also those who had earlier stated that the Negroes should be given the opportunity to be transplanted to a free country, where they might develop, without restriction (Woodson, 1919, p. 7).

During the first quarter of the Nineteenth Century, there were two effective forces gradually increasing the number of reactionaries who were in favor of prohibiting the education of people of color, in all places, except in urban areas where enlightened Negroes could provide schools to educate their own people. First, the world-wide industrial movement, which revolutionized spinning and weaving so much that there was an increased demand for cotton fiber, which in turn gave rise to the Plantation System in the South, resulting in the need for larger numbers of slaves (Woodson, 1919, p. 7). The second force was the circulation of antislavery accounts of inhuman treatment that slaves received, as well as the exploits of Toussaint L'Ouverture, who lead slave revolts. Moreover, the slaves began to develop an new taste for freedom, acquired from the stories told to them by refuges from Haiti, who had settled in Baltimore, Norfolk, Charleston, and New Orleans. These refuges told the slaves how Haitians had gotten their freedom. Further incitement came from certain abolitionists, who believed in and encouraged slaves to use the bloody methods used in the French Revolution. As a result, slaveholders lived in eternal fear of servile insurrection, and Southern states began adopting reactionary policies that made educating Negroes impossible (Woodson, 1919, p. 8).

Early Obstacles to Educating Blacks in America

One of the first legal setbacks to educating slaves came in the form of legislation passed by several of the colonial states. One such state to draft and pass legislation prohibiting the teaching of Black slaves was South Carolina. In 1740, the following law was passed.

"And Whereas the having of slaves taught to write or suffering them to be employed in writing, may be attended with great inconveniences; be it therefore enacted by the authority aforesaid, that all and every person and persons whatsoever, who shall hereafter teach, or cause any slave or slaves to be taught to write, or shall use or employ any slave as a scribe in any manner of writing whatsoever, hereafter taught to write; every such person and persons shall for every such offense forfeit that sum of one hundred pounds current money (West, 1972, p. 10)."

According to Anderson (1994) many states followed South Carolina's lead in prohibiting the education of slaves: 1) Missouri Literacy Law (1819) forbade assembling or teaching of black slaves to read or write; 2) Georgia Literacy Law (1829) provided fines and imprisonment for teaching blacks to read; 3) Kentucky Property Tax Law (1830) taxed blacks, forbade their voting, or attending school; 4) Alabama and Virginia Literacy Laws (1832) fined and flogged whites for teaching blacks to read or write; 5) Georgia Literacy Law (1833) provided fines and whippings for teaching blacks; and 6) Virginia School Law (1838) forbade blacks who had gone North to school to return.

More specific details on the laws prohibiting blacks from gaining an education in Georgia (1829) are as follows:

"Section 10. And be it further enacted . That if any slave, Negro, mustizzo, or free person of color, or any other person shall circulate, bring or cause to be circulated or brought into this state or aid or assist in any manner, or be instrumental in aiding or assisting in the circulation or

bringing into this state, or any manner concerned in any printed or written

pamphlet, paper or circular, for the purpose of exciting to insurrection,

conspiracy or resistance among the Salves, Negroes, or free persons of

color, of this state, the said person or persons offending this act, shall be

punished with death.

Section 11. And be it further enacted, that if any slave, Negro, or free

person of color, or any white person shall teach any other slave, Negro, or

free person of color to read or write, either written or printed characters,

the said free person of color, or slave, shall be punished by fine and

whipping, at the discretion of the court; and if a white person so offending,

he/she, or they shall be punished with fine, not exceeding five hundred

dollars and imprisonment in the common jail at the discretion of the court

before whom said offender is tried (West, p. 20)."

Additional specific details are offered in the North Carolina Laws of 1830,

enacted to prohibit the teaching of slaves. The laws were written as

follows:

Section I. Whereas the teaching of slaves to read and write has a tendency

to excite dissatisfaction in their minds, and to produce insurrection and

rebellion, to the manifest injury of the citizens of this state: Therefore, be

it enacted by the General Assembly of the State of north Carolina, and it is

hereby enacted by the authority of the same, that any free person, who

shall hereafter teach or attempt to teach, any slave within this State to read or write, the use of figures, exapted, or shall give or sell to such slaves any books or pamphlets, shall be liable to the indictment in any court of record in this State having jurisdiction thereof; and upon conviction, shall at the discretion of the Court, if a white man or woman, be fined not less than one hundred dollars, nor more than two hundred dollars, or imprisoned; if a free person of color, shall be fined, imprisoned, or whipped, at the discretion of the Court, not exceeding thirty-nine lashes, nor less than twenty lashes.

Section II. Be it further enacted, that the judges of the Superior Courts and the Justices of the County Courts shall give this act in charge to the grand jurors of their respective counties (West, 1972, p. 21)."

In furtherance of the prohibition to educating slaves, the citizens of Southampton,

Virginia enacted the following resolutions, in 1838:

- Resolved, that it is the duty of the citizens of this county to give an energetic support to the magistrates and constables in the execution of the laws for the suppression of meetings of Negroes by day or by night and for prevention of their having firearms and dogs.
- Resolved, that the education of persons of color is inexpedient and improper as it is calculated to cause them to be dissatisfied with their condition and furnishes the slave with the means of absconding from his master.

- Resolved, that the forgoing resolutions be transmitted to our Delegates in General Assembly and to the Executive of the State, and that they be printed in several newspapers in the state (West, 1972, p. 35).

In a very interesting legal move, Native Americans (Cherokees) themselves persecuted and oppressed by whites, passed an Act that prohibited the teaching of slaves. The Act of The Cherokee Nation, October 22, 1844, was written as follows:

Be it enacted by the National Council, that from and after the passage of this Act, it shall not be lawful for any person or persons whatsoever to teach any free Negro of Negroes not of Cherokee blood or any slave belonging to any citizen or citizens of the nation, to read or write (West, 1972, p.36)."

The education of slaves and free persons of color was a costly and dangerous undertaking. However some blacks received an education, in spite of the laws. One such person was Frederick Douglass. Born a slave in Talbot County Maryland, in 1817, Douglass' autobiography, "Narrative of the Life of Frederick Douglass, an American Slave," reveals some of the difficulties he encountered while trying to gain an education. He specifically recalls how his slave owner's wife Mrs. Auld was scolded by her husband for teaching him to read, when he was seven or eight years old:

314

"If you give a nigger an inch, he will take an elf. A nigger should know

nothing but to obey his master—to do as he is told to do. Learning would

spoil the best nigger in the world. Now, if you teach that nigger how to

read, there would be no keeping him. It would forever unfit him to be a

slave. He would at once become unmanageable, and of no value to his

master. As to himself, it could do him no good, but a great deal of harm.

It would make him discontented and unhappy (Douglass, 1973, p. 36)."

Douglass further writes,

"I now understood what had been to me a most perplexing difficulty- to

wit, the white man's power to enslave the black man. It was a grand

achievement, and I prized it highly. From that moment, I understood the

pathway form slavery to freedom... Though conscious of the difficulty of

learning without a teacher, I set out with high hope and a fixed purpose, at

whatever cost of trouble, to learn how to read... Form this time I was most

narrowly watched. If I was in a separate room any considerable length of

time, I was sure to be suspected of having a book, and was at once called

to give an account of myself. All this, however, was too late. The first

step had been taken. Mistress, in teaching me the alphabet, had given me

the inch, and no precaution could prevent me from taking the ell

(Douglass, 1973, p. 37)."

The Importance of an Education for Blacks
According to Dalton (1991) with the rise of the abolitionist movement,

debate centered more on the advisability of blacks learning to read and write, especially since it was forbidden by law in many slave-holding colonies and states

for slaves to acquire this knowledge. The Emancipation Proclamation and the

13th Amendment to the U.S. Constitution abolishing slavery in this country altered

the debate once again. No longer was it a question of ability or even advisability.

Rather it was a question of necessity and even urgency, for abolitionists and great

numbers of recently freed African-Americans saw literacy as the path to real

independence and full citizenship.

According to Quarles (1969) while benevolent societies, religious groups,

and government agencies proffered education as the appropriate tool for preparing

ex-slaves for citizenship, the former bondsmen hardly proved passive recipients,

for they recognized literacy as one of the principle means of improving their lot.

Despite their poverty and dislocation, black people throughout the South took the

initiative to insure their own education, both contributing to the Northern-

supported schools and establishing their own institutions. By late 1865 the

Freedmen's Bureau reported the quantitative effect of such efforts: 90,850 former

slaves were attending schools under its auspices, with 1,314 teachers using 740

buildings. But sheer numbers did not capture the intense motivation shown by

students of all ages. Quarles (1969) further wrote that J.W. Alvord, Inspector of

Schools and Finances of the Freedmen's Bureau, provided four reasons to explain

the Negroes enthusiasm for learning, in a report dated January 1, 1866. Alvord

reported the following:

1) They have the natural thirst for knowledge common to all men.

2) They have seen power and influence among white people always
   coupled with le-it is the sign of elevation to which they now aspire.

3) Its mysteries, hitherto hidden from them in written literature, excite
   them to the special study of books.

4) Their freedom has given wonderful stimulus to all efforts, indicating a
   vitality that augurs well for their whole future condition and character
   (p. 38).

Dalton (1991) also cited the May 3, 1873 issue of Harper's Weekly,
relative to the education of emancipated blacks. According to the Harper's
article:

One of the most remarkable and encouraging features attending the

emancipation of the colored race in our Southern States is the eagerness to

learn displayed from the earliest moment of freedom. Old and young

crowded to the schools opened for the benefit of the freedmen; and it was

not uncommon to see men and women who had nearly reached the allotted

term of their life poring over the spelling-book with all the eager interest

of children. Slowly and painfully, against every kind of discouragement,

they would master the A, B, C and learn to pick out simple words, until

they could read in the book, which thousands of them knew already by the

heart, the Bible (Harper's Weekly, 1873). As time passed, the education

of America's Black population was facilitated by the establishment of

numerous schools for free Blacks. In 1852, The Philadelphia Society of

Friends opened 'The Institute for Colored Youth." This was the first

coeducational classical high school for African Americans (King, 1995).

According to West (1969, p. 68), the Fisk School was established in 1866,

by the American Missionary Association and the Western Freedmen's Aid

Commission, for the purpose of educating the colored children of

Nashville and vicinity. School after school was opened, and funded, with

the intent of providing education to the newly freed Blacks (ex-slaves)

Although the idea of providing an education blacks was supported by

many, it was expressly understood that their education be facilitated in

schools separate from white children. This was not a philosophy that was

thought up over night. There was a great of thought put into how, where,

and what blacks should be educated to do. For the most part, blacks were

taught the religion of their former masters, as well as industrial trades.

These were things that would allow blacks to have a feeling of

independence, within their new state of emancipation, while at the same

time, allowing the former masters to maintain control over the lives of the

new freedmen.

Overall, the education of Blacks in Colonial American times, and beyond,

caused a great deal of frustration for Blacks, as well as the whites who attempted

to provide them with education. As previously mentioned, many of the slave

owners had family members who were initially entertained by the mimicking and

parroting skills possessed by their slaves. This, of course turned into a full-

fledged desire among the slaves to gain knowledge. As they began to develop intellectually, relative to their surroundings, they also saw that an education was

essential, if they were to ever break the chains that bound their bodies, as well as

their minds. Once the religious communities began advocating the education of

slaves, and others in bondage, it was only a matter of time before the notion of

total freedom, through education and religion was adopted and internalized by the

slave population. Clearly, the beginning of the end of slavery was insight.

Although the American systems (especially during Colonial times) of

government, and education have not been kind to its black population, or other

people of color, Black Americans have been most successful in pursuing,

obtaining, and disseminating knowledge gained through education. During the

years of America's infancy, (1600s) the Black Africans who were kidnapped, and

forced into involuntary servitude found a way of persevering. They overcame the

obstacles and took advantage

of the advocates of their education, under the most extreme conditions. With

that, they

have surely gained a place in American history as true pioneers.

The Intellectual Development and Education of Blacks Beyond Slavery
In the years since slavery was ended, Blacks in America, especially Black

males have had a horrendous time attempting to develop into intellectual beings.

Not only have Black males had to continue to battle the everyday obstacles of

racism, and discrimination within the context of American society, but they have

also had to endure the intricacies of the most potent form of educational

categorization, and classification into the classes and academic programs for the intellectually inferior, and the academically deficient, and chronically disruptive, or inattentive (i.e. special education, alternative schools). These programs have been operating decade after decade with the blessing of the U.S. Department of Education, individual states, and individual school districts, throughout the United States.

These programs have flourished because of an inherent misunderstanding, of how Black children learn; how they develop intellectually; what they should be taught; and how they should be taught. Moreover, as we begin to investigate these issues, we must also include a discussion on those who have been teaching Black children; how and why Black children have been diagnosed as having learning or behavior disorders, and what steps should be taken within the academic environment to insure success for Black children.

Cognitive Development and Culture

Most educators will admit that culture has a significant impact on the development of a child's cognitive skills. However, it's difficult to arrive at a group consensus when it comes to the intellectual development of Black (African-American) children. Particularly relative to learning styles and the teaching models. In an effort to truly discuss these issues thoroughly, it is necessary to examine the psychology of self realization, self-identity, and even self-worth. This can only be done honestly, by including the works of one of today's most noted experts in the field of "Black Psychology," Dr. Na im Akbar.

According to Akbar (1996) the development of African-Americans in today's society is directly linked to slavery. As I alluded to previously, slaves (particularly males) were taught to uphold any and everything white, while rejecting all things black. This has left a lasting negative image in the mindset of Blacks and Whites in America. Akbar (1996) goes on to assert that one of the most destructive characteristics carried over from slavery is a sense of our inferiority as African-American people. This also plays a major role in our intellectual development, especially in the academic environment. Akbar (1996) offered the following to explain the interesting impact and self-defeating long-term effect of being taught to be inferior to whites:

> The shrewd slave makers were fully aware that people who still respected themselves as human beings would resist to the death the dehumanizing process of slavery. Therefore a systematic process of creating a sense of inferiority in the proud African was necessary in order to maintain them as slaves. This was done by humiliating and dehumanizing acts such as public beatings, parading them on slave blocks unclothed, and inspecting them as though they were cattle or horses. They were forbidden to communicate with other slaves which would have been a basis for maintaining self-respect. Many historians and slave narratives report how young children were separated from their mother's because the mother's love might cultivate some self-respect in the child....Cleanliness and personal effectiveness are fairly essential in the maintenance of self-respect. The slaves were kept filthy and the very nature of physical restraints over long periods of time began to develop in the people a sense of helplessness. The loss of the ability to even cleans one's body and to

shield oneself from a blow began to teach the slaves that they should have no self-respect....These things, combined with the insults, the loss of cultural traditions, rituals, family life, religion, and even names served to cement the loss of self-respect. As the slave master exalted himself and enforced respect of himself, he was increasingly viewed as superior to the slaves. The superiority was based on the utter dehumanization of the Africans. The slave was forced to bow and bend to the slave owner and treat him as God. With the image of a Caucasian man even as God, and with all kinds of images of Africans as dirty and only half human, it was incvitable that a sense of inferiority would grow into the African— American personality (1996, p. 14).

Noted scholar and historian, Carter G. Woodson (1990) noted over a half century

ago:

...to handicap a student for life by teaching him that his black face is a curse and that his struggle to change his condition is hopeless, is the worst kind of lynching. It kills one's aspirations and dooms him to vagabondage and crime (p. 21)."

These opinions written by Woodson (1990) and Akar, (1996) et al, throughout the years have given us insight into why some Blacks intellectual growth is inadequate, deficient and sometimes appearing nonexistent! This issue further speaks to how Blacks as a people have sometimes fallen short, relative to

intellectual growth. Unfortunately, teaching Black inferiority, and White

superiority in schools has been a practice that has yet to be successfully

challenged and defeated. Moreover, this sense of self-worth, accompanied by

self-esteem can and has had an interesting effect on children. That point will be

discussed in detail, later.

Noted educator, and advocate for education reform, relative to Black

children, Jawanza Kunjufu (1995) offered some very important insight into the

development of cognitive skills in children. He especially provides valuable

insight relative to Black children. Kunjufu (1995) offered the following insight

into early childhood development:

The period between six months and four to five years of age is a very

important period. Many doctors and psychologists have pointed out the

brain's growth and development is greatest between infancy and three

years of age, with the next-greatest period being between three and six

years of age. It then becomes crucial that the African-American

community develop our children, especially our boys, during this critical

period of brain development and cognitive growth. This area of child

development is paramount in reinforcing fine motor and language

development....Instead, we have a frightening situation in which many of

our children live in homes where fine and gross motor and language

development is not encouraged. These are the reasons why many people

advocate Home Start, Head Start and other programs to develop these skills even before the child enters kindergarten. This reinforces the notion of professionals who say that the most important periods are between infancy and three, followed by three to five, in child development. These are times when parents should be cradling their children close to them; toys should be bought for their ability to stimulate cognitive and motor development as well as for fun. For example cradle gyms can be attached to the cradle to maximize development. It is remarkable how energetic and intelligent African American children are, especially if they are placed in environments with the proper nurturing, nutrition and guidance that all children should receive (p. 11).

When discussing the development of children, relative to fine motor, and gross motor skills, Kunjufu (1995) stated that schools must acknowledge that females and males mature at different rates. It's suggested that girls mature about two years ahead of boys. This, according to Kunjufi maybe due to the fact that at home and in school, girls are taught to play quietly by coloring or drawing, while boys are given trucks and footballs to play with. According to Kunjufu (1995) this problem could be addressed by schools if they were to realize that there are other ways of evaluating learning than utilizing left brain abstract exams. He suggests that we first stop comparing boys to girls. After all, the ideal student is actually the student who sits quietly and plays, as directed to. That student is the female.

Because of the types of activities engaged in during class assignments, girls tend to follow instructions more, and are less likely to be singled out for being disruptive. This practice of singling students out may be based on the school of thought developed by psychologist Alfred Binet (which involves classifying children into groups). However, a more favorable method of evaluating and serving students was developed by Maria Montessori, a medical doctor. The Montessori approach teaches that children develop at different rates (males vs. females, Blacks vs. Whites), and that there's nothing wrong with children developing or learning at different rates or with different styles. This style asserts that we should design homes and classrooms to allow for those differences and we should encourage children to expose themselves in ways that are comfortable. Unfortunately, the Montessori approach is least used in our schools; classification dominates, as a rule. Consequently, high numbers of male children are labeled hyperactive and dyslexic; then they are placed in remedial reading classes, and ultimately, special education. When examining how Black children are being educated in American schools, as well as how they are being categorized and placed in various classes and academic programs, one must also carefully examine the impact of diagnosing Black males with learning disabilities.

Attention Deficit Hyperactivity Disorder, Conduct Disorder and Black Males

In an effort to fully understand the plight of African-American males and their attempt to develop intellectually, via the American Educational System, one must include a discussion of the impact of "learning disabilities" and "disorders" that seem to attach themselves to Black male students. Those that seem to find Black male victims too often are: 1) Attention-Deficit Hyperactivity Disorder (ADHD), formerly known as Attention Deficit Disorder, and 2) Conduct Disorder

(CD). These two disorders can and have been very damaging to Black students...particularly males. According to Spencer and Oattes (1999), ADHD is defined symptomatologically. It is a behavior characterized by two separate subtypes: 1) inattention and 2) hyperactivity-impulsivity. ADHD with inattention describes in part a child who fails to pay close attention to details, has difficulty sustaining attention, does not seem to listen when spoken to, or who has difficulty organizing tasks and activities (DSM-IV, 1994). ADHD with hyperactivity-impulsivity describes a child in part who appears fidgety, leaves his/her seat in the classroom regularly without permission, runs about excessively, or blurts out answers before questions have been completed (DSM-IV, 1994). According to Barren (1994), 3 to 5% of all children have some form of a primary ADHD with or without hyperactivity. Clearly, with as the person in charge of the classroom itself, the teacher becomes instrumental in the detection of these disorders; the counselor evaluates them, and ultimately classifies the children who display these tendencies. It is the role of the teacher and school counselors that contribute to the diagnosis, and often the misdiagnosis of ADHD.

According to Kunjufu (1995), the word "hyperactive" is a value judgment. The word is based on an assumption that we have an understanding and knowledge of what normal activity represents. It may be that African American children, specifically males, are not hyperactive. It may be that the stimuli around them are simply not challenging enough. They choose to become involved with other activities that they find to be of greater interest. According to Kunjufu (1984), Yale University conducted a study that examined the popular television shows, Mr. Rogers and Sesame Street. Mr. Rogers is a slow moving show, where Sesame Street is more action oriented; the images change more frequently. This study revealed that African American children responded better to Sesame Street and European children responded better to Mr. Rogers. Kunjufu (1995) further offered that the average classroom moves at a pace similar to the Mr. Rogers show. Therefore, it may not be that African American children, especially males, are hyperactive. It may be that the methodology is too slow. Moreover, boys of all races do not seem to be hyperactive when they play video games or when they are involved in other activities that capture their interest. Kunjufu (1995) concludes that "..what children are involved with will determine their interest level. We may need to look at the stimuli we provide for children instead of labeling them hyperactive, when they do not respond as we deem appropriate (p. 17)."

When examining Conduct Disorder (CD) as a problem plaguing African American Children, especially males, we must understand first develop an understanding of its definition and nature. Conduct Disorder (CD) is characterized by as a repetitive and persistent pattern of behavior in which the basic rights of others or major age-appropriate societal norms or rules are violated (DSM-IV, 1994). ADHD is attributed to central nervous system dysfunction (Barren, 1994), whereas Conduct Disorder is mostly attributed to social maladjustment (Spencer & Oattes, 1999).

Spencer and Oattes (1999) offered the following explanation as to the misdiagnosis of African-American males as ADHD and CD:

"In many schools systems, teachers, administrators, and counselors serve as informal diagnostic teams in assessing student behavioral issues. This is particularly true of systems that have alternative educational settings for students who have been diagnosed with behavior problems or conduct disorder. There is a market disparity in the diagnosis of White males and African-American males with regard to ADHD and Conduct Disorder. In a society where negative stereotypes unfortunately still persist of African-American males, it is no wonder that Black males who exhibit Attention-Deficit Disorder characterized by lack of impulse control are often given an immediate and informal diagnosis of Conduct Disorder. A lack of clear understanding of our personal perceptions and prejudices coupled with a lack of knowledge of the DSM-IV criteria for diagnosis can result in misdiagnosis of African- American adolescent males."

According to Atkinson, Morton, and Sue (1998) there is a mistrust of counseling and service delivery systems by oppressed populations. This mistrust is based on some facts of past prejudices and mistreatment from institutions which were charged to serve oppressed people. Consequently, professional educators and counselors find themselves attempting to increase their knowledge and awareness of how oppression has impacted the perceptions of oppressed populations.

Spencer and Oattes (1999) have identified three significant factors that contribute to the misdiagnosis of African-American males: 1) schools that do not have a significant number of African- American teachers; 2) schools that favor

homogeneous or ability grouping over heterogeneous grouping; and 3) schools
that do not support a curriculum that promotes multicultural awareness and
sensitivity. Spencer and Oattes offer the following:

> "To the degree that schools do not actively seek to hire an appropriate
> number of African-Americans, Black male adolescents' self-concept and
> achievement are adversely impacted resulting in the African-American
> adolescent male becoming detached from the educational process and
> those charged with educating them (Blake & Darling, 1994). This
> detachment, which often becomes a way of interaction for these students,
> is often perceived by teachers as willful disobedience and defiance
> ironically both of which are characteristic of Conduct Disorder.
> Considering these points, schools that favor homogeneous grouping, a
> system whereby students are grouped together according to their ability
> levels, generally come across as promoting and perpetuating the status quo
> which further alienates African-American adolescent males. Grouping
> students in such a way tends to adversely affect the racial identity
> development of minority students (Davidson, (1997). This tracking tends
> to be more destructive than constructive as African-American adolescents
> become frustrated at the notion of being separated and grouped on the
> basis of special characteristics. This for them has the all too familiar
> appearance of segregation, as a result resentment builds. The combination
> of frustration and resentment manifests itself into authority figure defying
> behavior either overt or passive. Irrespective of that, African-American

males tend to receive informal diagnosis of Conduct Disorder.

Unfortunately, it appears that any misconduct displayed by African-American male adolescents is viewed as conduct disorder. Finally, schools that do not support a curriculum that promotes cross-cultural awareness and sensitivity send the message that there is but one culture that matters and that is the dominant one. Clearly, this message is met by even further African-American male resistance. Multicultural awareness and sensitivity are crucial to the development of an environment conducive to the understanding of the unique problems that plague minority and other special populations."

The American Educational System is Meant to Serve Whites

According to McIntyre (1996) culturally and linguistically different children are oftentimes mis-classified as having a disability. Differences in cognitive style between teachers and students may result in learners being perceived as less competent than they truly are (Anderson, 1988). This perception, combined with the commonly found cultural bias in assessment, can result in youngsters from culturally different backgrounds and households being labeled as having a disorder, when they do not. For example, most teachers' expectations for quiet, non-active student behavior would be in opposition to the more active and emotionally outspoken contributory styles common among students of Arab heritage (Nydell, 1997). In further example, consider a teacher who explains a task to an Asian- American student and then asks if the directions are understood. The student says "Yes." Upon later review of the assignment, the teacher finds that the instructions were not comprehended. The teacher may

believe that the student is dishonest, or just plain dumb. However, the student may

be attempting to "save face." Some students who hold to the "traditional" East

Asian ways it is a commonly held belief that one should save face, and at the

same time avoid conflict or public embarrassment (Leung, 1988).

James Turner (1971) defined traditional American education as

tantamount to "white studies." It has functioned to prepare Black people to accept,

value, and affirm white society. Turner adds the following to further illustrate his

point:

> White studies is a system of intellectual legitimacy which defines the
>
> activities and experiences of white Western people as the universal
>
> yardstick of human existence. Black studies challenges this assumption
>
> and asserts that white is not now, nor has it ever been either intrinsically
>
> right or complete. White students are educated to be the rulers and makers
>
> of their society. Black students are taught to synthesize the experiences
>
> and memorize the conclusions of another people. The consequence of
>
> such education is that many Blacks, if not most, are inclined to confuse the
>
> interest of our people, with that of our oppressor; creating a situation
>
> where we accept the white people's definitions of problems they cause for
>
> us and the situations they deem acceptable for Black people (p. 12).
>
> Clearly, the education of white children is relatively more successful than
>
> that of

Black children because the schools are designed for white education (Hale, 1986).

Providing additional discussion on this topic is Hakim Rashid (1981). He stated,

"Children from non-European lower socioeconomic status culture groups are at a

disadvantage in the schools because the American educational system has evolved

out of a European philosophical, theoretical, and pedagogical context (p. 57)."

If one were to accept this premise, it's not out of the bounds of logical

thought to also accept and expect the chauvinistic ethnocentrism that perpetuates

an image of normality in describing white children and of pathology in describing

Black children. They typically use harsh terms when describing a phenomenon

that affects Blacks and more neutral terms when discussing middle-class whites.

According to Hale (1986), this practice is regularly undertaken by white social

scientists. The following is an example:

> "Black children who skip school are truants, but upper-middle class white
>
> children might have "school phobia" and require treatment. While poor
>
> Black children who do not perform well in school are likely to be moved
>
> into classes for the mentally retarded, children from white upper-middle
>
> class families who perform poorly are designated "underachievers," in
>
> need of special counseling and educational services. We define and
>
> pinpoint their disabilities with diagnosis like dyslexia, and we create
>
> categories like, "learning disability" to differentiate their problems (p.
>
> 179)."

In an effort to further illustrate her point, Hale (1986) offered:

Black children are defined in white terms because white children are

considered by psychologists to represent the norm. That criterion for

normality pervades the description of psychomotor skills as well as

cognitive skills. Psychologists have developed a language and set of

standards with which we describe children from diverse ethnic groups

using a white frame of reference. When Black children do not

approximate the norms for white children, they are regarded as deficient,

deviant, or pathological, even when they exceed white children in some

dimension. For example Black children are disproportionately labeled

hyperactive because they exhibit different psychomotor skills and needs

than do white children (p. 180).

Special Education: A Formidable Opponent of African American Males

At this point, we have discussed many obstacles and pitfalls that permeate

the

African-American males plight to develop intellectually in the American

Educational

System. Institutions have continued to met out hostile treatment, in the form of

policies, that do nothing but degrade and humiliate Black males. In furtherance of

this hostility, is the process of placing Black children, especially males, in Special

Education classes and programs. This is perhaps one of the most damning and

destructive practices impacting Black youth. According to James M. Patton

(1998), there is a severe overrepresentation of African-Americans in certain special education programs, which in turn, negatively impacts their families, the field of special education and society at large. Patton (1998) further asserted that this disproportionate treatment and labeling can be traced back to 1619, when the first slaves were brought to American shores. Moreover, Patton (1998) wrote:

The current overrepresentation of African-Americans in Special Education classes perpetuates this socio-historical legacy by allowing the general and special education enterprises to continue the programmatic and classroom arrangements that jeopardize the life chances of large numbers of African-American youth.

Many of these students are inappropriately placed...Exacerbating this problem is the fact that many Black youth placed in these Special Education courses fail to receive quality and life-enhancing education in precisely those courses where they're inappropriately placed. In addition, the special education label borne by these students often serves as a stigma, producing negative effects on the bearer of the label and others interacting with the stigmatized individual. Furthermore, while these students are in special education courses, they miss essential general education academic and social curricula. This limited exposure with the core academic curriculum continues the spiral of "lower levels of achievement, and decreased likelihood of post secondary education, and more limited employment.

According to the Office of Civil Rights [OCR] (1994), in 1992, African Americans constituted 16% of public school population. According to Chinn and

Hughes (1987) an acceptable range would be between 14.4% and 17.6% of all children in Special Education programs. However, according to this same time period, African-American students made up 32%, or double the acceptable representative population of students in special education classes (OCR, 1994).

When viewing how and why African-American students are placed in Special Education courses, Michael Porter (1997) offered an interesting and detailed perspective. Porter describes what he calls the "conning" of African-American parents into signing their children up for Special Education classes. Porter stated:

> Many Caucasian, and some Black, teachers, counselors, principals, social workers, and psychologists con African-American parents, especially mothers on a daily basis. Money is not what they're conned out of, its their children—especially their sons and grandsons. The conning usually begins with one or more teachers, mostly Caucasian female, suggesting to the principal, counselor, or special education teacher that a particular child be screened for a behavior disorder. The child is usually a Black male, in an elementary school. After the school staff has observed the child, the parent, usually a single Black woman, is sent a letter to attend a meeting to discuss her child. The school and the special education staff have already decided that the boy be placed in the Behavior Disorders program. They are confident that they will convince the mother to sign the necessary forms giving them permission to test and place her son in the program. (The Meeting) The Black mother is lured unwittingly into the vampire's

den where her son's life-blood, and spirituality will be sucked out of him. These school representatives will throw their titles at the mother, which tend to intimidate her, especially if she hasn't attended college, or does not hold a professional position, that carries an impressive title. To avoid appearing dumb, the parent will usually agree with whatever is being recommended. They use such phrases as, "for the welfare of your child." The idea is to convince the already intimidated mother that they're on her side. After the mother has signed the papers that surround her, the wolves get more aggressive, with phrases like, "You may want to consider having your child evaluated for medication." They tell her that the drugs will help her child concentrate more and make better grades. By the time the parent leaves the meeting, she has signed away her son's life. She will take him to see a doctor, usually one recommended by the school, to have his medication prescribed. From here on out, he exists within a maze of guinea-pigism and bureaucratic paperwork designed to keep him forever a Behavior Disorder student. He and thousands of his BD peers will be the source of income for mostly middle-class Caucasian women, the topic of many doctoral dissertations, and human guinea pigs for medication administered by state mental health clinics and private physician (p. 10-12.)

After reviewing Porter's (1997) observation on the covert tactics used by

American educators and the system they work in, it's not too difficult to

understand how we come to have so many African-American students in these

special education courses. All too often, we are victimized, unwittingly, by our

own doing.

Conclusion and Recommendations for Change

As stated previously, no perpetrator has played a more villainous role in

maintaining the (Anglo-American) status quo than the American Educational

Institutions.

Through its policies, employees, and unethical (and sometimes criminal)

practices, America's Educational Institutions, have perpetrated a long-lasting

fraud on African Americans…especially African-American males. The fraud I

speak of is that of convincing African Americans that they are intellectually

inferior, to their white counterparts. Aiding, subsidizing, and perpetuating this

practice of instilling intellectual inferiority into African Americans is, none other

than, the United States Government.

For the most part, this sense of being intellectually inferior has claimed

perhaps hundreds of thousands, if not millions, of African American males, as

they struggle to develop intellectually, in a country that has never accepted them

as intellectual equals. Difficult as their plight may be, African American males

have, and will continue to develop into intellectual giants, with the aid of, or in

spite of America's Educational Institutions.

In the years since slavery was ended, Blacks in America, especially Black

males have had a horrendous time attempting to develop into intellectual beings.

Not only have Black males had to continue to battle the everyday obstacles of racism, and discrimination within the context of American society, but they have also had to endure the intricacies of the most potent form of educational categorization, and classification into the classes and academic programs for the intellectually inferior, and the academically deficient, and chronically disruptive, or inattentive (i.e. special education, alternative schools). These programs have been operating decade after decade with the blessing of the U.S. Department of Education, individual states, and individual school districts, throughout the United States.

These programs have flourished because of an inherent misunderstanding, of how Black children learn; how they develop intellectually; what they should be taught; and how they should be taught. Moreover, as we begin to investigate these issues, we must also include a discussion on who have been teaching Black children; how and why Black children have been diagnosed as having learning or behavior disorders, and what steps should be taken within the academic environment to insure success for Black children.

In an effort to assist African-American children, especially males, we must employ a multi-faceted approach to combating the system that has been so detrimental and damaging. Moreover, we must first acknowledge that children, especially Black children, and males in particular, have different learning styles and that they develop intellectually at a different pace. We must also change our classrooms to better accommodate all students. McIntyre (1996) offered the

338

following suggestions that I also believe would enhance the learning experience for all children:

1. Use an "advanced organizer" to provide a context for and conceptualization of the final product before beginning to teach the various segments of the lesson.

2. Make the lessons interesting.

3. Relate concepts and material to the students' experience.

4. Include student interests in lessons.

5. Use a variety of methods and modalities in presentation.

6. Re-explain material to perplexed students in the style in which they learn best.

7. Use Cooperative academic techniques to enhance the learning of culturally diverse students.

8. Higher Education faculty should teach prospective teachers how to interact, instruct, and discipline their students in a more culturally aware manner.

9. Educators at every level must undertake self-study regarding cultural background and its effect on learning (p.3)."

REFERENCES

Akbar, N. (1996). Breaking the chains of psychological slavery. Tallahassee, FL.: Mind Productions and Associates, Inc. p. 14-15.

Anderson, C. (1994). Black labor, white wealth: The search for power and economic Justice. Englewood, Maryland: Duncan and Duncan Publishers, Inc.

Atkins, D. R., Morten, G. & Sue, D. W. (1998). Counseling American minorities (5th Ed.), Boston, MA: Mcgraw-Hill Companies, Inc.

Baren, M. (1994). Hyperactivity and attention disorders in children. HIN, Inc.

Blake, W. M., & Darling, C. A., (1994). The dilemmas of the African-American Male. Journal of Black Studies, 24 (4), pp. 402-415.

Chambers-Dalton, K. C. (1991). The alphabet is an abolitionist: Literacy and African Americans in the emancipation era. The Massachusetts Review, Winter.

Douglass, F. (1973). Narrative of the life of frederick douglass: An American slave. New York: Anchor Books.

Good, H., and Teller, J. D., (1969). A history of western education. 3rd ed. London: The MacMillian Company.

Hale, J. E. (1986). Black children: Their roots, culture, and learning styles. Baltimore, Maryland: The Johns Hopkins University Press.

Harper's Weekly. (May, 1873). Straightening the crooked tree. p. 368.

King, W. (1995). Toward the promised land: From uncle tom's cabin to the onset of the Civil War, (1851-1861). New York: Chelsea House Publishing.

Kunjufu, J. (1995). Countering the conspiracy to destroy Black boys, (series). Chicago, IL.: African American Images.

--------------(1984). Developing positive self-images and discipline in Black children. Chicago, IL.: African-American Images.

340

Leung, E. (1988). Cultural and acculturational commonalities and diversities
among

Asian Americans: Identification and programming considerations. In A.
Ortiz & B. Ramirez (Eds.), Schools and the culturally diverse exceptional student:
(underbar) Promising practices and future directions. Reston, VA: The Council
for Exceptional Children.

McIntyer, T. (1996). Does the way we teach create behavior disorders in
culturally different students? Education and Treatment of Children, (August).

Patton, J. M., (1998). The disproportionate representation of African-Americans
In special education: Looking behind the curtain for understanding and
solutions. The Journal of Special Education, (Spring).

Porter, M. (1997). Kill them before they grow: Misdiagnosis of African-American
boys In American classrooms. Chicago, IL: African American Images.

Quarles, B. (1969). The Negro in the civil war. Boston: Harvard University Press.

Rashid, H. M. (1980). Minorities in educational research. Communication
Quartely.

Russo, C.and Talbert-Johnson, C. (1997). The overrepresentation of African-
American Children in special education: The re-segregation of educational
programming. Education and Urban Society, (February).

Sparks, J. (1836). Works of benjamin franklin, vol. II., Boston, Mass: Tappan and
Whittemore Publishers.

Spenser, L. and Oatts, T. (1999). Conduct disorder vs. ADHD: Diagnostic
implications For African-American males. Education, (Spring, 1999).

Turner, J. (1971). Black studies and a Black philosophy of education. Imani

August/September, pp. 12-17.

U.S. Department of Education, Office of Civil Rights (OCR) (1994). 1992 elementary and secondary school civil rights survey: National summaries. Washington, DC DBS Corporation.

Vaux, R. (1817). Memoirs of the life of Anthony Benezet. Philadelphia: James P. Parke.

West, E. H., (1972). The black American and education. Columbus, Ohio: Bell and Howell Company.

Woodson, C. G. (1968). The education of the Negro prior to 1861. New York, Arno Press and The New York Times.

Chapter 22

Where is my Child? Is the System Splitting my Family? The Future of African American Families?

Joseph L. Jefferson, Ph.D., LPC, NCC, LMFT, LCDC
Texas Southern University
Houston, TX

LaRonda Y. Ashford, M.Ed., LPC-I, ABD
Texas Southern University
Houston, TX

Abstract

African American juveniles are being separated more and more from their families due to criminal behavior. What effect does the juvenile criminal justice system have on theses families? How can families make the best of their situations? This discussion will explore the attitudes and ideas of the presenters, along with those of other professionals, parents, and juvenile offenders. The questions deal with culture, society, and education. Suggestions are offered to help all mental health professional and educators in working with these families individually and collectively.

Despite extensive sociological and psychological research, little evidence exists on how mental health professionals should work with African American families, involved with the juvenile justice system.

Overview

What effects does the criminal justice system have on African American families?

    I.   Rationale for concern

    II. How can families make the best of their situations?

    III. Suggestions for mental health professionals working with these families.

    IV. The future of African families

Myths about African Americans

Say the word "criminal," and the first image that pops into most people's mind is black teenage gangster with a gun. However, blacks don't even come close to the amount of crime that white commit in society.

Myth: If you are black and live in the U.S., things are getting better.

Reality: When told that a disproportionate number of minorities are behind bars, an all too common response is, "Well, don't they commit more crimes?" While it is true that arrest rates for most minorities is higher than for whites, arrest numbers alone do not tell the whole story.

Myth: America is close to realizing Dr. Martin Luther King's Dream

Reality: In March 1963, Dr. Martin Luther King, Jr. led 250.000 Americans to "dramatize a shameful condition" noting that he "refused to believe that the bank of justice is bankrupt." Dr. King's famous speech left people inspired and hopeful that his dream would be realized. We end this century with Dr. King's dream firmly handcuffed, hackled and locked down.

Where is my Child? Is the system splitting my Family?
The Future of African American Families?

Introduction

African American juveniles are being separated more and more from their families due to criminal behaviors. What effect does the juvenile criminal justice system have on these families? How can families make the best of their situations? This discussion will explore the attitudes and ideas of the presenters, along with those of other professionals, parents, and juvenile offenders. The questions deal with culture, society, and education. Suggestions are offered to help all mental health professional and educators in working with these families individually and collectively.

Despite extensive sociological and psychological research, little evidence exists on how mental health professionals should work with African American families, involved with the juvenile justice system.

Overview

What effects does the criminal justice system have on African American families?

I.   How can families make the best of their situations?

Families must first be willing to cooperate with the professional staff assigned to their child's case most likely in more than one setting (for example therapist, psychiatrist caseworkers, residential staff, attorneys). Lack of cooperation tends to add more time in which the family will be involved with the system, demonstrates an unwillingness to work on the identified problem areas for the individual and the family as a whole, and may even limit the quality of service the family will receive.

Families should accept the situation as a learning opportunity, they are exposed to professional staff that are specialized in numerous areas (for example counseling, law, social work, medical, administrative, etc), although not voluntarily, they are provided numerous occasions to interact as a family unit that may or may not have been present in their lives prior to entering the system, these families may also obtain valuable information that may have been detrimental to them in the long run.

II. Suggestions for mental health professionals working with these families.

Mental health professionals should be aware of the individual family's strengths and weakness, be sensitive to the values of each individual family; understand the family background, parenting style and lifestyle of each family. It is also important to get all the family members living in the home involved in the assessment of the individual and all counseling services that will be provided for the family.

Mental health professionals should dispel all myths, maintain their cultural sensitivity and be aware of their individual biases. In doing this the mental health professions should evaluate and assess these families according that families values system and not to that of the "majority." This will help the assessments and evaluations become more accurate and relevant for the families.

Mental health professionals must know that these families will more likely experience multiple negative feelings such as shame, hopeless, helpless, oppressed anger and hostility for their involvement with the system In order for families to be successful these feelings will need to be addressed and not ignored early in the working relationship.

III. The future of African American families.

African American families have a bright future in society as a whole; however in the criminal justice system the future seems dim. There is much more research needed in the areas of working with African Americans, especially those that are involved in the juvenile justice systems. Professional staff needs to be able to make more accurate, appropriate and justifiable assessments and evaluations of the individuals we work with. The juvenile offenders among African Americans will continue to rise and be disproportionate to the general population if we as professional do not educate ourselves to the best practices, commit ourselves to researching this population, and diligently working with this population with an unbiased attitude.

<u>Myths about African Americans</u>

Say the word "criminal," and the first image that pops into most people's mind is black teenage gangster with a gun. However, blacks don't even come close to the amount of crime that white commit in society.

Myth: If you are black and live in the U.S., things are getting better.

Reality: When told that a disproportionate number of minorities are behind bars, an all too common response is, "Well, don't they commit more crimes?" While it is true that arrest rates for most minorities is higher than for whites, arrest numbers alone do not tell the whole story.

Myth: America is close to realizing Dr. Martin Luther King's Dream

Reality: In March 1963, Dr. Martin Luther King, Jr. led 250.000 Americans to "dramatize a shameful condition" noting that he "refused to believe that the bank of justice is bankrupt." Dr. King's famous speech left people inspired and hopeful that his dream would be realized. We end this century with Dr. King's dream firmly handcuffed, hackled and locked down.

Myth: Minorities are incarcerated at higher rates because they commit crimes at higher rates.

Reality: Relative to their population, minorities commits larger numbers of serious crimes than whites – but not nearly enough to justify the disparities. African Americans are incarcerated at seven times the rate of whites. Minorities receive harsher treatment than whites at every stage of the process, from arrest to bail to sentencing. The injustice is greater in drug crimes. African Americans make up 12 percent of population, 13 percent of monthly drug users, 55 percent of those convicted of drug possession and 74 percent of those sentenced to prison for drug possession.

REFERENCES

U.S. Department of Justice, Office of Juvenile Justice and Delinquency Prevention: Juvenile Offenders and Victims: 1999 National Report.

Texas Youth Commission, 1999. Pamela Ward, Public Information Officer.

Bridges, G. S. and Steen, S. (1998, August). Racial disparities in official assessments of juvenile offenders: Attributional stereotypes as mediating mechanisms. American Sociological Review, 63, 554-570.

National Center on Institutions and Alternatives (NCIA). (1996, July and 1999 January). Myths about African Americans. Alexandria, Virginia.

Chapter 23

Afrocentric Education Consideration For Needs of Learning Disabled African American Students

Freddie Goss, MS

Jurupa Unified School District

Riverside, CA

American education has been under attack following the publication of A Nation at Risk and America 2000. The attack has come from parents, legislators, the business leadership and the religious communities. As a result, these groups supported major restructuring in America Schools. As evidence, consider the response to the American 2000 Gallop/Phi Delta Kappa Poll of 1991 discussed by Doyle (1991). In that article he said, "Event without asking specific questions about America 2000, the poll makes it clear that Americans overwhelmingly support the underlying concepts; choice, higher standards, radical reforms and national testing." (Doyle, 1991, p. 186)

Parents are demonstrating their support for restructuring by advocating such programs as open enrollment, charter schools, voucher systems, and neighborhood schools. The desire is simply to improve the quality of education for their children.

Like other ethnic groups, African Americans support the education reform movements spawned by the publication of A Nation At Risk and America 2000. Yet, at the same time, many African Americans reached the conclusion that America's traditional education cannot successfully achieve reform goals for African American students. "Some black parents believe the reform movement addresses schooling designed and controlled by Anglo Americans to benefit their cultural, political, and economic interests and individual groups connected to the Eurocentric power elite." (Ratteray, 1992, p. 138)

Education reform in the area of special education also has its critics. Social activist, writer and author Andrew Hacker echoes the sentiments of African American parents of learning handicapped students in his New York best seller, Two Nations Black and White. Separate, Hostile, Unequal. He says, "...many more black youngsters are assigned to special education classes...Even if their diagnosis are couched in clinical terms, too often the message is that their behavior fails to mirror middle-class demeanor. (Hacker, A. 1993. P.164) Additionally, the Bell Curve, anti-affirmative action mandates and the endangered species theory for Black men in America is generating increasing numbers of educators to look for new educational philosophy for American black children.

It is this writer's opinion that, of all the educational programs shaken by the shock waves from the reformist education movement of the 80's, special education has suffered the most. "In this regard, students are currently being under served and inappropriately served despite program IEP's and other legal regulations associated with Public Law 194-92. The main reason is the confusion and lack of training to implement the currently popular program of inclusion.

The purpose of the report is to discuss Afrocentric education as a tool for improving the academic and social skills of disabled African American students, particularly males in the public school systems. To this end, the report focuses in two directions. First the report goes back to the historical origin and philosophy of this ethnocentric education theory, and, second, this report comes forward to discuss currently successful programs and strategies used by public and private schools in the Afrocentric education movement.

This writer's hope is that special education administrators and teachers in tradition public and private schools may find something discussed in this report useful in understanding and serving all of their students in the special education environment.

"The history of Afrocentric education is the history of the attempt by African America educators to minimize the political, social, educational and economic negative effects resulting from slavery on the education and training of African American children since Reconstruction. Afrocentric education is a twenty-first century response to a debate that was befun by British educated and black nationalist Alexander Crummell and the brilliant Machavellian, Booker T. Washington in the 1880's and about the best education for Afro-Americans following Emancipation." (Moses, W. 1991.P.78)

Today's Afrocentrist cite Crumwell, W.E.B. Dubois, Marcus Garvey, Garland Penn, Silas X. Floyd and Carter G. Woodson as the leaders of the past who campaigned for Afrocentric education materials. (Harris, V. 1994, P.147) One of these early leaders merits special consideration in this report. He is the father of Negro History, Carter G. Woodson. Consider these words by Mr. Woodson that run through the spirit of the Afrocentric Education Movement. He writes, "…no systematic effort toward change has been possible, for taught the same economics, history, philosophy, literature and religion which have established the present code of morals, the Negro's mind has been brought under the control of his oppressor. The problem of holding the Negro down, therefore, is easily solved. When you control a man's thinking, you do not have to worry about his actions. You do not have to tell him not to stand here or go yonder. He will find his "proper place" and will stay in it. You do not need to send him to the back door. He will go without being told. In fact, if there is no back door, he will cut one for this special benefit. His education makes it necessary. The same educational process which inspires and stimulates the oppressor with thought that his is everything and has accomplished everything worthwhile, depresses and crushes at the same time the spark of genius in the Negro by making him feel that his race does not amount to much and never will measure up to the standards of other people. The Negro thus educated is a hopeless liability of the race." (Woodson, 1990).

The philosophy of Afrocentric education places the African American student at the center of all the activities within the educational experience by presenting a curriculum based on that learner's style. The aim of this curriculum is to improve the student's self-concept, teach historical accuracy, provide values clarification, and demonstrate community empowerment. (Lee, 1994, p.300) Equally important, the aim is to improve academic performance. In short, the goal of Afrocentrists is to do what mainstream American schools appear unable or unwilling to do – successfully educate a large majority of Black American youth with the required skills to succeed in this society. Again, there is overwhelming statistical evidence that this is the case. Jawanza Kunjufu reinforces this fact in his book Countering the Conspiracy to Destroy Black Boys. He says, "Black children constitute 17%of all students, but comprise 41% of all Special Education placements, primarily Educable Mentally Retarded (EMR), and Behavior Disorder (BD). Black boys are 85% of this figure and African American males lead the nation suspension." (Kinjufu, 1986, p.11)

Radical thinking Afrocentrists have adopted the philosophy that these unfortunate figures indicate that many African American students are lost in a Eurocentric world of education with an inadequate sense of self-esteem. Further, they use the information to raise questions about the role of too few racially similar teachers to Black children among school faculty. Afrocentrists cite that a lack of Black role models plays a major influence for some students who demonstrate school failure. Moreover, the claim is made special education is the only alternative provided in mainstream schools to service many African American students who don't fit the basic curriculum.

African American Afrocentric educators in public and private schools identify Molefi K. Asante as the brainchild and leader of modern Afrocentric educational philosophy. Professor Asante is the Chairperson of the Department of African American studies at Temple University in Philadelphia, PA. He is the author of more than twenty books and close to one hundred articles related to the subject of Afrocentricity and Afrocentric education. The major point to Asante's philosophy that guides Afrocentric education is his position that, "Education based on Europe and Euro-American subject matter is so deeply racist that only an Afrocentric Theory of education based on the Nilotic-Egyptian origins of civilization can mitigate the effects of racism on the psyches of Black school children." (Asante, 1992, p.5)

Finally, some Afrocentrists suggest a conspiracy the related to the mis-education of African American students. When explaining the success of his school program, Mr. Palmer answered this way – a 1986 Christi Screen Monitor feature story. "Primarily, it's a palpable quality of caring and involvement on the part of the teachers – a quality too often missing in public schools that serve black children." (Helmore,K., November 1986) To Dr. Palmer, the struggle for the minds of black children is real and must be taken seriously by black people, because the broader society does not want black children to succeed. As he stated in an interview for the Los Angeles Times: "black people were not brought here to be educated... We were brought here to pick cotton. They didn't tell us of our great culture, that we were the founders of man, of science and the arts. They did tell us that we were Crips and Bounty Hunters (youth gangs) and pimps and prostitutes. The schools are eliminating (our) young people as competitors in society. Most of these public school students are going to end up in prison, on drugs or welfare. People say the schools are failing. If you accept the premise that

this is a racist society, then they are not failing. They are doing their job.)
(Clegg,L., Sepia Magazine 1980, p.10)

Many Afrocentric schools follow the blueprint for academic instruction used by the Nairobi Day School that operated from 1966 to 1984 and was considered the best educational program for Black children according to the Institute of Child Development. A brief description of its curriculum is given. The pedagogy and philosophy included positive attitudes, high expectations, skills oriented instruction, the use of African American learning styles, and a caring commitment to the African American community through service was the foundation of the educational experience by the students. According to founder Gergrude Wilks, "The Nairobi Day School philosophy stressed that the motivation to learn the joy of learning comes from the culture itself – not from external rewards such as money, raisins, starts. The study of black history and culture was an integral part of the Nairobi Day School's pedagogy. Students and teachers at the school celebrated black history and culture in the form of politically oriented music, rhymes and short stories." (Hoover, 1992, pp. 204-207)

All of the tenets of the Nairobi School had their roots in the philosophy, liturgy and politics of the Black church. Consider the overwhelming influence of the Black church experience on Nairobi's founder as she describes the call-response assembly mode of instruction, paramount in the Black church, which was a fundamental strategy at Nairobi. The following excerpts from Hoover's (1992) article lay out specific examples of the Afrocentric curricula at Nairobi:

"We use the assembly for motivation. Assembly begins with the singing of "Lift Every Voice and Sing," which is sometimes referred to as the Black National Anthem. We continue with motivational songs, many of which are old familiar hymns tunes and spirituals with new words to stimulate the students in developing a positive attitude towards community. Typical songs

include: "I'm On My Way, Don't You Hinder Me", "I'm a Learning Man", "Good News, Freedom's Coming!", "Come and Go With Me to Nairobi School"..."

I use a lot of my father's plantation tricks. My father's a minister used to a lot of singing – to get folks together and organize churches. At the day school another unique example of teaching strategies use by the Nairobi School was the call and responses/audience participating mode of teaching. The method of instruction was based on research suggests that Black students tend to learn better in group activities. Daily assemblies were used to discuss current events, groups sang, as mentioned earlier, and recite poetry." (pp. 205-207)

The suggestion that the inspirational singing, response, and motivational assembly were special forces guiding Black students is something educators who push for prayer in the schools and who support the morning pledge of allegiance should study when seeking to improve Black school children's performance.

The Nairobi Day School used a holistic approach based on African-American learning styles in teaching reading. Students were taught to recognize syllable patterns through rhymes, "raps" and stories rather than sounding out each letter or memorizing words. These rhymes taught the pattern of spelling words and fostered political pride. "In grades four through six, the schools reading instruction was oriented toward problem solving, core subject vocabulary development, and reading for enjoyment." For example, to introduce the simple vowel pattern ([CVC] consistent pattern):

"Harriet Tubman

Harriet Tubman

Had a plan

To help blacks get to

The promised land."

-   to introduce the double vowel spelling pattern ([VV] – variable pattern):

"Old Prophet Nat

Not afraid to fight

To fight for right

Not afraid to lead

A hero indeed."

In 1995, the U.S. Department of Education named Chick Elementary School of Kansas City, Missouri a Certificate of Merit award winner in a Chapter 1 ESEA National Recognition Program. (Bullard, A., 1995, pp.15-16) Chick Elementary was established as an Afrocentric alternative to the Eurocentric mediocre school that was mis-educating its students. "Today the T.S. Chick School's African centered Shule (Swahili for school) is separate but better." (McCormick, J.,1994, P32) Under Afrocentrism it is no longer an inferior school without influence in the community. It is superior and now the guiding force of the community for issues and concerns related to Chick children, their families, and other community members.

Chick Elementary stresses the importance of improving student self-esteem as one of the major criteria for enhancing student academic achievement. In addition to Afrocentric study of history and culture, Chick uses morning assemblies similar to those used in the Nairobi Day School with call and response activities to motivate students toward pride and success. <u>Kansas City Star</u> reporter, L. Horsley, (1994) described an inspirational scene at a Monday morning assembly in this way:

"The music teacher, Mr. Bailey, plays "We Shall Overcome" on the piano. First graders stand to lead their peers and suddenly hundreds of children chant their personal pledge of allegiance" "I can be the best/by doing my best in everything I do and taking pride/in who I am/my faith will see me through.," This is the weekly Harambee – meaning coming together in Kiswahli. It expresses the tone for the entire week."

The Monday assembly experience is a major affirmation of the schools dedication to pride, dignity and personal responsibility. The mood described by Horsley suggests the tone and flavor of a religious rally. According to the principal Audrey Bullard (1995) students and staff are dressed in blue and white school uniforms or traditional African attire. Students chant, meditate and sing songs. Harambee take place Tuesday – Thursday by students quoting African proverbs and encouraging each other to have a positive day and to reach academic goals. Moreover, other on-going activities address affirmation and recognition for students. Some of those included self-management, self-esteem enhancement, value system restructuring, dress for success program, Khuuf Kash Village Store rewards and Afrocentric interface visits by professionals and community leaders. (1995, pp.3-5) All of the self-esteem, affirmation and recognition components of the curricula were reminiscent of what African American clergy have used for generations to guarantee the success of their ministries. It is significant that the same spirit can work to help students become effective learners in an Afrocentric education system.

Chick school administrators use the Iowa achievement tests to focus on the general academic goals for each year. The tests are conducted each Spring. Once the school year begins, teachers by grade level meet with resource teachers and Chapter 1 facilitators to prioritize goals and objectives to improving instruction and academic assessment. Monthly objective tests are assessed the last Friday of each month. Students are required to achieve 80% mastery of the material tested. Otherwise, the teacher, Chapter 1 paraprofessionals, tutors, parents and volunteer elders re-teach until the material is mastered. In addition, supplementary academic support is provided in the form of a read-at-home program with incentives for student and parent participation. Moreover, regular classroom teachers provide after school tutoring Monday through Thursday. Close coordination is provided between the regular day classroom activities and those after school sessions to increase the chances of students mastering curriculum objectives. Finally, the Chick Saturday academy affords another opportunity for students to gain mastery of subject matter in the area of reading, math and language arts.

Many Afrocentric educators want to identify specific and realistic pedagogy that will be acceptable to all ethnic groups in many pluralistic public educational settings mainly located in integrated suburbs of America and those inner city schools overwhelmingly black. However, under the current social climate and considering that fewer African Americans are entering the teaching profession, Afrocentrists like Carol Lee believe Afrocentric pedagogy still has a chance of impacting many American public schools. She and others have written philosophical agendas that mainstream educators can use as a blueprint when possible. She insists that any attempt to implement an African centered pedagogy requires teachers who support and possess the following principles and a reservoir of knowledge.

1. The social ethics of African culture as exemplified in the social philosophy of Maat.
2. The history of the African continent and Diaspora.

3. Political and community organizing within the African American community.

4. The positive pedagogical implications of the indigenous language, African American English.

5. Child development principles that are relevant to the positive and productive growth of African American children.

6. African contributions in science, mathematics, literature, the arts, and societal organizations.

7. Teaching techniques that are socially interactive and positively affective.

8. The need for continuous personal study.

9. The African principle that "children are the reward of life."

The African principle of reciprocity; that is, a teacher sees his or her own future symbiotically linked to the development of students. (Lee, C.,1994, p.307)

BIBLIOGRAPHY

Asante, M. K. (1988). Afrocentricity. Trenton, NJ: Africa World Press, Inc.
Bullard, A. (1995). Chick elementary parent student handbook.

Doyle, D. P. (1991, November). America 2000. Phi Delta Kappan., 184-210.

Hacker, A. (1992). Two nations black and white, separate, hostile, unequal. New York: Balantine Books.

Harris, V. J. (1994). Historic readers for African American children (1864-1944) of uncovering and reclaiming a tradition of opposition. In Mwalimu J. Shujaa (Ed.), Too much schooling, too little education, (pp. 143-173). New Jersey: Afrika World Press, Inc.

Hoover, M.E.R. (1992). The Nairobi day school: An Afrikan American independent school, 1966-1984. The Journal of Negro Education, 61 (2), 201-209.

Kunjufu, J. (1966). Countering the conspiracy to destroy black boys. Chicago: African American Images.

McCormick, J. (1994, May 16). Separate but equal again. Newsweek, 26.

Moses, W. J. (1991). Eurocentrism, afrocentrism, and William H. Ferris, The African abroad: 1911. The Journal of Negro Education, 173 (1), 76-90.

Ratteray, J. D. (1992). Independent neighborhood schools: A framework for the education of African Americans. The Journal of Negro Education, 61 (2), 138-147.

Woodson, C. G., Jr. (1990). <u>The miss-education of the Negro.</u> Nashville, TN: Wisnton Derek Publishers, Inc.

Chapter 24

Emerging Profiles of High Achieving Hispanic American and African American Women Scholars

Angela Clark-Louque, Ed.D.
California State University – San Bernardino
San Bernardino, CA

Helen M. Garcia, Ph.D.
California State University – San Bernardino
San Bernardino, CA

Introduction/statement of the problem

The present status of Hispanics and Blacks in higher education illustrates the limited numbers of individuals who are college and university administrators, full time faculty, and students, and reveals the paucity of degrees awarded to Hispanics and Blacks. For example, in 1995, Hispanics numbered 3,795 and Blacks numbered 12,657 of some 140,990 executive, administrative, or managerial positions. Of full-time faculty, Hispanics comprised 12,942 and Blacks comprised 26,835 of some 550,822 positions. 1994-95 degree data indicates that Hispanics received 54,201 and Blacks received 87,203 of some 1,160,134 bachelor's degrees; 12,907 and 24,171 of some 397,629 master's degrees; 3,231 and 4,747 of some 75,800 professional degree; 984 and 1,667 of some 44,446 doctoral degrees, respectively. Hispanic women received 496 and Black women received 936 of all doctorates conferred (The Chronicle of Higher Education Almanac Issue, August 28, 1998).

Models explaining underachievement

The academic and social problems that ethnic minority students experience in schools and the theory of school failure have been widely discussed by educators and social scientists spanning well over a century. Of the school failure theories, the deficit model has held the longest currency (Valencia, 1997). "The deficit thinking model at its core, -- positing that the student who fails in school does so because of internal deficits or deficiencies. Such deficits manifest, it is alleged, in limited intellectual abilities, linguistic shortcomings, lack of motivation to learn and immoral behavior…genetics, culture and class and familial socialization have all been postulated as the sources of alleged deficits expressed by the individual student who experiences school failure" (Valencia, 1997, p. 2). In keeping with this theory, educators have often utilized cultural deficiency models espoused by social scientists to explain the problems of Hispanic and Black underachievement in education (Valencia, 1997; Nieto, 1996; Baca-Zinn, 1989; Banks, 1988; Escobero, 1980). The basic tenets of these models rest on the works of such noted social scientists as Ruth Benedict, Talcott Parsons, and Florence Kluckhohn (Del Castillo & Torres, 1988). This literature, some of which dates back to the early 1930s, has sought to explain Hispanic and Black school failure by focusing primarily on the inadequacy of student' cultural backgrounds, home environment, and the community's belief and value systems (Nieto, 1996).

Benedict (1934) applied universal personality types to minority cultures, and thereby made assumptions about patterns of minority cultural values, which were primarily based on personality characteristics, such as low self-esteem (Del Castillo & Torres, 1988).

Parsons (1935) developed a typology of social structures to articulate his perspective on Hispanic value systems. This paradigm compared Anglo-American society's value systems with those of Hispanic willing to delay gratification, and goal-oriented. In contrast, Hispanics are portrayed as undisciplined, demanding immediate gratification, and lacking purpose (Del Castillo & Torres, 1988).

Kluckhohn's (1961) concept of value orientation states that "values which assume greater cultural priority can be understood to designate the respective culture." Within this conceptual frame, she described Hispanic culture as "present-time oriented, fatalistic, traditional, and irrational" (Del Castillo & Torres, 1988, p. 41). These ascribed values were based on analysis of 23 Hispanic persons' value orientations, residing in a community of 150 inhabitants, located in the Rimrock, New Mexico area (Del Castillo & Torres, 1988).

In sum, the early research of Benedict, Parsons, and Kluckhohn has substantially contributed to the negative stereotypic descriptions of Hispanic and Black culture and normative behavior. These theorists' interpretations of ethnic minority cultural value patterns, systems, and orientations are the prototype of cultural deficiency models (Del Castillo & Torres, 1988).

More Recent Applications of Cultural Deficiency Models to Hispanic Americans and African Americans

By the 1960s, and into the 1970s, educational researchers such as Grebler (1970), Schwartz (1969), and Madsen (1961) had published seminal work on the educational value orientations of Hispanics, borrowing theories and models extensively from early social science literature on Hispanic value patterns, systems, and orientations, they sought to explain how value orientations are correlated with Hispanic academic achievement. True to the theoretical constructs upon which their work was framed, all of these researchers found that Hispanic students' family background, language, and cultural value systems were detrimental to educational achievement (Del Castillo & Torres, 1988).

Of special interest are the works of Schwartz and Madsen because they include valuable information on Hispanic females. For example, Schwartz (1969) found that Hispanic girls are "more profoundly victimized" by Hispanic values than Hispanic males. And Madsen (1961) concluded that Hispanic women "are not only overly passive and fatalistic, but sadomasochistic as well since wife beating for them represents profound love" (Del Castillo & Torres, 1988, p. 43).

Furthermore, in a study that reviewed the research on the underachievement of Black students, Baratz and Baratz (1971) found that like Hispanic students they have also been characterized as "deficient in language, social development, and intelligence...In effect, Baratz and Baratz found that the homes and backgrounds of Black children and poor children in general were classified in such research as sick, pathological, deviant, or underdeveloped" (Nieto, 1996, p. 244).

Regrettably, much of the social science literature on Hispanics and Blacks over the past century has sought to explain cultural norms and behavior via the pervasive use of such negative stereotypes and misconceptions as these. This orientation has ultimately been utilized to blame Hispanics and Blacks for their low academic aspirations and poor academic achievement at all educational levels.

Given the dismal statistics regarding Hispanic and Black attainment in education and the disparaging pronouncements made by theorists about Hispanic and Black underachievement, "the fact that some stigmatized minorities do manage to negotiate the American educational system successfully becomes a matter of consequence" (Achor & Morales, 1990, p. 269). Much research has documented the problems, barriers, and deficiencies of Hispanics and Blacks that have hindered their educational attainment. Few studies have focused on successful Hispanics and Blacks. Fewer studies have concentrated on Hispanic and Black women, and even fewer on academic success in higher education

(Wolf-Wendel, 1998; King et. al., 1996; Nieve-Squires, 1991 & 1992; Nettles, 1990; Clewell, 1987; and Achor & Morales, 1990). "This research has yielded a litany of reasons for educational failure but has produced few insights into the process of educational success" (Gandara, 1982, p. 168). One might conclude, then, that a main reason for the failure of theoreticians to understand the dynamics of educational attainment within the Hispanic and Black communities may be because of the over reliance on research that centers on underachievers and/or underachievement. Since most studies have focused on Hispanic and Black underachievers, to the exclusion of other types of students, little is known about the influences that stimulate academic achievement in Hispanics and Blacks, particularly females.

The present study

The present study investigated the dynamics of educational attainment by Hispanic American and African American women who have obtained the Ph.D. degree. A paucity of useable research studies had investigated the educational experiences of Hispanic American and African American women. Even fewer studies have examined the educational experiences of these women at postsecondary levels. Of particular concern is the apparent lack of research on Hispanic American and African American women at post-baccalaureate levels, especially doctoral education (Wolf-Wendel, 1998; King et. al., 1996; Nieves-Squires, 1991 & 1992; Del Castillo et. al., 1998; Clewell, 1987; Ortiz, 1986; Casas & Ponterotto, 1984; de los Santos et. al., 1983; Gandara, 1982; Vasquez, 1982; and Escobero, 1980).

Del Castillo et. al. (1988) has cited several reasons for this lack of useable information on the educational experiences of Hispanic American women. First, of the studies that have examined the educational experiences of Hispanic Americans, few have described or analyzed the educational condition of women.

"Scholars interested in Hispanic women are confronted with a mass of information which appears to assume that the educational process is the same for Hispanic males and females" (p. 7). Second, of the few studies that have examined Hispanic American women's educational issues, most have focused on secondary or undergraduate levels, with the exclusion of graduate and professional levels. Third, much of the research on Hispanic Americans is conceptualized from cultural deficiency model perspectives, which assume that Hispanic Americans are lower class, lack motivation, and are limited English proficient. Fourth, the Hispanic American culture has been consistently portrayed as extremely patriarchal, socializing females into submissive, passive, and maternal roles. In short, this group has been characterized as possessing negative cultural traits that account for their alleged anti-intellectual values and attitudes toward education. Fifth, aggregating data on different Hispanic American subgroups or socioeconomic levels and generalizing findings to all Hispanic Americans assumes a homogeneous population, and neglects important differences such as historical traditions, geographic location, and political alliances. Finally, there appears to be no operational theoretical framework by which to guide and explain the educational experiences of Hispanic American women.

Additionally, Nieto (1996) has stated that the deficit theories popularized in the 1960s-1970s are largely responsible for much of our current educational policy. She asserts that deficit theories also portray Black students as possessing poorly developed language skills, inadequate mothers, and too little stimulation in the home. The depictions blame students for school failure. And assume that students from culturally diverse families are genetically, culturally, and linguistically inferior to students from the dominant culture.

These studies completely overlook students who succeed in spite of overwhelmingly negative caricatures of their culture and home environments by educators and social scientists.

Therefore, a study that examined the educational success of Hispanic American and African American women who had attained the Ph.D. degree did provide crucial information on academic achievement. The effectiveness of education for Hispanic American and African American women will be improved by what we have learned about those individuals who have experienced academic success at the highest levels of the educational system.

Purpose

The purposes of this study were to examine the factors that contribute to the attainment of the Ph.D. degree by Hispanic American and African American women, to provide insights about high achieving Hispanic American and African American women that reflect contemporary values about education, to compare Hispanic American and African American women's' educational experiences across both cultures, and to further our understanding of academic achievement by learning from the women who have attained this level of academic success. In order to address these purposes a theoretical framework composed of five strands of research was constructed. This research had previously identified factors that influenced the academic achievement of traditional college students, nontraditional college students, Black college students, and successful minority students.

Framework

Salient components of each model guided the study, in order to relate aspects of these theories to the groups in question, Hispanic American and African American women Ph.D. recipients. Because of the inadequacy of previously discussed cultural deficiency models, and the absence of theoretical framework that explicitly addresses Hispanic American and African American women's' educational success more contemporary models concerning college persistence and minority student school success were adapted to the population. The research of Vincent Tinto, John Bean and associates, Alexander Astin, William Sedlacek and associates, and John Ogbu served as the guiding principles of the study. These theoretical formulations were considered pertinent because they posed factors/variables that predict academic success for different groups. The five strands reviewed here as a cogent theoretical framework did provide a solid foundation from which to conduct the study. (See Illustration A, for a breakdown of the factors/variables cited in the aforementioned literature as predictive of persistence).

Tinto's theoretical model (1975), posits that the process of interactions between the individual and the academic and social systems of the college and the individual's integration into those systems influences persistence or withdrawal. The model discusses interaction and integration as underlying contributors to persistence. (See Illustration A). And Tinto's stages of student departure (1988), separation, transition, and incorporation are premised on rites of passage rituals, whereby individuals move from one developmental stage in their lives to another. In essence, a college or university is an institution indicative of a rite of passage ritual, in that it functions in a similar manner. Individuals who pass through the various stages become incorporated into the institution. Success is predicated on the individual's capacity to become academically and socially integrated into the institution, and to detach from previous communities. (See Illustration A).

While the academic/social integration models exemplified by Tinto's emphasize the importance of social integration into the college community, nontraditional student models such as Bean's focus on factors external to the college environment. These environmental variables; finances, hours of employment, outside encouragement, family responsibilities, opportunity to transfer, and student satisfaction were found by Bean and associates (1985 & 1994) to have a significant direct effect on non traditional student persistence. (See Illustration A).

Astin's student involvement theory "refers to the quantity and quality of the physical and psychological energy that students invest in the college experience" (Astin, 1984, p. 307). The theory is based on research by Astin that investigated factors about the college experience that significantly influenced student persistence. The basic elements of the theory are place of involvement, and involvement in student government. (See Illustration A).

Sedlacek has proposed eight non-cognitive variables as predictive of persistence for Black college students (1976, 1984, 1985, & 1987). These non-cognitive variables were found to be more important than traditional academic measures in the academic success of Black students. The following non-cognitive variables were incorporated into this study: positive self-concept, understands and deals with racism, realistic self-appraisal, prefers long-range goals to short-term or immediate needs, successful leadership experience, demonstrated community service, availability of strong support person, and nontraditional knowledge. (See Illustration A).

Ogbu's theoretical approach to minority school performance is based on the presupposition that autonomous, immigrant, and caste like minorities have identifiable distinguishing features that either promote school success or school failure based on their position in a typology that he proposes. (See Illustration A).

Autonomous minorities, the first category, are typically represented in the United States by Jews and Mormons groups whose cultural frame of reference, encourages school success. Immigrants, the second group, tend to overcome their academic problems, adjust socially, and do well academically. They are represented in the United States by groups such as the Chinese and Punjabi Indians. The caste like minorities—peoples brought to the United States involuntarily, or through conquest or colonization—are represented by American Indians, African Americans, and Mexican Americans. Ogbu found that these groups usually experience more academic difficulties and school performance problems than the other minority groups (Ogbu, 1987). In light of this proposition, the present study incorporated several important concepts from Ogbu's work: acquiring standard English, adopting the folk theory of success of the dominant culture, having favorable impressions of the dominant culture's institutions, adjusting to the social environment, and exhibiting appropriate behaviors and attitudes.

Methodology

Hispanic American Sample

Originally, this was a study of fifteen women—fifteen Hispanic American women from the Southwestern United States, who provided data about the accomplishments of women who have achieved the highest level of academic success by attaining the Ph.D. from well regarded American universities between 1983 and 1995 (Garcia, 1996). They variously identified themselves as Chicana, Hispanic, Mexican, Mexican American, and Navajo/Mexican-American. Of the fifteen women, six identified themselves as Chicana, six identified themselves as Hispanic, one identified herself as Mexican, one identified herself as Mexican American, and one identified herself as Navajo/Mexican-American. The terminology that was used to identify racial/ethnic identity by the informants was varied and based on personal preference, political ideology, and historical background.

The following three quotations illustrate different explanations for the particular terminology that they used to identify themselves:

"I'm a Chicana, because I have the best, what I think, and I don't mean to ethnocentric, the best of both worlds. I am bilingual and my first language is Spanish. I grew up on the border where I assumed everyone was bilingual and bicultural...I grew up feeling very comfortable about who I was...even the White kids spoke Spanish, were bilingual, and bicultural in many ways...As I began to study the history of my people and understand my place is that I have both the Mexican side of me, which is in my blood, but I also have the Anglo side of me that has been in my socialization. I feel very comfortable in recognizing that I've got both histories—both histories are part of my history. So I am Chicana and I call myself a Chicana."

"If you ask me in Spanish what I am, I'll tell you Mexican. If you ask me in English, we usually use Hispanic. That's just something we grew up with...Some people say Chicana, that's fine, although that's one that I least prefer because it has some radical undertones, in my opinion...When I was very young it was Spanish..."

"I am half Navajo on my dad's side, and I'm half Mexican American on my mother's side. I generally identify with the Navajo more than I do the Mexican because I was raised with my dad and not my mom. Although, in the last couple of years, since I've moved, I've become a little bit more familiar with my mom. I have done a lot of work in the Hispanic community. Part of the reason that I identify as being principally Navajo is that the Hispanic community is absolutely intolerant of having dual identity, especially if it's Indian...The native American community is equally intolerant. If you're a quarter Indian and want to identify as an Indian, that is fine. You identify as an Indian, the other three-quarters of you is just not acknowledged..."

This was also a study of a small group of women who are the daughters of farm workers, sheepherders, railroad workers, laborers, clerks, mechanics, ranchers, motel maids, kitchen workers, laboratory workers, factory workers, attorneys, engineers, teachers, professors, architects, and small business owners. They grew up in lower class, middle-class, and upper-middle-class homes, but they share the common characteristic of having achieved a Ph.D. degree.

All of the participants in this study were born between 1941 and 1966. Thirteen of the fifteen women were born in the United States. They received their undergraduate/graduate educations between 1963 and 1995.

All came from families with varying degrees of education, e.g., a father who never attended school, to a father with a Ph.D.; a mother with a first grade education, to a mother with a J.D.

The two religious preferences were Catholic and Methodist, with a large majority citing Catholic as their religious affiliation while they were growing up.

They are America's new generation of Hispanic American women scholars. They are mostly social scientists and educators, with the notable exceptions of a scientist, mathematician, and a woman from literature. They are college deans, college and university professors, and university museum curators.

To summarize, the Hispanic American women Ph.D. recipients described in this study do not represent a monolithic culture. At times social scientists have attempted to portray Hispanics as if they were not a diverse group with intercultural as well as intra-cultural variability. The evidence for intra-cultural variability is demonstrated over and over again in the informants' own words.

This is a diverse group of women who mostly share a common language and religious experience, who identify themselves in multiple ways, who come from various socioeconomic backgrounds, who have parents with little to no formal education, to parents with doctorates, but who share the common experience of holding Ph.D.s.

African American Sample

This is a preliminary study of five women—five African American women who exemplify the accomplishments of African American women who have achieved the highest level of academic success by attaining the Ph.D. from well regarded American universities between 1977 and 1998 (Louque & Garcia, 1999). They variously identified themselves as African American and African American/Black. Of the five women, four identified themselves as African American and one identified herself as African American/Black. The terminology that was used to identify racial/ethnic identity by the informants was varied and based on custom, personal preference, political ideology, historical background, and ancestry.

The following three quotations illustrate different explanations for the particular terminology that they used to identify themselves:

"I use the term African American, but I also use the term Black, so I use the terms interchangeably, only because African American is a new term for us, and I have grown accustomed to using the term Black."

"Right now I use the term African American. It may change as it has for Blacks over the last 25 years. We were Coloreds, we were Negroes, we were Afro-Americans, we were Blacks, and now we're African Americans."

"I think that it is important for me and other African Americans to identify ourselves with our place of origin... So, let's make it African American."

This is also a preliminary study of a small group of women who are the daughters of Navy officers, hospital workers, factory workers, realtors, riverboat workers, and meat packers. They grew up in lower class and upper-middle-class homes, but they share the common characteristic of having achieved a Ph.D. degree.

All of the participants in this study were born between 1936 and 1957. And all of the women were born in the United States. They received their undergraduate/graduate educations between 1956 and 1998.

All came from families with varying degrees of education, e.g., a father who never attended school, to a father with some college; a mother with a 9th grade education, to mothers with high school diplomas.

The three religious preferences were Pentecostal, Baptist, and Protestant, with the largest majority citing Baptist as their religious affiliation while they were growing up.

They are America's new generation of African American women scholars. They are mostly social scientists and educators, with the exception of woman from literature. They are college and university professors and mental health specialists.

To summarize, the African American women Ph.D. recipients in this study are a diverse group of women. They exemplify a range of values and beliefs, share a common language, identify themselves as African Americans, come from lower and middle class backgrounds, have parents with little to no formal education, to parents with some college, but who share the common experience of holding Ph.D.s.

Data Collection

The criteria for including informants in this study and that are relevant to this particular discussion of Hispanic American and African American achievement are as follows:

Hispanic American

(1) Hispanic American woman – defined as having Mexican American/Mexican, Chicano/Chicana, Latino/Latina, Spanish American/Hispanic or Hispano/Hispana ancestry. Because of the variation in the terms used by Hispanic Americans currently residing in the Southwest to identify themselves, this study selected those women who designated themselves by the aforementioned terms, excluding those women of other Hispanic subgroups from the study (Gandara, 1995; Martinez, 1995; Garza, 1994; Zimmerman et.al., 1994; Aguirre & Martinez, 1993; de la Torre & Pesquera, 1993; Nieves-Squires, 1992; Deutsch, 1987; Hayes-Bautista & Chapa, 1987; Trevino, 1987).

(2) Currently residing in the States of California, Arizona, and New Mexico. Some 40% of the total Hispanic population lives in the states of California, Arizona, and New Mexico (NCLR, 1990). This study selected individuals from the available pool of Hispanic American women who have Ph.D.s and live in Southern California, Arizona, and New Mexico.

(3) Fluency in English and Spanish. Because language proficiency is a key factor in educational attainment, this study attended to that factor by selecting a group of individuals who identified themselves as English as a first language users, and a group of English as a second language users (Casas & Ponterotto, 1984).

(4) Socioeconomic status has been cited by some social scientists and educators to be correlated with academic success, the study addressed this variable by making every effort to include individuals from each of the lower, middle, and upper classes to assess the influence of SES on the attainment of the Ph.D. (Gandara, 1995; Nettles, 1990; Casa & Ponterotto, 1984; Escobero, 1980).

(5) An earned bachelor's degree and Ph.D. from a recognized college or university in the United States. In view of the fact that some college and university programs do not require a master's degree for entrance into the Ph.D. program, this study acknowledged receipt of the master's degree, but did not require it for participation in the study. As the M.D. and J.D. are professional degrees, and the Ed.D. may be both an academic or professional degree, depending on the institution and the program, this study confined itself to the Ph.D.s, in keeping with the statement of the problem.

(6) Completion of the Ph.D. within the past twenty years. A follow-back, retrospective method, as described by Gandara (1995), was used to collect data. As this was an in-depth interview study and the informants were asked to recall life events that occurred prior to the interview, this method provided a range of information, from the most current, to events that took place long before the interview.

African American

(1) African American/Black woman – is defined as having a race and/or a cultural basis by which to identify themself (Nieto, 1996).

(2) Currently residing in California. This study selected individuals from the available pool of African American women who have Ph.D.s and live in Southern California.

(3) Fluency in English and African American Language (AAL). Because language proficiency is a key factor in educational attainment, this study attended to that factor by selecting a group of individuals who identified themselves as English as a first language users, and a group of individuals who classified themselves as AAL, i.e., Ebonics or Black English users (Nieto, 1996).

(4) Socioeconomic status has been cited by some social scientists and educators to be correlated with academic success, the study addressed this variable by making every effort to include individuals from each of the lower, middle, and upper classes to assess the influence of SES on that attainment of the Ph.D. (Gandara, 1995; Nettles, 1990; Casas & Ponterotto, 1984; Escobero, 1980).

(5) An earned bachelor's degree and Ph.D. from a recognized college or university in the United States. In view of the fact that some college and university programs do not require a master's degree for entrance into the Ph.D. program, this study acknowledged receipt of the master's degree, but did not require it for participation in the study. As the M.D. and J.D. are professional degrees, and the Ed.D. may be both an academic or professional degree, depending on the institution and the program, this study confined itself to Ph.D.s, in keeping with the statement of the problem.

(6) Completion of the Ph.D. within the past twenty years. A follow-back, retrospective method, as described by Gandara (1995), was used to collect data. As this was an in-depth interview study and the informants were asked to recall life events that occurred prior to the interview, this method provided a range of information, from the most current, to events that took place long before the interview.

Selection Process

The sources for obtaining the names of potential informants included the following: (1) National listings; (2) College and university research offices; (3) Individuals who came into contact with Hispanic American and African American women scholars and professionals; (4) Women's organizations; and (5) Referrals by other informants.

An initial selection of individuals—chosen via a criterion-based selection strategy, and then other individuals located via a variation of criterion-based selection known as network selection guided the selection process.

Criterion-based selection necessitates establishing a set of preconditions that list criteria, attributes, or dimensions that the individuals in the study must possess. The investigator then searches for individuals who typify the particular characteristics of the group being studied. The research problem, questions, theoretical framework, and identification of empirical factors considered to influence the problem and questions form the basis of the set of attributes (Goetz & LeCompte, 1984). "Criterion-based selection requires only that the researcher create a recipe of the attributes essential to the selected unit and proceed to find or locate an unit that matches the recipe" (Goetz & LeCompte, 1984, p. 77).

Network selection is a variation of the criterion-based selection strategy in which successive informant is named by the preceding informant. The researcher thus collected a selection of informants on the basis of participant referrals (Goetz & LeCompte, 1984). For example, Hispanic American and African American women Ph.D. recipients possessing the attributes under investigation suggest other with similar characteristics. The process of linking based on similarity of profiles called network configuration provides access to like informants (Goetz & LeCompte, 1984).

Research Approach

The research approach that was used in this study was ethnography. "Ethnography is the work of describing culture. The essential core of this activity aims to understand another way of life from the native point of view...Rather than studying people, ethnography means learning from people" (Spradley, 1979, p. 3). The informant's frame of reference or wold view is explored and described, thereby communicating her/his cultural knowledge to the researcher.

Underlying the proposed research was the guiding assumption that the culture of the schools, and the culture of the women work interdependently to frame core values and beliefs about educational success (Del Castillo & Torres, 1988). Since cultural norms and values are being increasingly recognized as crucial for understanding educational effectiveness; it is advantageous to know how those factors interact to promote educational success. Thus, the primary research task was to provide detailed information about the linkages and processes within the culture of the schools and the culture of the women that encourages success.

In short, an ethnographic approach assessed the background characteristics, qualities, events, and experiences, which were crucial to the understanding of education success, form the informant's frame of reference, within her cultural context. Moreover, a cultural perspective permitted scholarship that was thorough, rich, and detailed in its description of the culture of the school and the culture of Hispanic American and African American women as they influence educational attainment.

Instrumentation

This study employed in-depth interviews with twenty of those individuals who met the criteria established for inclusion in the study. The purpose of the interviews was to determine the factors or variables considered most crucial in contributing to the individual's academic success. Interviews provided a way for informants to discuss the background characteristics, qualities, events, and experiences that were instrumental to their academic attainment.

The factors or variables articulated by Tinto (1975, 1988); Bean and Associates (1985, 1994); Astin (1984); Sedlacek (1976, 1984, 1985, 1987); and Ogbu (1987) as being predictive of academic success provided the basis for the construction of the interview schedule. (See Illustration A).

Data Analysis

The ten categories of variables that were identified as factors that were linked to student persistence by these aforementioned researchers; demographic characteristics, academic integration, social integration, separation, transition, incorporation, environmental variables, factors of involvement, non-cognitive variables, and classification of minority types were analyzed using Spradley's (1979) comprehensive and systematic procedure called "The Developmental Research Sequence Method," (D.R.S. Method) which provides a step-by-step approach to construction and analysis of an ethnography and was adapted to the study (p. 224-226).

The variables that emerged as the major factors contributing to the academic success of both Hispanic American and African American women with Ph.D.s and that are pertinent to the discussion regarding academic achievement were family background, grade performance, finances, outside encouragement, family responsibilities, understanding and dealing with racism (sexism), successful leadership experience, demonstrated community service, strong support person, and acquiring standard English. The factors/variables were identified as crucial to academic success by an overwhelming majority (and in some cases by all) of the informants (Garcia, 1996; Louque & Garcia, 1999).

From Tinto's work on academic integration, family background and grade performance emerged as crucial to academic achievement. Of Bean and associates' environmental variables, finances, outside encouragement, and family responsibilities were found to be important in academic success. Four of Sedlacek's non-cognitive variables—understanding and dealing with racism (sexism), successful leadership experience, demonstrated community service, and strong support person—were shown associated with these women's achievement. (The two categories of nontraditional knowledge—culturally relevant ways of obtaining information and demonstrating knowledge—were addressed by asking the informants to describe culturally specific ways that they learn and demonstrate knowledge. Although his question yielded much valuable information, a better question would have been to ask the informants not only to describe culturally specific ways that they learn and demonstrate knowledge, but to ask the influence of those factors on the attainment of the Ph.D. What may be inferred from the data about cultural knowledge is only that it appears to have had an influence on the attainment of the Ph.D. for Hispanic American and African American women). Ogbu's emphasis on acquiring (standard) English was established as a critical feature for these academically successful Hispanic American and African American women.

These particular variables are clearly related to the achievement of the Ph.D. by Hispanic American and African American women. Therefore, they are congruent with influencing Hispanic American and African American women's academic achievement.

In conclusion, this study has found that several of the factors/variables identified by the leading researchers as predictive of academic success for other types of populations were relevant to this group of Hispanic American and African American women.

Major themes/findings

The finding and their interpretation are presented in this section based on the in-depth interview data collected from high achieving Hispanic American and African American women scholars currently residing in the American Southwest. Six major themes emerged from the interviews and are as follows: cultural value system, language, academic achievement, faculty/student interaction, finances, and personal attributes.

In each of the following sections the discussion of the major themes includes selected quotations to illustrate a particular point of view, to typify similar responses, or to show diversity of responses within a theme.

Cultural Value System

Within cultural value system are the following categories: family values, family support, and family responsibilities.

Hispanic American

"Education," "Religion," "Moral imperatives," "Mother's support," "Family encouragement," and "Woman's work" forms the foundation for a cultural value system whose core beliefs about family are crucial to academic success. Family is the central theme of the cultural value system.

Family Values

When the informants were asked to describe their family's cultural value system terms like respect, traditions, hard work, fairness, religion, compassion, community, education, and deference to mother were cited consistently by the majority of the informants as forming the core family values.

The following quotations illustrate the effect of family on the attainment of the Ph.D.:

"...I would say that education has probably been the most highly valued quality in our family or attribute, if you will. Also, religion, my parents are both traditional and nontraditional Catholics...I was brought up to be much more of a thinking Catholic and be aware of Catholicism as not just ritual but also a moral imperative, care for the poor, sick, underprivileged, be aware of those less fortunate than you are. All of those moral imperatives."

"Hardworking, honest, positive, education was very important in our family. I think the work ethic was a very important on and not screwing people over...My family really valued the issue of being a good person, treating people with respect."

Family Support

The informants were asked to explain how their families felt about heir pursuit of a doctoral education. Most cited family support as including immediate and/or extended, such as support from husbands, life partners, children, mothers, fathers, siblings, and other relatives.

The following three quotations show the importance of family support in achieving the Ph.D.:

"...I had a heavy reliance on my family. My mother helped me with the babysitting. She gave me psychological and emotional support. My family gave me psychological and emotional support...I probably would have not been successful without their help."

"I got a lot of pressure from my husband. He really wanted it for me. My kids and my husband—yeah, definitely."

"I got encouragement from my family. My mother was very supportive. I don't know that she really understood everything that was entailed in the doctoral work, but she would always tell me something about—when I would get discouraged, and there were about three or four times—I was even thinking of dropping out of the program—She listened to me and told me that I was almost done, to be patient, that I could do it, and to go do my estudios. She was very supportive, and I think my family was also very supportive."

Family Responsibilities

The informants were asked to discuss the kinds of family responsibilities they had during their doctoral programs. The majority cited responsibilities such as, wife and mother, daughter, granddaughter, and caretaker for parents and in-laws, suggesting that commitment from the family and to the family in a reciprocal relationship forms the foundation from which to achieve high levels of academic success.

The following three quotations illustrate the effect of family responsibilities in the attainment of the Ph.D.:

"I take care of both of my parents now, and I did during my doctoral program... Women do the work, take care of everything, have a career and do everything else...So, I took care of my parents, my children, my husband, extended family--...my husband's mother...I tell everybody...that is my job and I darn well not forget it."

"...My responsibilities would be to my folks, visit my grandmother. I had a responsibility to her. She's an old lady. She loves me. She calls me up. She's always like a little cheerleader. I felt lots of responsibility for her, to always let her know what I was doing..."

"...My father became ill and died when I was in graduate school, as well as my mother... There was less impact when my mother died than when my father died because my stepmother needed a lot of help because she was ill for a while. I had to go and help—going to the hospital to visit and financially I had to help her during that time and after. I kind of financially supported my stepmother."

African American

"Worship," "Music," Extended family," "Nonverbal communication," "African American history and culture," "Father," "Mother," "Food," "Education," and "Strict discipline," were various descriptions of family values ascribed to African Americans by the informants and appear to be crucial to academic success. Family is a main theme of the cultural value system.

Family Values

When the informants were asked to describe their family's cultural value system terms like tradition, tied to the church, community, education, deference to mother, father, and extended family, song, dance, and body language were cited by the informants as forming the core family values.

The following quotations illustrate the effect of family on the attainment of the Ph.D.:

"...I would say that a lot of our cultural values were tied to our church values because church was such an influential part of my childhood..."

"...It was very traditional, very strict, highly authoritarian..."

Family Support

The informants were asked to explain how their families felt about heir pursuit of a doctoral education. Most cited family support as including immediate and/or extended, such as support from husbands, life partners, children, mothers, fathers, siblings, and other relatives.

The following two quotations show the importance of family support in achieving the Ph.D.:

"My mother was very, very proud. My mother was always my number one pep team, fan club. So she was extremely supportive, very proud..."

"...In my family...I've been the one of which a lot was expected...I think the success that I had was expected..."

Family Responsibilities

The informants were asked to discuss the kinds of family responsibilities they had during their doctoral programs. All five cited responsibilities such as mother suggesting that commitment from the family to the family in a reciprocal relationship forms the foundation from which to achieve high levels of academic success.

The following two quotations illustrate the effect of family responsibilities in the attainment of the Ph.D.:

"I was raising a child. When I started he was 5, when I finished, it was just before he graduated from high school."

"Normal ones related to children."

Summary

It is clear that family values, family support, and family responsibilities are very influential in attaining the Ph.D. for Hispanic American and African American women. The relationship between family values, family support, and family responsibilities forms the core cultural value system.

Language

Within the language theme are the following categories: language background, language proficiency, and acquiring (standard) English. These are the elements that form a language system that is fundamental to the academic success of Hispanic American and African American women.

Hispanic American
Language Background

For Hispanics, "language has long been thought to be the chief barrier to educational and occupational advancement...More recent research has dispelled the myth that bilingualism, or the us of Spanish in the home, is a source of Latino underachievement" (Gandara, 1995, p. 79 & 80). This particular study supports current research on this subject with the following data: For example, of the fifteen Hispanic American women in this study only 2 of the informants classified their home language as primarily English. 6 of the informants classified their home language as primarily Spanish. And 6 of the informants classified their home languages as bilingual. 1 informant classified her home languages as English, Spanish, and Navajo. Clearly, growing up in a Spanish-speaking home or bilingual home was not impediment to attaining a Ph.D. for these women.

This particular group of high achieving Hispanic American women further illuminates our current understanding of home language(s) and academic achievement by demonstrating that speaking Spanish or being bilingual did not inhibit academic attainment.

Language Proficiency

Of the fifteen informants 5 rated their proficiency in English as "excellent," 8 rated their proficiency in English as "above average," and 2 rated their proficiency in "English as "average," demonstrating that coming from a Spanish dominant background or bilingual background did not impede progress in developing English language proficiency.

Acquire Standard English

Being from a Spanish-speaking background or a bilingual background did not appear to constrain these informants from acquiring (standard) English. On the contrary, all fifteen of the informants said that acquiring (standard) English was "very important" to attaining the Ph.D.

Again, data from this study seem to provide more evidence that coming from a Spanish-speaking home or bilingual home does not hinder acquiring (standard) English.

African American
Language Background

For African Americans, being reprimanded for speaking Black English (AAL) is common practice within the schools. Powerful messages are sent that the language variety that they speak is not valued, has little prestige, and is to be silenced. Rather than use this information in teaching about the role of language and culture in society, African Americans are frequently forced to cope with the stigma attached to the language that they speak (Nieto, 1996). Evidence from this study and many others seem to support the thesis that lack of (standard) English skills is not an impediment to academic achievement. For example, of the five African American women in this study only 3 of the informants classified their home language as (standard) English. 2 of the informants cited their home language as Ebonics and Southern English. Clearly, growing up in homes where Black dialects were predominant was not a handicap to attaining a Ph.D. for these women.

Language Proficiency

All five of the informants rated their proficiency in English as "excellent," demonstrating that coming from a AAL dominant background did not hinder developing English language proficiency.

Acquire Standard English

Being from an AAL background did not constrain theses informants from acquiring (standard) English. On the contrary, all five of the informants said that acquiring (standard) English was "very important" to attaining the Ph.D.

Again, data from this study seem to provide more evidence that coming from an African American Language home does not deter individuals from acquiring (standard) English.

Summary

All of the women in this study were aware of the value of strong proficiency in English and acquiring (standard) English to achievement in academia. In addition, there is no evidence from this study that the language of the home influenced achievement in a negative way.

Academic Achievement

Within academic achievement are the following categories: academic background and culture specific ways of learning/demonstrating knowledge. Undergraduate and graduate grade point averages and nontraditional knowledge combine to form the major theme, academic achievement.

Hispanic American
Academic Background

The grade point averages range from 2.9 to 3.8 at the undergraduate level, from 3.0 to 4.0 at the master's level, and 3.5 to 4.0 at the doctoral level for this group of women. Obviously, these grade point averages reflect a high level of academic achievement all levels for all informants, providing data about the influence of high grade point averages on academic achievement for Hispanic American women.

Cultural Knowledge

The following culturally specific characteristics were identified by the informants as crucial to leaning: "self-discipline," "sense of duty," "thinking in Spanish," "watching very carefully," "following examples," "seeing interrelationships," "looking for all the possibilities," "thinking in a circular manner," and "taking initiative."

In addition, the following culturally specific ways of demonstrating knowledge were noted by the informants as equally important for shaping their cultural knowledge systems: "recognizing the connection between language and culture," "modeling behavior and treatment of others," "caring for others," "story telling," "interaction and communication style," "speaking and writing Spanish," "cultural/world view," and "sharing the old traditions."

The following three quotations exemplify the informants rich descriptions of cultural knowledge:

"I mentioned the whole thing of oral tradition. A lot of the ways that I know I communicate, and I'm sure the way that I learned is something that's unique or specific to Hispanic culture, where everything is explained through example...like dichos and cuentos,... a lot of it is done orally."

"I think that I tend--...I use more examples that might appear to be story-like...They like that in New Mexico—It seems like the student in New Mexico like that..."

"I think that people have commented in my teaching particularly that I have personalismo, I have a tendency to use personal examples and funny stories. Sometimes it irritates the Anglos, but I think it draws in the people of color in my classes. I think it's a culture specific way of being. I think my understanding of the culture is actually quite critical to my entire research on. I think it's because I know what I mean in our culture that helps me actually, and informs my research in ways that few other people in the field can really grasp."

African American
Academic Background

The grade point averages range from 3.0 to 3.9 at the undergraduate level, from 3.0 to 3.9 at the master's level, and 3.0 to 3.9 at the doctoral level for this group of women. Obviously, these grade point averages reflect a high level of academic achievement at all levels for all informant, providing data about the influence of high grade point averages on academic achievement for African American women.

Cultural Knowledge

The following culturally specific characteristics were identified by the informants as crucial to leaning: "music," "songs," "education," "extended family," "mother," "African American organizations," and "family."

In addition, the following culturally specific ways of demonstrating knowledge were noted by the informants as equally important for shaping their cultural knowledge systems: "talk, act, dance and sing things out," "African American history and culture," "speaking to African American experience," and "communicating through body language."

The following two quotations exemplify the informant rich descriptions of cultural knowledge:

"...I think that...because African Americans tend to be expressive, not all, but many, that giving African American children the opportunity to talk things out, act things out, sing things out, and dance things out, are important to their education...and those kids would learn information quicker through those vehicles of presentation versus just a straight lecture or textbook."

"...Education was very highly valued by my mother, who had been a country school teacher...she prized education very highly, and everyone was supportive of me getting an education...my family was always very supportive of that."

Summary

The informants' perceptions about the influence of their cultural knowledge systems on leaning overwhelmingly supports the contention that family, language, and culture are sources of strength, rather than the so-called "cultural deficits, language deficits, learning deficits, knowledge deficits, and academic deficits" that have been historically associated with Hispanic American and African American education. These results offer new hope that we can move beyond "deficit model thinking" to a more enlightened view that emphasizes a cultural knowledge perspective that is so powerful as to overcome the most racist, sexist, impoverished, and adversarial educational experience.

Faculty/student Interaction

Within faculty/student interaction are the following categories: male/female relationships and gender/racial discrimination. The informant's responses to questions regarding their relationships with male Hispanic and Black faculty are emphasized, and their experiences with gender/racial discrimination form the major theme faculty/student interaction.

Hispanic American

While 9 of 15 informants had male Hispanic professors, variously identified as Chicano, Hispanic, and Latino, 5 of the informants experienced negative behaviors and attitudes that ranged from ignoring the informant, and humiliating the informant, to overt displays of gender discrimination. Four of the informants had positive experiences with their mail Hispanic professors.

The data on this theme are mixed. Male Hispanic professors are portrayed as supportive and kind, gentle yet firm, providing guidance, helpful, approachable, patient, and politically astute. Yet, they are also graphically describes as "sleazebags," men who do not take women seriously, men who behave unprofessionally, men who sleep with women students, men who are prejudiced against women, men who are just not helpful, and men who humiliate women.

The data are compelling, yet troubling. More in-depth interviews with other Hispanic American women scholars on this particular issue could provide additional evidence as to the gravity of the problem, and appropriate ways to address the very serious allegations that were made by five of nine informants in this study who had contact with Hispanic male professors.

Other noteworthy data about faulty/student interactions are that only two of the fifteen informants reported not having experienced racial and/or gender discrimination during their doctoral programs.

African American

While 3 of the 5 informants had Black professors; informants' experiences ranged from somewhat negative attitudes towards them to positive feelings about their relationships with their professors. For example, comments ranged from "did not remember much about him/her," "liked him," "not wowed by anyone," "not the best teacher," and "not a scholar."

The data on this theme are mixed. Although, Black professors are portrayed in a somewhat negative way, more in-depth interviews with other African American women scholars on this particular issue could provide additional evidence as to the role that African American professors played in their academic lives.

Other noteworthy data about faculty/student interactions are that only two of the five informants reported not having experienced racial and/or gender discrimination during their doctoral programs.

Summary

A pattern of racial/gender discrimination has been established in that sixteen of twenty informants experienced varying degrees of such discrimination in their doctoral programs. Some subtle, some overt, yet all of it transcended, as evidence by their academic achievements.

Finances

Within finances are the following categories: financial aid and the effects of financial problems. Informants were asked questions regarding the influence of financial aid on achieving the Ph.D. and if they ever considered dropping out of their doctoral programs because of financial problems. Their statements about financial matters became the basis for the major theme, finances.

Hispanic American

Financial aid was identified as instrumental to attaining the Ph.D. by 14 of 15 informants. 14 informants reported receiving fellowships of various types; scholarships, tuition waivers, grants, loans, stipends, teaching, research, or graduate assistantships, Title III funds, and Title VII funds.

Only three of the informants ever seriously considered dropping out of their doctoral programs because of financial problems, and of the three, one was the informant who was not receiving any financial aid. Obviously all managed to overcome financial adversity to attain the Ph.D.

African American

Financial aid was identified as instrumental to attaining the Ph.D. by 3 of 5 informants. All of informants reported receiving various types of fellowships, grants, loans, and stipends.

Only two of the informants ever seriously considered dropped out of their doctoral programs because of financial problems.

Summary

These data overwhelming support the influence of financial aid in the achievement of the Ph.D. for Hispanic American and African American women.

Personal Attributes

Within personal attributes are the following categories: leadership and personal theory of success. Defining leadership qualities and theory of success combine to form the major theme personal attributes.

Hispanic American

Leadership

When asked about leadership, informants cited a number of specific factors that they felt defined leadership for them and that were attributes that they themselves possessed. Among the list of lengthy responses were strength, survival skills, visibility, political involvement, vision, social justice, being bilingual, willing to take an unpopular position, strong convictions, community involvement, taking responsibility, caring about others, empathy, teaching, understanding how to work with others, and trust. Most of these qualities were highly individualistic and were seldom mentioned by more than two of the informants.

Personal Theory of Success

When the informants were asked to articulate their personal theory of success and its relationship to academic success, most emphasize the importance of family and/or community as crucial factors in their personal success and/or academic success:

The following three quotations vividly describe their feelings about personal success and academic success:

"My definition of success is being involved in teaching classes and doing research that's relevant to making a difference in the community because if it's not something that's going to do anything for women or people of color, why get involved...?"

"I suppose that I would use success in very personal terms, not necessarily monetary or material terms...I think that I view success in terms of being loved and loving others, having friends, doing something that you feel is important to you and important for other people—that makes a difference in the world."

"As far as success, I'm very conscious about not being a brown statistic. I like to show mainstream America that Chicanos/Chicanas can do well at their game. I love to see the look on their faces. That's also gratification that I get...That is fuel for my fire...because there is so much work to be done for the community."

Two additional distinctive comments are valuable because they offer a different kind of insight on the idea of success. The informants make special note of the fact that personal success has nothing to do with academia.

"My personal theory of success would be to be a good person, a contributing person to society, and having raised good healthy children, to be productive however you want to define productive. However you want to define good. Somebody who gives back to the community a little bit of what they have taken. That's my idea of success, which has nothing to do with academe."

"...I think success for me has increasingly become whether or not I can have a reasonable family life...I think for a lot of people in academe, the typical Anglo American might be something to do with success in their careers. That's not my primary agenda. I like the work that I do, but it's not the main focus of my life. I don't believe it ever really has been...It's whether or not I can raise my child and be there for my mother."

African American
Leadership

When asked about leadership, informants cited a number of specific factors that they felt defined leadership for them and that were attributes that they themselves possessed. Among the list of responses were not being a follower, being driven by a goal, working for the good of others, healthy vision, acquiring resources, put ideas into practice, convince others to do things, passion, sense of own power, self-directed, working toward a mission, mentoring, making a difference, inspiring courage, community leadership, and writing a book. Most of these qualities were highly individualistic and were seldom mention by more than one of the informants.

Personal Theory of Success

When the informants were asked to state their personal theory of success and its relationship to academic success, most focused on the importance of family and/or community as crucial factors in their personal success and/or academic success:

The following two quotations vividly describe their feelings about personal success and academic success:

"...One who has used talent, the resources, the opportunities that are available to improve the quality of his/her life and the lives of less fortunate individuals."

"...Someone who engages in some type of decision-making about where they want to be in life and what kind of contribution that they want to make to the social-political entity for which they are a part..."

What is of consequence about these data are that success is indelibly linked to family and community. Once again family values, family support, and family responsibilities, the essential components of the cultural value system, are the salient factors in achieving personal and/or academic success for Hispanic American and African American women.

Summary

The personal attributes that influenced the attainment of the Ph.D. for Hispanic American and African American women in this study were their leadership traits and personal theory of success.

With respect to leadership and by a large margin the informants believed that they were leaders and that they possessed the qualities that have traditionally been associated with leadership. Additionally, several other qualities were stated by the women to be indicative of leadership such as: survival skills, political involvement, pursuit of social justice, being bilingual, passion, mentoring, and inspiring courage, characteristics generally not found on a typical list of leadership traits.

Finally, when the informants were asked to articulate their views on personal and academic success, they overwhelmingly identified family and community involvement as way to assess not only their personal and academic success, but self-worth.

Summary and Conclusions

First, the profile that emerges of these high achieving Hispanic American and African American women is one characterized by a cultural value system that believes in education. For the most part, especially the mothers of the informants were influential in cultivating and sustaining their support for education all through their daughter's lives. Family support was mentioned over and over by the informants as crucial to the attainment of the Ph.D. That support may have come form loving husbands or life partners, mothers, fathers, sisters, brothers, grandmothers, grandfathers, aunts, uncles, cousins, or their children. Whatever the specific case may have been, all experienced some sort of family support. But this was a reciprocal relationship; the expectations for a daughter, wife/partner, mother, or caretaker were never relinquished for the informant because she was in school. The family held very high expectations for her fulfilling her family responsibility at whatever her age. Second, Hispanic American women came from overwhelmingly Spanish dominant homes or bilingual homes. And of the African American women two of the informants came from African American Language (AAL) homes. Although a multitude of research studies have correlated Spanish usage in the home and Black dialect with achievement, more recent studies, (including this one) would argue that being bilingual or speaking Black English is not a "deficiency" to be overcome but indeed might be advantageous, for example in increasing cognitive and linguistic abilities in both languages. Third, these women excelled academically, as evidenced by their undergraduate and graduate records. Finally, personal and educational success is intimately connected to family and community value systems.

Thus, the portrait that emerges of the Hispanic American and African American woman with a Ph.D. is that she is an individual who has a positive and strong sense of ethnic identity, that she is family and community oriented, that being from Spanish dominant, bilingual, or Black English home was not detrimental to her cognitive and linguistic abilities, that she grew up in lower-class, middle-class, and upper-class families, that she was an outstanding student in undergraduate and graduate school, and that success is measured by what "we can give back to our community and to our society and to our world" (Garcia, 1996, p. 90).

This profile, along with other contemporary reconceptualizations of ethnicity and ethnic identity inform a paradigm shift that seems to be emerging from cultural anthropology, various ethnic minority scholars, and critical cultural theorists, and does contain "some of the best critiques of poverty/deficit thinking" (Foley, 1997, p. 122). "Presently, many behavioral and social scientists hold the deficit thinking model in disrepute – arguing that it is unduly simplistic, lacks empirical verification, more ideological than productive educational prescriptions for school success" (Valencia, 1997, p. 2).

Consequently, proponents of cultural deficiency models who argue that the cultural value systems of Hispanic Americans and African Americans are characterized by low aspirations, low levels of motivation, and "psychological characteristics that inhibit their achievement and produce behavioral deficiencies..." (Baca-Zinn, 1989, p. 857) and continue to posit language, culture, family background, parental values and attitudes as instrumental to Hispanic and Black social, educational, and economic immobility simply seem to ignore the new empirical studies, paradigms of culture, empowerment and school success theories in favor of these racist, classist, and sexist theories that portray women of color in a pathological fashion (Valencia, 1997; Del Castillo & Torres, 1988).

Illustration A

The following list summarizes the factors (or variables) cited by these scholars as predictive of academic success.

Tinto's Integration Variables

Academic Integration	Social Integration
Family background	Informal peer group
	Associations
Grade performance	Extracurricular activities
Pre-college schooling	Friendship

Tinto's Stages of Student Persistence/Departure

Separation

Disassociate from membership in past communities

Parting from past habits and patterns of affiliation

Transition

Passage between the old and new

Passage between the associations of the past and hoped for associations with communities of the present

Adjusting to the social and intellectual life of the college

Incorporation

Passage through the stages of separation and transition

Integration into the college community

Adopting norms appropriate to the new college setting

Establishing competent membership in the social and intellectual communities of college life

Bean and Associates

Nontraditional   Undergraduate   Student   Attrition/Persistence
Variables

   Environmental Variables

   Finances

   Hours of employment

   Outside encouragement

   Family responsibilities

   Opportunity to transfer

   Student satisfaction

Astin's Factors of Involvement

   Place of residence

   Honors program

   Student-Faculty interaction

   Athletic involvement

   Involvement in student government

Sedlacek's Noncognitive Variables

   Positive self-concept

   Understands and deals with racism

   Realistic self-appraisal

   Prefers long-range goals to short term or immediate needs

   Successful leadership experience

   Demonstrated community service

   Availability of strong support person

   Nontraditional knowledge

Ogbu's Classification of Successful Minority Types

Autonomous Minorities & Immigrant Minorities

>Acquire (standard) English
>
>Adopt the folk theory of success of the dominant culture
>
>Have favorable impressions of the dominant culture's institutions
>
>Adjust to the social environment
>
>Exhibit appropriate behaviors and attitudes

REFERENCES

Achor, S., & Morales, A. (1990). Chicanas holding doctoral degrees: Social reproduction and cultural ecological approaches. Anthropology & Education Quarterly, 21, 269-287.

Aguirre, A. Jr., & Martinez, R. O. (1993). Chicanos in higher education: Issues and dilemmas for the 21st century (Report No. 3.) Washington, D. C.: The George Washington University School of Education and Human Development. (ERIC Document Reproduction Service No. ED 365 207).

Almanac. (1998, August, 28). The Chronicle of Higher Education, 26 & 30.

Astin, A. W. (1984). Student involvement: A developmental theory for higher education. Journal of College Student Personnel, 25, 297-308.

Baca-Zinn, M. (1989). Family, race, and poverty in the eighties. Signs: Journal of Women in Culture and Society, 14, 856-874.

Banks, J. A. (1988). Multiethnic education: Theory and practice. Boston, MA: Allyn and Bacon, Inc.

Bean, J. P., & Metzner, B. S. (1985). A conceptual model of nontraditional undergraduate student attrition. Review of Educational Research, 55, 485-540.

Bean, J. P., & Vesper, N. (1994). Gender differences in college student satisfaction. Tucson, AZ.: University of Arizona. (ERIC Document Reproduction Service No. ED 375 728)

Casas, J. M., & Ponterotto, J. G. (1984). Profiling an invisible minority in higher education: The Chicana . The Personnel & Guidance Journal, 62, 349-353.

Clewell, B. C. (1987). Retention of Black and Hispanic doctoral students (Report No. 83-4R.) Princeton, NJ: Educational Testing Service.

de la Torre, A., & Pesquera, B. M. (Eds.). (1993). Building with our hands: New directions in Chicana studies. Berkeley and Los Angeles, CA: University of California Press.

de los Santos, A. G. Jr., Montemayor, J., & Solis, E. Jr. (1983). Chicano students in institutions of higher education: Access, attrition, and achievement. Aztlan, 14, 79-110.

Del Castillo, A. R., Frederickson, J., McKenna, T., & Ortiz, F. I. (1988). An assessment of the status of the education of Hispanic American women. In T. McKenna & F. I. Ortiz (Eds.), The broken web: The educational experience of Hispanic American women (pp. 3-24). Encino, CA: Floricanto Press.

Del Castillo, A. R. & Torres, M. (1988). The interdependency of educational institutions and cultural norms: The Hispana experience. In T. McKenna & F. I. Ortiz (Eds.), The broken web: The educational experience of Hispanic American women (pp. 39-60). Encino, CA: Floricanto Press.

412

Deutsch, S. (1987). No separate refuge: Culture, class, and gender on the Anglo-Hispanic frontier in the American Southwest, 1880-1940. New York, NY: Oxford University Press, Inc.

Escobero, T. H. (1980). Are Hispanic women in higher education the nonexistent minority? Educational Researcher, 9, 7-12.

Foley, D. E. (1997). Deficit thinking models based on culture: The anthropological protest. In R. Valencia (Ed.), The evolution of deficit thinking: Educational thought and practice (pp. 113-131). London: The Falmer Press.

Gandara, P. (1982). Passing through the eye of the needle: High-achieving Chicanas. Hispanic Journal of Behavioral Sciences, 4, 167-179.

Gandara, P. (1995). Over the ivy walls: The educational mobility of low-income Chicanos. Albany, NY: State University of New York Press.

Garcia, H. M. (1996). Factors influencing academic attainment for Hispanic-American women Ph.D. recipients. Unpublished Doctoral Dissertation, University of Arizona, Tucson.

Garza, H. (1994). Latinas: Hispanic women in the United States. New York, NY: Franklin Watts.

Goetz, J. P., & LeCompte, M. D. (1984). Ethnography and qualitative design in educational research. Orlando, FL: Academic Press, Inc.

Hayes-Bautista, D. E., & Chapa, J. (1987). Latino terminology: Conceptual bases for standardized terminology. American Journal of Public Health, 77, 61-68.

King, S., Chepyator-Thomson, & Jepkorir, R. (1996). Factors affecting the enrollment and persistence of African-American doctoral students. The Physical Educator, 53, 170-180.

Louque, A. & Garcia, H. M. (1999). Profile of African-American women Ph.D. recipients: A case study approach. Manuscript in preparation.

Martinez, E. (1995). In pursuit of Latina liberation. Signs: Journal of Women in Culture and Society, 20, 1019-1028.

National Council of La Raza. (1990). Hispanic education: A statistical portrait 1990. Washington, DC: Office of Research, Advocacy, and Legislation.

Nettles, M. T. (1990). Success in doctoral programs: Experiences of minority and White students. American Journal of Education, 98, 494-522.

Nieto, S. (1996). Affirming diversity: The sociopolitical context of multicultural education. White Plains, NY: Longman Publishers.

Nieves-Squires, S. (1991). Hispanic women: Making their presence on campus less tenuous. Washington, DC: Association of American Colleges.

Nieves-Squries, S. (1992). Hispanic women in the U. S. academic context. In L. B. Welch (Ed.), Perspectives on minority women in higher education (pp. 71-92). New York, NY: Praeger Publishers.

Ogbu, J. U. (1987). Variability in minority school performance: A problem in search of an explanation. Anthropology & Education Quarterly, 18, 312-334.

Ortiz, F. I. (1986). Hispanic American women in higher education: A consideration of the socialization process. Aztlan, 17, 125-152.

Sedlacek, W. E., & Brooks, G. C. Jr. (1976). Racism in American education: A model for change. Chicago, IL: Nelson-Hall.

Spradley, J. P. (1979). The ethnographic interview. Orlando, FL: Holt, Rinehart and Winston, Inc.

Tinto, V. (1975). Dropout from higher education: A theoretical synthesis of recent research. Review of Educational Research, 45, 89-125.

Tinto, V. (1988). Stages of student departure: Reflections on the longitudinal character of student leaving. Journal of Higher Education, 59, 438-455.

Tracey, T. J., & Sedlacek, W. E. (1984). Noncognitive variables in predicting academic success by race. Measurement and Evaluation in Guidance, 16, 171-178.

Tracey, T. J., & Sedlacek, W. E. (1985). The relationship of noncognitive variables to academic success: A longitudinal comparison by race. Journal of College Student Personnel, 26, 405-410.

Tracey, T. J., & Sedlacek, W. E. (1987). Prediction of college graduation using noncognitive variables by race. Measurement and Evaluation in Counseling and Development, 19, 177-184.

Trevino, F. M. (1987). Standardized terminology for Hispanic populations. American Journal of Public Health, 77, 69-72.

Valencia, R. R. (Ed.) (1997). The evolution of deficit thinking: Educational thought and practice. London: The Falmer Press.

Vasquez, M. J. T. (1982). Confronting barriers to the participation of Mexican American women in higher education. Hispanic Journal of Behavior Sciences, 4, 147-165.

Wolf-Wendel, L. (1998). Models of excellence: the baccalaureate origins of successful European American women, African American women, and Latinas. The Journal of Higher Education, 69, 141-186.

Zimmerman, P. S., Vega, W. A., Gil, A. G., Warheit, G. J., Apospori, E., & Biafora, F. (1994). Who is Hispanic? Definitions and their consequences. American Journal of Public Health, 84, 1985-1987.

Chapter 25

The Dilemma of Diversity

Blanche Jackson Glimps, Ph.D.
Kentucky Christian College
Grayson, KY

Theron Ford, Ph.D.
The Ohio State University
Columbus, OH

Cultural diversity, or multiculturalism, as it is sometimes called, is a process designed to promote awareness, understanding and appreciation among people of various cultures. Multiculturalism in less than three decades has become a word immediately recognized by policy makers, social commentators, academic and the general public in certain countries (Multiculturalism: A Policy Response to Diversity, 1995). However, there is currently a backlash against multicultural education (Limerick, 1994; Siegel, 1991; Chavez, 1996; Famularo, 1996; Whitfield, 1996;). The topic of diversity frightens colleges and university administrator and many would like the issue to go away (Levine, 1991).

Education for diversity is perhaps one of the most misunderstood educational concepts in recent times. Is it truly such a difficult concept to comprehend or is it that the potential for powerful systemic change, which is at the core of the concept, is understood too well and is therefore, feared and rejected? Students and educators alike sometimes embrace and quote diversity at national holidays and participate in the consumption of traditional dishes from exotic nations. They rarely know that they have merely taken one small step on a journey that literally requires circumnavigation of the planet while viewing it through critical lens.

What is needed is a clear articulation of the goals of diversity education prior to any discourse purporting to tell why it should or should not be embraced and canonized. Gotfredson, Murray, Nettles, and McHugh (1992) identify major themes of multicultural education to include presenting a balanced view of history, matching instruction with children's learning styles, equalizing learning opportunities for all children, promoting multicultural ideals and inter-group respect. Miller-Lachmann and Taylor (1995) translate theses themes into the following goals: change in the total school environment to create a climate that appreciate diversity, change in the curriculum making it more inclusive and relevant, use of instructional approaches that reflect the unique needs of students, changes in the values that schools promote, and greater diversity among educational personnel including teachers, administrators, and staff.

These goals are straightforward and theoretical and should not be seen as threatening to any constituency. After all, this is America, a nation that expounds its virtue when it comes to democracy and equality. In reality, however, goals two and five are actually extremely threatening to our very continuance of the American social structure as it exists today. These two goals would move school systems away from the current curriculum with its extensive focus on European ideology and require systems to staff schools with personnel that reflect our diverse society.

Ours is a social structure premised upon "white" supremacy. Thus, this paper posits that it is exactly because the potential of multicultural education is understood so extremely well, that critics have been so virulent in their attacks and have successfully perverted the resulting discourse.

In the eye of the critics, the only beneficiaries of multicultural education would be persons of color generally, and African Americans specifically. Many European Americans hold that perception in large part because of their relationship with African Americans. It is at once intimate, alien and long standing, stretching back since the nation's inception. Thus the perception of multicultural education is linked almost exclusively with African American issues. It is somehow "a Black thing."

But how did that happen? It certainly was not by accident. There was a systematic course of attack that sought to slur and destroy this movement. Any movement that seeks to create a society that has equity in the balance of power and resources would be viewed as radical, revolutionary and dangerous. Indeed, that is exactly how the British government viewed the upstart American colonies' demand for equity within the context of taxation and voting rights. Flash forward some 200 hundred years and you find another group of revolutionary thinkers who, if their movement is successful, would topple another unjust society that is also founded upon the principle of inequity much as the colonial British was.

Multicultural education is a danger to many because it would make level fields of economic opportunity, expand the cannons within the educational sphere and impact the political realm. Multicultural education would strip European Americans of the power and privilege that accrue not meritoriously, but merely because of skin color.

Perhaps the most powerful and frightening aspect of multicultural education is that it would achieve its goals, not through armed conflict of revolutionary war, but throughout the enlightening experience of an education process that re-examines the cannon (Howe, 1991; Hughes, 1992), critiques the teaching process (Nelson, 1996) and asks that educators themselves explore their own curricular limitations.

Critics like Ravitch and Schelessing respond simply and directly. They linked multicultural education to the Afrocentrism movement and attacked vehemently. In effect, the linkage is most efficient, as it would kill two birds with one stone. The ridicule that has been heaped upon Afrocentric education has at its core a deeply held racism that spills freely on to multicultural education.

Two separate and distinct movements with different goals are conflated. Perhaps the commonality between Afrocentrism and Multiculturalism is that both seek to expand the traditional cannon and the worldview. Moreover, both Afrocentrism and Multiculturalism have witnessed the emergence of powerful, skilled intellectual African American writers such as Asant, Banks, and Grant.

Any movement in American that is not led or cooped by European American is viewed with suspicion and assured that major attempts will be made to discredit or marginalize it. Thus the need and the convenience of attacking multicultural education and the Afrocentric movement have created the current discourse parameters. Critics say that Afrocentricity merely replaced one hegemony with another (Dyson, 1992; Hunges, 1992) Many, who consider themselves Afrocentric, according to critics, often don't have much knowledge of African culture and place a distorted emphasis on Egypt. In order for a clear image and meaningful discourse on multicultural education, the two movements must be disaggregated and each viewed within the context of its own theoretical frame.

Opponents of multiculturalism fear the lost of unity in the country as a result of the emphasis on differences (Miller-Lachmann and Taylor, 1995). A tour of K-12 schools, institutions of higher education, and local communities in this country emphasizes that unity has a negligible appearance. Such a tour would reveal pockets of separation, in urban and suburban areas, based on ethnicity and income levels that begs the question of the existence of national unity. The executive office of this country has never had a president who was not a male and from European ancestry. Such a fact does not reflect representativeness. When unity does not exist, it cannot be lost.

There is a certain lack of seriousness in the way multiculturalism is being taught. Whereas it's assumed that faculty have had some formal education in Shakespeare before they teach it, people are teaching texts from other ethnic and national groups without any understanding of the histories and cultures which inform them. Related to this is the problem of professional development, or the retooling of teachers so that their own outlook is more multicultural. The resistance to this may be political on the one hand, but it also has to do with languorousness. There is an enormous amount of new material to read and a lot of people just don't want to read it. Some professors don't read that much after finishing their dissertations.

There is a lot of exhaustion among the people who are "doing" multiculturalism, especially those who are doing it on top of their traditional teaching load, because they are being called on to participate in conferences, write and edit books and papers, and do a lot of mentoring and informal consulting. This responsibility of promoting multiculturalism is obviously not being shared equally.

There are almost as many definitions of multiculturalism as there are multiculturalists. But, nearly all agree on three things. First, multiculturalism would be characterized by tremendous diversity. Second, it would-must-include a commitment to economic justice. And, third, it would encourage European Americans to define themselves as something other than just "white" (New Options, 1990).

The goal of multiculturalism is to prepare us all for a wider world—without the haughty stance of political correctness (Ehrenreich, 1991). The real issue on campus and in the classroom is not whether there will be multiculturalism, but what kind of multiculturalism there will be. Two versions presently compete for dominance in the teaching of American culture. One approach reflects culturalism and accepts diversity as a fact; the other represents particularism and demands loyalty to a particular group. The two coexist uncomfortably, because they are opposite in spirit and purpose. The pluralist approach to American culture recognizes that the common culture is shaped by the interaction of the nation's many diverse cultural elements. It sees American culture as the creation of many groups of immigrants, American Indians, Africans, and their descendants. The particularist approach to American culture can be seen most vividly in ethnic studies programs whose goal is to "raise the self-esteem" of students by providing role models to attach their students to their ancestral homelands as a source of their personal identity and authentic culture (Ravitch, 1990).

Multiculturalism is often defined in terms of what it is not or as a corrective reaction to Eurocentric bias; but also to ethnocentrism, Afrocentrism, monoculturalism, and any kind of particularism.

Americans know that the Declaration of Independence gives grounding to equality. But, Americans are not identical. Individually and as groupings, Americans bring distinct values, morals, and customs. In an interdependent world, whether it is on the campus, or in civic or religious communities, such variety greatly enhances the quality of life. There is recognition that as others' ways of living are learned, individuals come to appreciate their own and others' culture at deeper levels. There is no longer "one right answer." A giant leap is made from perhaps intolerance to tolerance and often to appreciation and affirmation. Such expansion of our cultural horizons leads to a new sense of freedom and to new ways of living.

The major responsibility of schooling in the United States is to prepare students for effective participation in our American society and the global community. Such education includes a thorough understanding of the history of the people of the world, geography, the humanities, and America's history, including the language of the Constitution and the Bill of Rights as the foundations for cultural diversity. Schools must simultaneously honor diversity, while building democracy. Schools must assist future generations of students in creating a more just society.

How does this translate into an action agenda for higher education institutions? Daniel Yankelovich's firm conducted the first-ever national poll on diversity in higher education for the Ford Foundation's Campus Diversity Initiative (Campus Diversity Initiative, 1998). Results indicated that two in three Americans feel it is very important that colleges and universities prepare people to function in a diverse society. Fifty-five percent feel that every college student should have to study different cultures in order to graduate. Seventy-one percent feel that diversity education on college and university campuses helps bring society together. Ninety-one percent feel that because our society is multi-cultural, the more Americans know about each other, the better they will get along.

Across the curriculum diversity is an approach that has the potential for facilitating the acquisition of skills in diversity. Such an approach could integrate the disciplines to allow the student and faculty to have a basic knowledge of how it all fits into the "big picture." Because of the approach it builds confidence in students to go on to higher leveled courses and other disciplines thus assisting retention efforts. When students graduate, who have been exposed to diversity across the curriculum, they have an advantage over other students because they can effectively interact with members of other cultures and thus assume leadership roles and be more marketable. Diversity across the curriculum would attract those individuals committed to a diverse world and who are capable of being socially conscious and active.

The metaphor of the melting pot is no longer functional. Students challenge this assimilationist model. Students seek acknowledgement through campus programming and curriculum that there are multiple cultural traditions in this country that all have value (Schneider, 1997). A true learning environment is diverse, integrating people of various ethnic, political, geographic, and philosophical backgrounds into the university community. To achieve this learning environment, colleges must internationalize the curriculum and attract a representative cross-section of our society as students, faculty, staff members, and administrators.

The results of diversity education have enormous implications for meaning in the United States. Each day we send students to their fields of professional preparation without the necessary self-knowledge and skills to achieve "otherness." We assume that by immersing them in the diverse cultures of the workplace, they will be able to build the intercultural bridges necessary to understand and work effectively in structuring an environment rich with diversity in which they will succeed.

We must give students the necessary skills to facilitate cultural understanding. Johnson (1999) suggests that colleges establish a goal of enabling all students to see how they and their nation are linked to others in dynamically changing contemporary global context. With such a goal, courses would be established that focus on world systems and global issues. The primary goal of globalizing the curriculum is to enlarge one's sense of humanity, enhance the understanding of different cultures, sharpen critical perspective, and change the way one thinks (Bullock, 1999)." Culture is not limited to the West, or Europe or a white skin or Christianity. Culture, in its truest sense is the expression of the personality of a people" (Jewell, 1993).

REFERENCES

Americans see many benefits to diversity in higher education, finds first-ever national poll on topic. (1998, October 6). *Campus Diversity Initiative* [Online]. Available: http://www.inform.umd.edu/diversityweb/RLL/polirelease.html.

Chavez, Linda. (1996, May 1). Multiculturalism is driving us apart. *USA Today Magazine 39*, 124.

Dyson, Michae. (1992, February). Melanin madness: A struggle for the black mind. *Emerge*, 32-37.

Famularo, Thomas. (   ). The intellectual bankruptcy of multiculturalism. *USA Today Magazine*.

Howe, Irving. (1991, February 18). The value of the canon. *The New Republic*, 40-47.

Hughes, Robert. (1992, February 3). The fraying of America. *Time* , 44-49.

Jewell, Terri. (1995). *The black woman's gumbo ya-ya* Freedom, California: The Crossing Press.

Johnson, Joseph. (1999, Winter). Missing the Peer big picture: General education and global system of interdependence. *AACU Review, 1*, 3-5.

Levine, Arthur. (1991, September/October). The meaning of diversity. *Change*, 4-5.

Limerick, Patricia. (1994, May 4). Some advice to liberals on coping with their conservative critics. *The Chronicles of Higher Education*, B1-B2.

Multiculturalism: A policy response to diversity. (   ). [Online]. Available: http://www.unesco.org./most/sydpaper.htm.

Nelson, Craig. (1996, November/December). Student diversity requires different approaches to college teaching, even in math and science. *American Behavioral Scientist*, 40, 165-175.

Ravitch, Diane. (1990, October 24). *Chronicles of Higher Education*.

Schneider, Carol. (1997). Whatever happened to the goal of integration? *Diversity Digest* [Online]. Available:
http://www.inform.umd.edu:8080/DiversityWeb/Digest/Sm97/integration.html

Siegel, Fred. (1991, February 18). The cult of multiculturalism. *The New Republic*, 34-40.

Whitfield, Stephen(1996, June 1). The mystique of multiculturalism. *Virginia Quarterly Review*, 72, 429.

Chapter 26

A rationale for multiculturalism and diversity in collegiate education: How the debate is framed and why it continues to be controversial

<u>An Abstract</u>

Blanche Jackson Glimps, Ph.D.,
Kentucky Christian College
Grayson, KY

Theron Ford, Ph.D.
The Ohio State University
Columbus, OH

There is a mistaken assumption among many educators and the general public that a focus on, "diversity" will in and of itself reduce the national crisis of hate crimes and lead to a "kinder, gentler nation." It is time that we approached the issue of the world's perception of "America" and Americans. Such an effort requires that we step outside of our narrowly defined social and cultural borders and begin to view the world through the eyes of the "other." This will prove a difficult, yet fulfilling experience, if we have the will to confront ourselves, our values, and our prejudices. Once that is undertaken, then we can begin to truly reconstruct this nation as one that is culturally diverse as it strives in earnest to be genuinely multicultural. We can then more effectively prepare students to live harmoniously and productively in a multi-class, multi-ethnic, multi-cultural, multinational world.

There is a mistaken assumption among many educators and the general public that a focus on, "diversity" will in and of itself reduce the national crisis of hate crimes and lead to a "kinder, gentler nation." Nothing could be further from the truth. Diversity, namely the process of bringing people of varied age, ethnicity, gender, religion, sexual orientation, ability level, linguistic background and other distinguishing characteristics, together in schools and the workplace, does not automatically ensure that the school or work environments will simultaneously become multicultural. The presence of Asian Americans, the physically disabled, and females in a given environment usually just means that a diverse group of individuals have been charged with "fitting" into a mono-cultural setting that is dominated by and disproportionately rewarding to European American males. The icons and the canons of the environments are grounded in a Western European, English language, and patriarchic tradition.

It is perhaps precisely because critics are too aware that one can achieve diversity within the work place without forfeiting one inch of territory where multiculturalism is concerned that the concept is less objectionable and maligned than multiculturalism. In three decades, the concept of multiculturalism has really become a viable burning issue. However, policymakers, social commentators, academicians, and the general public have become very familiar with the term and critics have sprung like bad leaks from every joint of a rusted pipe (Limerick, 1994; Siegel, 1991; Chavez, 1996; Famularo, 1996; Whitfield, 1996). In fact, the topic of diversity frightens many colleges and university administrator and creates in them a desire to eliminate the issue (Levine, 1991).

Why is multiculturalism one of the misunderstood social and educational concepts in recent times? Is it truly such a difficult concept to comprehend? Definitions of multiculturalism are as varied as there are multi-culturalists. But, nearly all agree on three things. First, multiculturalism would be characterized by tremendous diversity. Second, it would-must-include a commitment to economic and social justice. Third, it would encourage European Americans to define themselves as something other than just "white." Simultaneously, it would call into question certain terminology used in connection with the discussion on diversity. The word "minority" is one such example often used in reference to individuals from traditionally underrepresented groups. This term conveys a sense of marginalization. Its use raises the question of exactly who is a "minority." Importantly, in many geographic areas of this country and the world the use of the term "minority" for the previously mentioned group is indeed a misnomer.

What is needed is a clear articulation of the goals of multicultural education prior to any discourse purporting to tell why it should or should not be embraced and canonized. Sleeter and Grant (1994) noted that, in 1980, Gollnick described five goals of multicultural education that today are still relevant and desirable. Those goals include promoting: the strength and value of cultural diversity; human rights and respect for those who are different; alternative life choices for people; social justice and equal opportunity for all people; and equity in the distribution of power among groups.

These goals are straightforward and theoretical and should not be seen as threatening to any constituency. After all, this is America, a nation that expounds its virtue when it comes to democracy and equality. In reality, however, goals two and five are actually extremely threatening to the very continuance of the American social structure as it exists today. These two goals would necessitate that school systems move away from its current curriculum and workforce that extensively reflect a Western European ideology.

Additionally, Gotfredson, Murray, Nettles, and McHugh (1992) identify major themes of multicultural education to include presenting a balanced view of history, matching instruction with children's learning styles, equalizing learning opportunities for all children, promoting multicultural ideals and inter-group respect. Miller-Lachmann and Taylor (1995) translate these themes into the following goals: change in the total school environment to create a climate that appreciate diversity, change in the curriculum making it more inclusive and relevant, use of instructional approaches that reflect the unique needs of students, change in the values that schools promote, and greater diversity among educational personnel including teachers, administrators, and staff.

The rationale for multicultural education and diversity is viewed within the context of our social structure that is premised upon "white" supremacy. One is hard pressed to deny the assertion given in the Constitution's own valuation of enslaved African Americans as three-fifths of a human being or the bias in favor of land owning white males. Thus, this paper posits that it is exactly because the potential of multicultural education is understood so extremely well, that critics have been so virulent in their attacks and have successfully perverted the resulting discourse.

In the eye of the critics, the only beneficiaries of multicultural education would be persons of color generally, and African Americans specifically. Many European Americans hold this perception in large part because of their relationship with African Americans. It is at once intimate, alien and long-standing, stretching back since the nation's inception. Thus the perception of multicultural education is linked almost exclusively with African American issues. It is somehow "a Black thing!"

But how did that happen? Certainly this perception did not develop by accident. There was a systematic course of attack that sought to slur and destroy this movement. Any action that seeks to create a society that has equity in the balance of power and resources would be viewed as radical, revolutionary and dangerous. Indeed, that is exactly how the British government, 200 years ago, viewed the upstart American colonies' demand for equity within the context of taxation and voting rights. Flash forward some 200 hundred years, to the present day, you will find another group of revolutionary thinkers who, if their movement is successful, would topple another unjust society that is also founded upon principles of inequity.

MELLEN STUDIES IN EDUCATION

24. Rose M. Duhon-Sells and Emma T. Pitts, **An Interdisciplinary Approach to Multicultural Teaching and Learning**

25. Robert E. Ward, **An Encyclopedia of Irish Schools, 1500-1800**

26. David A. Brodie, **A Reference Manual for Human Performance Measurement in the Field of Physical Education and Sports Sciences**

27. Xiufeng Liu, **Mathematics and Science Curriculum Change in the People's Republic of China**

28. Judith Evans Longacre, **The History of Wilson College 1868 to 1970**

29. Thomas E. Jordan, **The First Decade of Life, Volume I: Birth to Age Five**

30. Thomas E. Jordan, **The First Decade of Life, Volume II: The Child From Five to Ten Years**

31. Mary I. Fuller and Anthony J. Rosie (eds.), **Teacher Education and School Partnerships**

32. James J. Van Patten (ed.), **Watersheds in Higher Education**

33. K. (Moti) Gokulsing and Cornel DaCosta (eds.), **Usable Knowledges as the Goal of University Education: Innovations in the Academic Enterprise Culture**

34. Georges Duquette (ed.), **Classroom Methods and Strategies for Teaching at the Secondary Level**

35. Linda A. Jackson and Michael Murray, **What Students Really Think of Professors: An Analysis of Classroom Evaluation Forms at an American University**

36. Donald H. Parkerson and Jo Ann Parkerson, **The Emergence of the Common School in the U.S. Countryside**

37. Neil R. Fenske, **A History of American Public High Schools, 1890-1990: Through the Eyes of Principals**

38. Gwendolyn M. Duhon Boudreaux (ed.), **An Interdisciplinary Approach to Issues and Practices in Teacher Education**

39. John Roach, **A Regional Study of Yorkshire Schools 1500-1820**

40. V.J. Thacker, **Using Co-operative Inquiry to Raise Awareness of the Leadership and Organizational Culture in an English Primary School**

41 Elizabeth Monk-Turner, **Community College Education and Its Impact on Socioeconomic Status Attainment**

42. George A. Churukian and Corey R. Lock (eds.), **International Narratives on Becoming a Teacher Educator: Pathways to a Profession**

43. Cecilia G. Manrique and Gabriel G. Manrique, **The Multicultural or Immigrant Faculty in American Society**

44. James J. Van Patten (ed.), **Challenges and Opportunities for Education in the 21st Century**

45. Barry W. Birnbaum, **Connecting Special Education and Technology for the 21st Century**

46. J. David Knottnerus and Frédérique Van de Poel-Knottnerus, **The Social Worlds of Male and Female Children in the Nineteenth Century French Educational System: Youth, Rituals, and Elites**

47. Sandra Frey Stegman, **Student Teaching in the Choral Classroom: An Investigation of Secondary Choral Music Student Teachers' Perceptions of Instructional Successes and Problems as They Reflect on Their Music Teaching**

48. Gwendolyn M. Duhon and Tony Manson (eds.), **Preparation, Collaboration, and Emphasis on the Family in School Counseling for the New Millennium**